ISBN 978-1-331-55853-8
PIBN 10205711

FB &c Ltd, Dalton House, 60 Windsor Avenue, London, SW19 2RR.
Company number 08720141. Registered in England and Wales.

For support please visit www.forgottenbooks.com

THE SPIRITS IN PRISON

And Other Studies on the

LIFE AFTER DEATH

BY THE LATE

E. H. PLUMPTRE D.D.

DEAN OF WELLS

NEW AND REVISED EDITION

SEVENTH THOUSAND

NEW YORK
THOMAS WHITTAKER
2 & 3, BIBLE HOUSE
1894

THE LOVED AND HONOURED MEMORY

OF

FREDERICK DENISON MAURICE

PREFACE.

THE Sermon which gives its title to this volume was preached at St. Paul's, April 30th, 1871. I said, in a short Prefatory Note to the edition then published, that "I hoped before long to show that nothing I had said on the question discussed in it had been said hastily, and that there were ample grounds for every statement I had made as to the teaching of Scripture, or the belief of the Church, or the opinions of her great teachers."

That hope has, up to the present time, remained unfulfilled. Other work and other cares pressed upon me. My time was fully occupied with labours in other regions of theology, which have not, I hope, been altogether unfruitful. What I had sketched out mentally in outline has remained for more than the proverbial nine years, not unthought of, but also not filled up. At last a time of a little more leisure has come, and I wish, before it passes from my hands, to say what I have to say on the grave questions of which the Sermon treats

Meanwhile the attitude of men's minds towards

those questions has widened with the years. When I wrote in 1871, the two chief epochs in the recent history of the controversies which I then discussed were (1) the expulsion of Mr. F. D. Maurice from King's College in 1853, which made him, so to speak, the proto-martyr of the wider hope; and (2) the excitement caused by the publication of *Essays and Reviews* in 1860, and the judgment pronounced by the Judicial Committee of Council in the case of *Fendall* v. *Wilson* in 1864. Since that date Dr. Farrar's Sermons, published under the title of *Eternal Hope*, may fairly be looked on as an "epoch-making" book, both in the wide circulation it has attained and the discussion of which it has been the starting point.

It lies in the nature of the case that much that I had intended to say, that I had in fact at that time prepared for publication, has now been, wholly or in part, said by others. Were I to yield to the impulses which are the penalty of procrastination, I might be tempted to take up the anathema, *Pereant qui nostra ante nos dixerint.* As it is I am content to follow in the track of others, gleaning where they have reaped, and plucking a few grapes as from the topmost bough.

Of the *Studies* that are now published with the Sermon, some, such as those on *The Eschatology of the Early Church*, the *Letter to Dr. Farrar*, the *Correspondence with a Roman Catholic Priest*, have already appeared in print. That on *The Descent into Hell* was written, though not published, some years ago. For others, materials were gathered but the papers themselves did not assume their present form till the present volume was in contemplation.

The nature of the subjects discussed, no less than the *genesis* and growth of the book now laid before the reader, has involved a certain measure of over-lapping, but I have thought it better to incur at times the reproach of repetition rather than that of incompleteness. At the best, however, and after all labours that I, or others abler than myself, can bring to the problems which I have undertaken to investigate, one feels that that last reproach of incompleteness is, in the nature of the case, inevitable. It is something, at least, to begin and end with a profound sense of the limits of our knowledge. I can but hope that within those limits I have travelled on the right track, applied a true method, and attained, at least approximately, to the clearer vision and the wider charity, and the forbearance that grows out of mutual reverence, to which it is the object of this volume to lead others.

E. H. P.

DEANERY, WELLS,
October 22nd, 1884.

PREFACE TO NEW EDITION.

THE fact that, after a sale of four thousand copies of this work, I have been asked to prepare a fresh issue, leads me to think that it has met a want more or less widely felt. The many letters which I have received from correspondents personally unknown, but whose minds had been drawn to the contemplation of the great problems of which I have ventured to treat, confirm that impression and are a more than sufficient reward for whatever labour I have bestowed on them. I am largely indebted to those correspondents for the facts, references, and quotations which will be found in the *Additional Notes*.

Acting on the suggestion of some of my reviewers and of personal friends, I have, I hope, added to the usefulness of the book by the addition (1) of a fuller analytical Table of Contents, and (2) of somewhat copious *Indexes*. For both of these I am indebted to the kindness of the Rev. H. W. Pereira, M.A., of whose scholarly accuracy in such work—a work, perhaps, of greater labour than that of the writer—sufficient evidence will be found, if any were wanted besides that thus given to the reader, in his thoughtful and exhaustive volume, *A Commentary on the Office for the Ministration of Holy Baptism*. I know no work on that subject in English theological literature more abounding in a wealth of illustrative quotations from Scripture, Ancient Liturgies, and the writings of Catholic Fathers, Doctors, and Divines.

E. H. P.

DEANERY, WELLS,
April 21, 1886.

CONTENTS.

SHORT STUDIES.

"THE SPIRITS IN PRISON."

b

"THE SPIRITS IN PRISON."

"He went and preached unto the spirits in prison."
1 PETER iii. 19.

THERE is one article of the Creed which, strange as it may seem, for some centuries past, has practically fallen into the back-ground, and lost its hold on the thoughts and affections of mankind. We repeat the words which tell us that Christ "descended into hell," but they do not move us. Our thoughts about them are indistinct and dim. They bring no strength or comfort to us. To the untaught they probably suggest the dark and monstrous belief that, in order to complete the work of a penalty vicariously borne, the agony of the Garden and the passion of the Cross were followed by the endurance, for a few brief hours, of the torments of the lost.[1] Those who have been taught better know that the "hell" of which the

(1) This was the view actually held by Calvin (*Instit.* ii. 16) and his followers. The entire absence of any teaching as to the purpose of the Descent, which now characterises the Third of the Thirty-nine Articles, as contrasted with the explanation given in the Articles of A.D. 1542, was probably due to the influence of Calvinistic theology on the Elizabethan divines. See Study III., *The Descent into Hell.*

Creed speaks is Hades, the unseen world wherein are the souls of the dead, not Gehenna, where "the worm dieth not and the fire is not quenched," but do not advance one step beyond that negation of an error. Even the great masters of theological science among us teach on this point with stammering lips and uncertain speech,[2] afraid to speak with the bolder, more articulate utterances of the Church's earlier faith. Those who contend most for the letter of Scripture, as the one authoritative rule of faith, close their eyes to its clearest and most direct statements. Those who turn to the witness of primitive Christianity, the *consensus*, in thought and worship, of the ages that were nearest to the teaching of the Apostles and their Master, are too often content to accept the narrower thoughts of a later, more speculative, less loving, and less hopeful time.

And yet, we may be quite sure, that if the Descent into Hell had brought to men's minds no other thoughts than those which we commonly attach to it, it would never have gained a place in the Creed of Christendom, or seized, as it did for centuries, on men's thoughts and feelings. To those who so received it it spoke of a victory over death, which was the completion of the sacrifice of the cross. It told

(2) It is not without reluctance that I write the great name of Pearson as one of those who are open to this charge, but I am constrained to say that few theological studies seem to me less satisfactory than the section of his work *On the Creed* which deals with this clause of it. I share Bishop Harold Browne's regret that he should on this matter "have written less lucidly than was his wont" (*Thirty-nine Articles*, Art. III., *ad fin.*).

them that He who came to seek and save the souls He loved on earth had continued that divine work while the body was lying in the rock-hewn grave. He had passed into that unseen world as a mighty King, the herald of His own conquests; and Death and Hell had trembled at His coming; and the bands of the prisoners were broken, and the gates of the prison-house were thrown open. There the banner of the King was unfurled, and the cross set up, that there also, even there, the souls of those who were capable of life might turn to it and live. There had He gathered round Him the souls of those righteous ones, from Abel onwards, who had had the faith which from the beginning of the world has justified, and had confessed that they were strangers and pilgrims upon the earth. These He had delivered from the passionate yearning of expectancy, and the pain of unsatisfied desire, and had taken them to rest till the Resurrection in that paradise of God where He had promised to be with one whose lawless life had melted at the last hour into some touch of tenderness, and awe, and pity.[3] Others, worthy of but a lower place, had yet found mercy. They had perished in God's great judgment, when the flood came upon the world of the ungodly, but they had not hardened themselves against His righteousness and love, and therefore were not shut out utterly from hope. In His Father's house there were many mansions, and there was a place found there for them. Such at one time

(3) See Study III., *The Descent into Hell.*

was the Creed of Christendom. It retained its hold on the minds of the great masses of mankind for fifteen centuries; mingled itself with strange and fantastic imaginations; was embodied in legends, false gospels, poems, dramas, hymns. Men clung to it instinctively as suggesting a wider hope than their dogmatic systems seemed to render possible. In part, at least, it retained its hold on our own Church even at the Reformation. This, at one time, was the authorised formal exposition of the words, "He descended into hell." [4] The paraphrase which turned the Creed into a hymn taught men that the end and purpose of that descent was that Christ the Lord might be

"Of them who long in darkness were,
The true light of their hearts." [5]

---

(4) The form of the Third Article in 1553 was as follows: "As Christ died and was buried for us: so also is it to be believed that he went downe into Hell. For the bodie laie in the Sepulchre, untill the resurrection, but his Ghoste departing from him, was with the Ghostes that were in prison, or in Helle, and didde preache to the same, as the place of S. Peter dooeth testifie."

(5) The quotation is taken from the paraphrase of the Apostles' Creed commonly found with Sternhold and Hopkins's version of the Psalms, in Prayer Books of the sixteenth and seventeenth centuries. Another version in 1641 gives—

"His soule did after this descend
Into the lower parts;
A dread unto the wicked spirits,
But joy to faithful hearts."

The selection of 1 Peter iii. 17—22 as the Epistle for Easter Eve, and of Zech. ix. (obviously chosen for the verse which speaks of the "prisoners" who were "in the pit wherein is no water," and yet were "prisoners of hope") as the First Lesson for the morning of that day, is sufficiently suggestive as an indication of the though s of the Edwardian reformers. The latter retains its place, it may be noted, in the revised Lectionary.

It has not been without a witness even among ourselves. The writer of the *Christian Year* follows in the footsteps of the earlier, not the later, interpreters of the Church's faith. He had spoken of the Lord Jesus as "sleeping, a silent corpse." He draws back from that thought as poor and unsatisfying, and asks :—

> "Sleep'st Thou indeed, or is Thy spirit fled,
> At large among the dead?
> Whether in Eden-bowers Thy welcome voice
> Wake Abraham to rejoice;
>
> "Or in some drearier scene Thine eye controls
> The thronging band of souls;
> That as Thy death won earth, Thine agony
> Might set the shadowy world from sin and sorrow free."[6]

It is clear that the whole current of thought thus suggested sets in the direction of wider hopes than that which has been almost the stereotyped belief of most Protestant Churches during the last three centuries. The dread of the Romish doctrine of purgatory, with all its monstrous claims and manifold superstitions, has made men close their eyes to the truths which lay beneath it, and which it had distorted and obscured. And so the gloom which had settled on the theology of Western Christendom since the dark shadow of Augustine[7]—dark, in spite of all

(6) *Christian Year*, "Easter Eve."

(7) The phrase may seem harsh, but it must be remembered that it was owing to the influence of Augustine that the doctrine of the absolute necessity of baptism as a condition of salvation was formally impressed on the teaching of the Western Church. The kingdom of Heaven was closed not only to the millions of the heathen world who lived and sinned in ignorance, but to the unbaptised children

the nobleness of the man—had rested on it, accepted without that which half deprived it of its horrors, was deepened into the blackness of midnight by the dogmas of Calvin; and the belief of men in the everlasting love of the Father and the universality of the redeeming work of Christ, was either utterly crushed out, or emptied, by restrictions and limitations, of all comfort and life and hope. Let us think for a moment what those restrictions are in the systems which bear the impress of either or both of those great teachers, and which refer them all, in their remotest and most awful issues, to the dread decrees of the

alike of heathens and of Christians; and to those who were not in that kingdom there remained nothing but the pains of Gehenna. (Aug., *Serm.* cxxxviii.) Their damnation might be *levissima* as compared with that of others. (Aug., *Contr. Julian.* v. 44.) Their existence in that state might even be better than their ceasing to exist might be (*ibid.*), but for them there was no possibility of pardon, or growth, or ultimate acceptance. The picture which Dante draws of the outer *limbus* of the *Inferno*, in which

"No other plaint rose up than that of sighs,"

and where were found the souls of those who, because they lacked baptism, bear the wrath of God,

"And without hope, live ever in desire"
(*Inferno*, iv. 24—40),

embodies the dogma of mediæval theology in the form of poetry. Protestantism, as it rejected the Romish doctrine of purgatory, rejected also the belief in this *limbus infantum* as an unscriptural figment. Practically it ceased to teach even gradations of punishment, and ignored the intermediate state between death and judgment. Hell, in all the horrors which imagination could picture to itself, was, for the Calvinist, the portion of all who were not predestined to life, and therefore were ordained to condemnation. The sacramentalism of Augustine enabled the Christian parent to hope that a baptized child dying in infancy was saved by his baptism. Calvinism left even that in doubt. Augustine recognised a *levissima damnatio*. Popular Calvinism thought of hell as one and the same thing for all but the elect.

Eternal Sovereignty. There are still, it may be feared, tens of thousands among us who hold that the whole heathen world, with all its strivings after light and good, in all its countless multitudes, with the myriads who have but breathed and died, is sentenced to an eternity of torment. "There is none other name," men tell us, and tell us truly, "given among men whereby they must be saved, save only the name of Christ;" and ignorance of that name, they add, and add falsely, closes therefore for ever the gates of everlasting life.[8] Even the children of believing parents, snatched away before the baptismal waters have passed over them, are, according to the pitiless, relentless logic of the dogmatist, doomed to condemnation, shut out for ever from the kingdom and the life of God. The mourning mother was left, like Rachel of old, to weep for her children, whom she was never to see again, refusing to be comforted. Nor was this all. Accuracy and precision in following the intricate mazes of theological speculation were thought of as essential to any participation in the blessedness beyond the grave; and the spirit which still breathes, or seems to breathe,[9] in the warnings of the Athanasian Creed, has led, on many questions, and in many different directions, to a yet narrower circumscription of the grace and love, the everlasting charity of God. All error has been thought of as heresy, and all heresy as fatal. Romanists and Pro-

(8) See Study VI., *The Salvation of the Heathen.*
(9) See Study XV., *The Damnatory Clauses of the Athanasian Creed.*

testants have hurled their anathemas at each other, with the conviction that they were but proclaiming the decrees of the Divine Judge.[10] Both have made common cause against the seekers, strugglers, wanderers who could attach themselves to neither.

As if this were not enough, men have gone further. A triumphant utterance of personal assurance, the acceptance of some doctrine of justification or some forensic theory of atonement—these also have been made conditions of salvation, and, where they have been absent, men who thought themselves orthodox believers have sorrowed, or have *not* sorrowed, as without hope, for the souls that were thus found wanting. And through all, or nearly all, of these convictions there has been the common thought that change and progress are excluded altogether from the state into which men pass at death. At whatever age and in whatever way death may come, it is thought of as stereotyping for ever the state upon which it falls. Fuller knowledge may come to those whose lives were spent in the ignorance that God winked at, but it brings with it no capacity for living in the light which is at last seen without the refraction of human errors. "In the place where the tree falleth, there it shall be,"[1] has been trans-

(10) See Study V., *The Mutual Anathemas of Romanists and Protestants.*

(1) Eccles xi. 3. The current application has the authority of the *Book of Homilies* ("Concerning Prayer," part iii.), but is, I think, clearly untenable. The true meaning of the text in question, determined by the context, is obvious enough. The writer of *Ecclesiastes* passes out of his pessimism and practical epicureanism into the

ferred from its true region to the unseen world into which we pass at death. "There is no repentance in the grave" has been accepted as though it were an oracle from God.

We may thank God, even though the protest has come in the form of wild dreams and fantastic speculations, that the natural instincts of men have risen up in revolt, and protested against conclusions so irreconcilably at variance with all belief in the love of Christ and the Fatherhood of God. The devout Romanist, when his thoughts dwell upon the dead whom he has loved and cared for, soothes his anxious fears by his belief in purgatory,[2] practically thinks of all or nearly all baptized members of his Church as

temper which sees in doing good, as far as lies in our power, the golden rule of life, "Cast thy bread upon the waters and thou shalt find it after many days. Give a portion to seven and also to eight." And this is to be done without regard to immediate results or anxious hesitation, "for thou knowest not what evil shall be upon the earth." We are to accept the changes and chances of life that lie beyond our control with a calm equanimity. "If the clouds be full of rain they empty themselves upon the earth; and if the tree fall towards the south or towards the north, in the place where the tree falleth there it shall be." The course of nature goes on according to its own laws. If we are always "observing the wind" and "regarding the clouds," as in temper

"over-exquisite
To cast the fashion of uncertain evils,"

we shall neither sow nor reap as God wills us to do. We must "accept the inevitable" and do our work as we best can. Thus taken, all is harmonious and coherent. The popular interpretation, on the other hand, introduces an alien dogmatic element, foreign alike to the sequence of thought, the immediate context, and to the whole scope of the book. (See the present writer's *Commentary on Ecclesiastes*, in the *Cambridge School Bible.*)

(2) See Study X., *The Doctrine of Purgatory*.

sentenced to no severer penalties, hopes even for heretics and unbelievers that the plea that they erred in an ignorance which was inevitable and invincible, may avail to lighten their condemnation. That belief has been associated, it is too true, with many dark superstitions. Men have thought of a given quantity of pain as the fit and adequate punishment of sin ; have held that it belonged to the Bishop of Rome to remit or protract the penalty, that all power was committed to him in heaven and in earth, and that he could bind and loose even the "spirits in prison." The monstrous dream that there was an accumulated treasure of the merits of the saints, which he could transfer at his pleasure to those who needed it, with all the abuses of purchased indulgences and masses for the dead that grew out of it, brought yet greater discredit on the truth which was thus distorted, and our minds shrink back, with an almost morbid dread—morbid in degree, however natural and inevitable—from any real or apparent approximation to a doctrine which has been so fruitful in evil. And yet with the holier and nobler members of that Church we can hardly doubt that the belief in a progressive purification after death, with growing clearness of vision and stronger yearnings after good as yet unattainable, has brought with it, in their thoughts of themselves and others, a consolation which Protestants have often envied. Is it quite impossible that those who hold truth to be more than comfort, may yet be able to rest on the one without surrendering their hold upon the other?

Others there are, we know, who have found refuge in the belief that sooner or later, after, it may be, the lapse of ages numbered beyond human ken, all souls will rest, purified and renewed, in the bosom of the universal Father, that the Divine Purpose of love, which hateth nothing that it has made, and will have all men to be saved and to come to the knowledge of the truth, will not always be frustrated by man's resistance. That larger hope—call it, if you will, that glorious dream—has never been without its witnesses.[3] The noblest, loftiest, most loving of the teachers of the ancient Church (I am not afraid to speak thus of Origen) embraced it almost as the anchor of his soul. It was cherished by the theologian (Gregory of Nyssa) to whom we owe the fullest defence of the Nicene Confession of our faith, and was at least widely spread among the Churches of the East. In later times among ourselves it has been first condemned by the authoritative formularies of the Church of England, then apparently tolerated by the withdrawal of the condemnation, then declared by the highest judicial authority in the Church to be compatible with her dogmatic teaching. It has had many individual witnesses, some in the high places of the Church, some among her noblest thinkers and most loving hearts. It has been, and is, the creed of the great poets whom we accept as

(3) See Study IV., *The Eschatology of the Early Church.*

the spokesmen of a nation's thoughts. Traces of its latent influence are to be found in those who shrink from openly avowing it. It tends to gain, and will probably continue to gain yet more, in our country and in others, a place in the popular belief like that which purgatory occupies in the belief of Romanists.[4]

These facts, striking as they are, not to be ignored or overlooked, are, of course, no criterion of the truth of the opinion. And in this case the hindrances to the reception of the theory as true are, to say the least, very serious. It dwells with a passionate eagerness exclusively on the loving purpose of God, and turns its eyes from the terrible, inalienable prerogative of man's freedom, by which that purpose may be, and daily is, frustrated. It fails to prove that the element of duration is, as has been maintained, altogether absent from the word which defines the divine law of retribution as eternal in its issues.[5] It forgets that the teaching of our Lord and his Apostles gives a strange, awful prominence to the fact of a separation between the evil and the good as the last closing scene in the divine drama of the world's history, beyond which there lies only a darkness which we cannot penetrate. If here and there we meet with divine words which speak, or seem to speak, of a final victory, when God shall be all in all, and all shall be as God wills, all concluded in un-

(4) See Study VII., *The History of the Wider Hope in English Theology.*

(5) See Study XIV., *The Meaning of the Word "Eternal."*

belief, that He may have mercy upon all,[6] when one accordant song of praise and thanksgiving shall rise from the universe which He created, we cannot shut out from our thoughts those other words, which tell us of the sin that hath never forgiveness, and the worm that dieth not and the fire that never can be quenched, and the great chasm which none can pass. We must be content to leave this seeming contradiction as part of the great mystery of evil from which the veil has never yet been lifted. We can but say that it has its parallel in that other mystery of the seemingly irreconcilable antagonism between God's foreknowledge and man's free-will, the election before the foundation of the world, which works according to God's good pleasure, and the power to forfeit that election so that it is impossible for those who have so fallen to renew themselves to repentance. We can but hold and teach that the punishment of evil must be, in the nature of the case, everlasting—more keen and sharp as the soul recognises it more clearly in its essential hatefulness, and judges it as God judges. All experience shows that if punishment, accepted as the chastisement of a righteous Father, may lead men to repentance, it may also harden them into the sullen resistance of the rebellious slave. But here also, it may be, we have, as before, the distortion of a truth, the half-truth which becomes a falsehood, that which men's thoughts have fastened on with a passionate

(6) Rom. v. 1—20; xi. 32; 1 Cor. xv. 28.

eagerness, because that which might have fed and sustained them has been denied.

There is not much need to dwell on another phase of thought which yet has found supporters among earnest and God-fearing men, who shrank from the popular belief as to the nature and duration of the punishment of sin. To them it has seemed that immortality is no natural, indefeasible inheritance of man's soul, that God alone has it as His possession, and that He bestows it on those only who seek it by patient continuance in well-doing; that for others there is the doom of an everlasting destruction from the presence of the Lord,[7] and that this destruction involves the loss, not only of all blessedness, but of all conscious being, the utter irretrievable annihilation of that which had been made in the image of God. Whatever support that view may derive from a narrow and almost slavish literalism in its interpretation of Scripture, it must be rejected as at variance with the intuitive beliefs which all God's later revelation presupposes, at variance also with the meaning of Scripture when we pass beyond the letter to the truths which it represents.[8]

Are we, then, to rest in the confession that God's judgments are a great deep, and that we cannot fathom them? Is our cry to be—

"Alas! we know not anything,"

---

(7) 1 Tim. vi. 16; Rom. ii. 7; 1 Thess. i. 9.
(8) See Study XI., *Conditional Immortality*.

when we are half-drawn to

"Faintly trust the larger hope"?

Must we content ourselves with the thought that there is a mystery behind the veil, and wait till the veil be withdrawn? Has no glimpse behind the veil been given us? Has no forerunner passed there whose footsteps and whose work we may follow afar off? Or is there not another course? May we not give up our morbid fears and our dark dreams, our dread of superstition, our controversial jealousies, and turn for guidance and comfort to that which I had well-nigh called the *lost* article of the Creed, of which I spoke at first, and to the words of the oracles of God which connect themselves more or less closely with it? They, it may be, will direct our way, be a light unto our feet, and a lamp unto our path, when the traditions of men fail us.

And (1) let us look more closely at the words[9] which helped at once to fix the truth in men's minds, and to determine the thoughts which they connected with it. The Apostle has been led through what seemed at first a train of simply ethical counsels,[10] to the example of the meekness and patience of Christ. But he cannot rest—no Apostle could—in the thought of his Lord's passion as being only an example, and so he passes on to speak of its redeeming power. "It was a sacrifice for sins; in some mysterious, transcendent way, vicarious.

(9) 1 Peter iii. 19, 20.
(10) 1 Peter iii. 8—17.

Its purpose was nothing less than to bring us,—Jew and Gentile alike, as both embraced by the atoning love—to bring mankind, to God. But then the thought rose up before him that the work looked backward as well as forwards; that those who had fallen asleep in past ages, even under conditions that seemed most hopeless, were not shut out from hope. Starting either from a wide-spread belief among the Jews as to the extent of the Messiah's work; or from the direct teaching of his Master after that Resurrection; or from one of those flashes of truth which were revealed to him not by flesh and blood, but by his Father in heaven, he speaks of that wider work. The Lord was "put to death in the flesh," but was "quickened in the spirit." That cry, "Father, into Thy hands I commend my spirit," was the beginning of a new activity. He passed into the world of the dead to be the herald of His own victory. As our Lord, in speaking of God's judgments in the past, had taken the days of Noah and the destruction of Tyre and Sidon, and the cities of the plain, as representative instances of what was true of countless others, so does St. Peter. The spirits of whom he thought as hearing that message were those who had been unbelieving, disobedient, corrupt, ungodly; but who yet had not hardened themselves in the one irremediable antagonism to good which has never forgiveness. The words, taken by themselves, might leave us in some doubt as to the nature and effect of that proclamation. But it is surely altogether monstrous to think, as some have thought, that He who a short time before, had breathed the prayer, "Father, forgive them, for they know not what they do;" who had welcomed, with a marvellous tenderness, the cravings of the repentant robber; who had felt, though but for a moment, the agony of abandonment, as other children of God have felt it without ceasing to be children—should pass into the world of the unseen only to tell the souls of the lost of a kingdom from which they were excluded, a blessedness in which they had neither part nor lot, to mock with the proclamation of a victory those who were only to be crushed under the chariot wheels of the conqueror. We have not so learnt Christ as to think of that as possible. But whatever doubt might linger round the words is removed by the reiterated assertion of the same truth a few verses further on.[1] That which was "preached also to them that are dead" was nothing else but a gospel—the good news of the redeeming love of Christ. And it was published to them, not to exempt them from all penalty, but that they, having been judged, in all that belonged to the relations of their human life, with a true and righteous judgment, should yet, in all that affected their relation to God, "live in the spirit." Death came upon them, and they accepted their punishment as awarded by the loving and righteous Judge, and so ceased from the sin to which they had before been slaves,

(1) 1 Peter iv. 6.

and thus it became to them the gate of life. So, the Apostle says to his disciples, it should be with them, in times of calamity and persecution. They were to arm themselves with that thought, and so to cease from sin, as those who were sharers in the sufferings and death of Christ, crucified, buried, risen again with Him, accepting pain, privation, ignominy, as working out a like purification even in this present life.

(2) The teaching of St. Peter helps us to understand what else would seem a strange interruption to continuity of thought in the passage in which St. Paul speaks most clearly of Christ's descent to Hades.[2] He is dwelling mainly on the gifts that had been bestowed upon the Church by her risen and ascended Lord. But that word "ascended" leads him to pause abruptly. Men were not to think that the work of Christ in the unseen world was limited to that which followed His ascension. "Now that He ascended, what is it but that He also descended first into the lower parts of the earth? He that descended is the same also that ascended up far above all heavens, that He might fill all things." Hades and the Heaven of heavens, had alike felt the glory and the blessing of His presence. At His name had bowed every knee, not of men only on the earth, or angels in heaven, but those who were, as men thought, beneath the earth, the spirits of the dead.[3]

The words, then, of the Apostles lead us to the

(2) Eph. iv. 9, 10.
(3) Phil. ii. 10.

belief of a capacity for repentance, faith, love—for growth, discipline, education, in those who have passed away. We have no sufficient grounds for limiting the work on which they dwell to the representative instance or the time-boundaries of which they speak.

(3) Our Lord's personal teaching, as might be expected, is less explicit. He had many things to say to His disciples which they could not bear while He was yet with them,[4] and this might well be one. It was not till the work had been accomplished that in this, as in other things, they could enter fully into the mystery of the Cross. Yet hints, suggestions, glimpses of the truth there are, which receive a new significance when we look at them in the light of the later teaching. Now we see more clearly than we did before what He meant when He taught His disciples that there is one sin only which "has never forgiveness, neither in this world nor in the world to come;"[5] how it is that the servant which knew not his Lord's will, and did it not, "shall be beaten with few stripes;"[6] or the condemnation of those who never listened to a preacher of repentance be "more tolerable" than that of those who have sinned against light and knowledge:[7] how in the "many mansions" of his Father's house there may be room for souls in all stages of grace, strength, illumination.[8]

(4) John xvi. 12. (5) Matt. xii. 31; Mark iii. 28.
(6) Luke xii. 48. (7) Matt. x. 15; xi. 22, 24.
(8) John xiv. 2.

(4) It will hardly be questioned that the conclusion to which we are thus led is in harmony with all that analogy would lead us to expect, with all the guesses and the hopes that have been present to the thoughts of the great masters of those who know, Christian and pre-Christian, at whose feet we are content to learn. Prior to revelation all our thoughts of a life to come rest on our belief in the law of continuity. We are living, conscious beings, capable of willing, thinking, loving, acting, up to the hour of death. What is there in the fact of bodily death that should lead us to think that it stops that conscious and energetic life of the soul? And if the soul's existence continues, must we not think of it as passing into its new phase of being with the same capacities, with the character, plastic and capable of re-formation, in the same measure as at the hour of death? The character of evil or of good may, indeed, be stamped indelibly, irrevocably, on the soul. There may be, even in this life, that terrible hardening of the soul and searing of the conscience—that antagonism of the soul to light as light, good as good, God as God, which in its own nature excludes repentance, and therefore forgiveness also. But with the vast myriads who depart this life it is not so. Thousands are born and die without a single conscious act of will: thousands pass through life in absolute idiocy, or in an ignorance almost animal; thousands, with poor, stunted, feeble souls, that have never taken in a clear thought of God, or exercised a deliberate choice between good and evil.

On thousands the touch of fever or delirium has for the last days or months or years of life turned the harmonies of the soul, like "sweet bells jangled out of tune," into a strange and appalling discord. Shall we say that in cases such as these there is to be a special energy of the Divine Omnipotence, transforming the whole nature as with a lightning flash, and raising the soul in a moment to the completeness of the glorified saint who has been made perfect by suffering? Shall we say that those who thus depart, having had the seal of baptism stamped upon their souls, are admitted to the paradise of God, while for all others there is the doom of those who languish for ever in the darkness where no hope enters? Shall we refer baptized and unbaptized alike to the immutable decree which adjudges some to the right hand and others to the left, in order to proclaim the sovereignty of the Will from which it issues? If neither of these solutions satisfies us, will it not be truer to our intuitive convictions, to the teaching of Scripture, to the analogy of God's moral government in this life, to the lessons of experience, to believe that the state into which the soul passes at death is one which admits of discipline, change, progress—that there also the love which does not will that any should perish, but that all should come to repentance, proclaims evermore to the "spirits in prison," as during those hours of the descent into Hades, the glad tidings of reconciliation? Even the "prisoners in the pit where there is no water," those who are exiles from their home in a dry and thirsty land, may be as prisoners of hope, not without the stronghold in which they may find refuge.[9] May we not believe, rejecting with a righteous protest the dark dreams of the popular theology of Rome, that there (as one has said whose thoughts are higher than his system) the memory of the past, with all its shame and sadness—the prospect of the future, with all its hope and brightness—will work together to an issue which no material fires could accomplish—

> "That these two pains, so counter and so keen,
> The longing for Him when thou see'st Him not,
> The shame of self at thought of seeing Him," [10]

shall act to purify what is base in us, and illumine what is dark? If the future is to be the development and continuation of the present, if we are not to pass from a life of ever-varying relations with our fellow-men, each bringing with it opportunities for self-discipline and for serving God, to an absolute isolation, may we not go yet one step further and believe, as some did in the earliest ages of the Church, and as others have thought of late, that those whose joy it has been in life to be fellow-workers with Christ in leading many to righteousness, may continue to be fellow-workers there, and so share the life of angels in their work of service as in their ministries of praise?[1] The manifestation of God's righteous judgment and

(9) Zech. ix. 12; Ezek. xvii. 68; xx. 13, 14. See Study I., *On the Teaching of the Old Testament as to the Life after Death.*

(10) Cardinal Newman: *Dream of Gerontius.*

1) See Study XVI., *On the Activities of the Intermediate State.*

of His changeless love may thus, using men and angels as His instruments, help to renew throughout His universe all who are capable of renewal. These things lie behind the veil, and we see but as in a glass darkly; but that thought of the developed energies and ripened growth of the saints of God is at least truer to the laws of our spiritual life, than the belief in a dreamless sleep till the morn of the resurrection, or in long ages passed in self-centred contemplation, or even in the ceaseless utterance of the great Hallelujah of the spirits before the Throne.

(5) One witness, at least, to the truth of wider, happier thoughts as to the state of the dead than have recently prevailed among us, was borne, with no faltering voice, in no indistinct accents, by the Church of the first ages.[2] In every form, from the solemn liturgies which embodied the belief of her profoundest thinkers and truest worshippers, to the simple words of hope and love which were traced over the graves of the poor, her voice went up, without a doubt or misgiving, in prayers for the souls of the departed. Those prayers were indeed part of the inheritance which she had received from an older system. For more than two centuries before the conqueror over Hades was revealed, they had entered into the worship of all true Israelites, had been part of the services of Temple and synagogue.[3] They passed, to say the least, unblamed by Him who laid His finger with such unsparing

(2) See Study IX., *On Prayers for the Dead.*
(3) 2 Macc. xii. 44, 45.

severity on the corrupt traditions of Pharisaism; by the Apostle, who had no words too sharp for the weak and beggarly elements which he had left behind when Christ was revealed in him. We have good grounds for believing that they mingled with the thankfulness and hope with which St. Paul thought of the souls that had gone before.[4] From East and West, with a consent which is at least as strong as that in favour of Infant Baptism, they rose up in the assemblies of the faithful and from the hearts of mourners. They were associated all but indissolubly with the rite which was thought of as the highest act of worship and intercession, as a commemorative and Eucharistic sacrifice. And whatever else they implied, however undefined may have been the theory which supervened on the emotions out of which they rose, they at least bore their witness to the continuance of sympathy, communion, interdependence, between the living and the dead, to the belief that the state of the latter was one of discipline and progress. The prayers of the faithful might hasten their progress upward, or make them more capable of the Divine compassion, or help them to a higher or earlier place in the first resurrection, or mitigate, in some mysterious way, the keenness of their pain. It was an evil day when the hopes and sympathies which thus found utterance were wedded to the dark fancies and corrupt imaginations of the Romish theory of purgatory, and so came themselves to be looked on as corruptions of the simplicity which

(4) 2 Tim. i. 16—18.

is in Christ. It may be that our own Church, when she was called to the task of reforming those corruptions, had no alternative but to exclude from her public worship what had become associated in men's minds, it might well seem, associated inextricably, with so much that was evil. The traffic in indulgences and masses was so monstrous an abuse that it was well to get rid of it, even at the cost of leaving affections stifled in their natural utterances, and abandoning the traditions of the earliest ages of Christendom. All this we may acknowledge and accept; but the fact that it was once otherwise remains to bear a witness that we cannot and ought not to reject. It reminds us that it was part of the life of the first believers to think of themselves and of the dead as bound together by ties of fellowship and sympathy, of the state of souls departed with any capacity for repentance, as one of progressive peace, purity, illumination.

I have thought it right, friends and brothers, to bring these thoughts before you. It may be that they will seem to many of you strange, new, at variance with their traditional belief. But to not a few also they will come, if I do not greatly err, as strengthening their feeble hopes and helping them to sustain a burden which has often weighed on their hearts as too heavy to be borne. You have shuddered in awe and terror as you have looked into the abyss of God's judgments—have felt unable to reconcile the everlasting Righteousness with the everlasting

Love. Your hearts have ached as you have thought of the destinies of the millions of the great human family; or have followed with a yet more intense and agonized anxiety the pathway of a soul that you have loved—loved in spite of ignorance, passion, failures, sins—into the twilight region that lies beyond the grave. I, at least, can feel for and with you. For one who has been led to apprehend what seems to him a priceless, but forgotten, truth, in harmony with the mind of Christ, with the witness of His Church, and with the wisdom of the wise, steering a middle path between the falsehood of extremes, embraced by the profoundest thinkers of a Church whose witness against Rome is as distinct and unfaltering as our own;[5] for such an one, who has known the pain of those hot thoughts and the wretchedness of those dark visions, it was a simple duty to utter the truth according to his power—to endeavour at least to comfort others with the comfort wherewith he himself has been comforted of God.

(5) See Study VIII., *On Modern German Thought as to the Life after Death.*

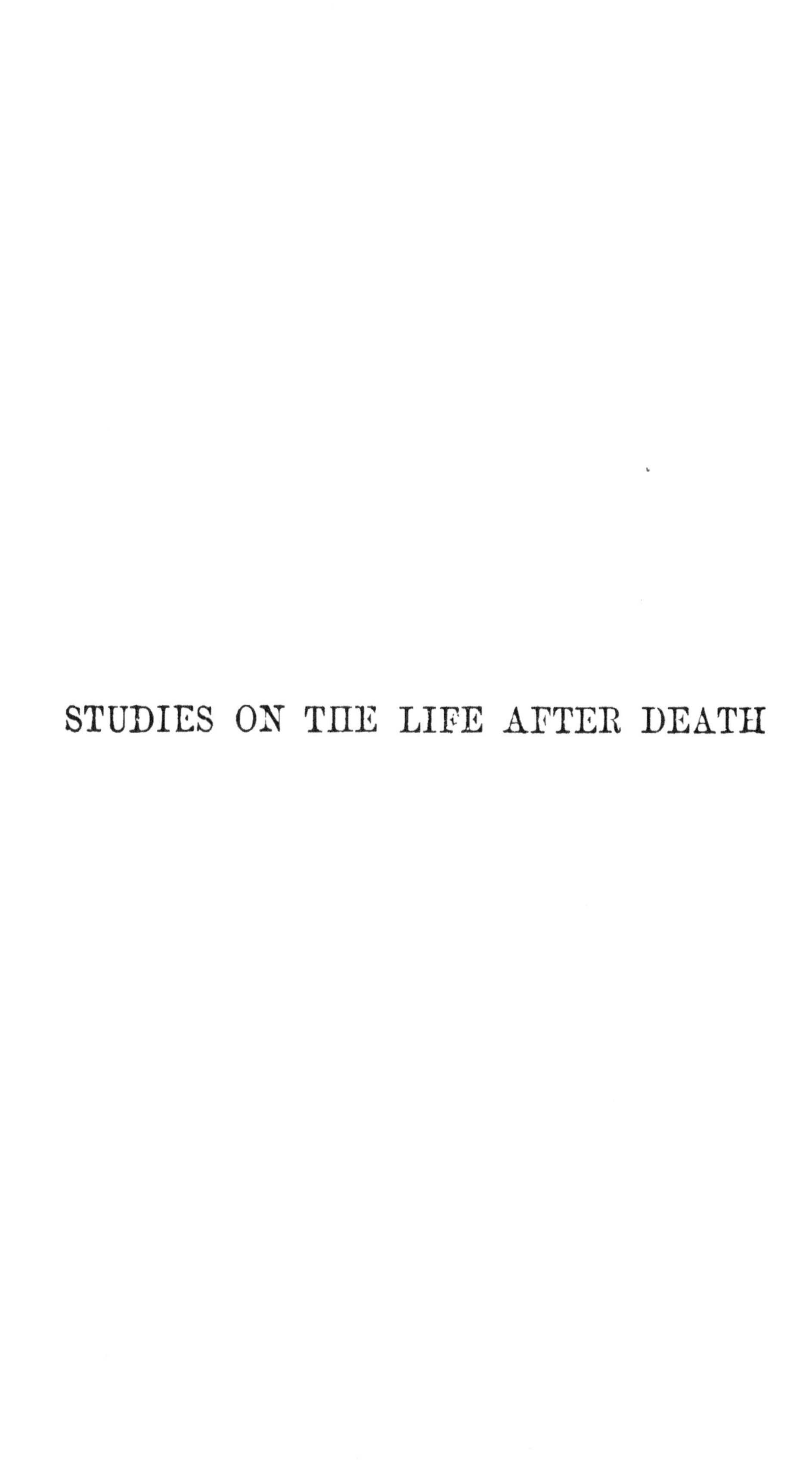

STUDIES ON THE LIFE AFTER DEATH

THE OLD TESTAMENT IN ITS BEARING ON THE LIFE AFTER DEATH.

THE Old Testament, as a whole, does not lend itself readily to dogmatic statements on either side, as to the nature or duration of the rewards, still less of the punishments, of the future state of man. As in other things, so pre-eminently in this, its teaching was germinal and rudimentary, given "in many different forms and in many different measures" (Heb. i. 1), as men were able to receive it. Each part of the book has accordingly to be studied in the light of its surroundings, as part of the plan of a divine, but very gradual, education. Such hints as were given may be read in the light of the truths into which they afterwards developed, still more in the light of the higher revelation which completed and combined them. In some instances even the after-thoughts of a later age will not be without interest, as showing what the thinkers of that age brought with them, and read, as it were, between the lines of what they found there.

The first of such suggestive hints is seen in the great

protevangelium, the first gospel promise of redemption and deliverance, in Gen. iii. 15. The absence of any reference to that promise in the later books of the Old Testament leaves us to conjecture what impression it made on the minds of men at the time or afterwards. But we can hardly err in thinking that it must have spoken to the compiler of Genesis, to whom it came as a tradition from the remote past, of a long conflict between mankind and the evil power, of which the serpent, in the thoughts of other nations as well as of the Jews, was the mysterious symbol,[1] and of a final victory. The "seed of the woman," till the event showed that there was to be another and a higher fulfilment in one who was *the* seed, gathering up in Himself, as the representative of the race, the Humanity which was common to all, would seem to include the whole family of man. The seed of the serpent would represent all forces of spiritual evil, and of wisdom and subtlety alienated from God. And the promise that the seed of the woman should be bruised in its heel, should suffer, *i.e.* partially and in its lowest and weakest part, while it was, in its turn, to bruise the serpent's head, must, at least, have suggested the thought of an ultimate reversal of the apparent triumph of evil which the history of the world presents. Would it have seemed, we may ask, to those who read the promise, that it would have

(1) Comp. Wisd. ii. 24. "Through the envy of the devil came death into the world." So in the *Zendavesta*, iii. 62, Ahriman appears in the form of a serpent (Hengstenberg's *Christology of the Old Testament*, i. p. 7. Engl. translation, 1854.) Comp. Rev. xii. 9, xvi. 20

found an adequate fulfilment in the irretrievable condemnation of the great majority of the human family, and the deliverance of a few? Does not that first primeval gospel fall in more harmoniously with the wider hope of the later ages of Christendom, than with the ever-recurring limitations which have been dominant during its history?

I pass to the next great promise which goes beyond the maintenance of the physical order of the world against the recurrence of a new catastrophe like the traditional deluge, and I find there also, as St. Paul afterwards found, the note of universality. "In thy seed shall all the nations of the earth be blessed" (Gen. xii. 3; xxii. 18). Of this also there were "springing and germinant" accomplishments. And during the history of Israel, till the true seed had come, it would suggest the thought that the children of Abraham were to be light-bearers, witnesses of the truth, to the nations with which they came in contact, so far as those nations were willing to receive their witness. Higher thoughts of God, truer thoughts of the worship due to Him, a deeper reverence for the laws of truth, kindness, purity, righteousness—this was what they were to carry with them through their long career. Did those who were the immediate heirs of the promise confine themselves to that aspect of its fulfilment, or had they glimpses of a higher and more permanent blessedness? The answer to that question must be given, I believe, in the affirmative. To the wanderer and the exile, not without his share in the sins and sorrows of mankind, God, the Eternal, was "his shield," and his "exceeding great reward" (Gen. xv. 1); and that thought sustained him because it brought him also into the region of the eternal. We may say of him, with no strained interpretation, that he "rejoiced" to see the "day" (John viii. 56) of Him, the Eternal Word, who came to manifest to men that eternal life which consisted in knowing God (John i. 2; xvii. 3), who was Himself that life (John xiv. 6; 1 John i. 2). When his grandson stood in the presence of the Egyptian king, his grey hairs all but bowed down with sorrow to the grave, and spoke of the few and evil days of the years of his pilgrimage (Gen. xlvii. 9), he could not have quite forgotten that in the visions of the night (Gen. xxviii. 12) he had had glimpses of a life which others saw not; of a country other than that promised to his descendants, towards which the closing years of his life were bringing him nearer; of everlasting arms which were ready to receive him when his pilgrim days were over; of a "salvation" for which he had waited all his life long (Gen. xlix. 18).

The absence of any reference to the rewards and punishments of the life after death in the stage of the education of Israel represented by the law of Moses is every way suggestive. We ask whether the omission involved the rejection, or, at least, the non-recognition, of immortality? Was belief in that immortality reserved for the fuller revelation that was to be given in the Christ? Had the patriarchs believed only in "transitory promises," or if their faith had had a higher aim, was the teaching of the law, in this as in other things, distinctly retrograde? Are we to accept Warburton's hypothesis, that the absence of any reference to this truth is the strongest proof we could have of the "Divine Legation," of the Jewish lawgiver, who was content to appeal to the rewards and punishments which followed close upon the heels of good or evil deeds, manifest in the sight of all men, instead of following the example of other legislators and holding forth the hopes and terrors of a distant and a shadowy future?[2] The fact that the judgments of that unseen future were conspicuously prominent in the religious system of the people in whose wisdom the Hebrew lawgiver had been trained, introduces a new element into the problem, and may, perhaps, give the key to its solution. The *Ritual of the Dead,*[3] the sculptures and paintings which it inter-

(2) See Warburton's *Divine Legation of Moses, passim.*

(3) See the *Book of Hades* in *Records of the Past*, x. 79—134, and the *Funereal Ritual* or *Book of the Manifestation to Light* in Le Normant's *Manual of Ancient History*, i. 308. (English translation, 1869.) The *Apologia* put into the lips of the soul that is destined to blessedness is worth giving, as showing the width and height of Egyptian ethics:—"I have not blasphemed; I have not stolen; I have not smitten men privily; I have not treated any person with cruelty; I have not stirred up trouble; I have not been idle; I have not been intoxicated; I have not made unjust commandments; I have shown no improper curiosity; I have not allowed my mouth to tell any secrets; I have not wounded any one; I have not put any one in fear; I have not slandered any one; I have not let envy gnaw my heart; I have not spoken evil, either of the king or of my father; I have not falsely accused any one; I have not withheld milk from the mouths of sucklings; I have not practised any shameful crime; I have not calumniated a slave to his master." The catalogue of the evil deeds from

prets for us, show what was the belief of every Egyptian. When he died his soul was carried over the waters of the dark river to *Amenti*, the land of the dead. It appeared before Osiris as its judge, and was compelled to confess its sins. Its good and evil deeds were weighed in the balance and its fate determined according to its deserts. May we not legitimately think of the divine education through which Moses was led as involving a reaction against the system in which he had grown up? He had seen how powerless that system was to raise men out of evil, how little the vague terrors of the future, even where men believed them, availed to restrain them, how they had become instruments of oppression in the hands of a priesthood who did *not* believe them. What was wanted was the belief in an ever-present God, governing and guiding *now*, rewarding the righteous, pardoning the penitent, and punishing the guilty. This government was to be seen partly in the general laws by which good and evil work out their own natural consequences of blessedness or misery, partly in the special enactments of the Mosaic code; partly also in the fact that in the theocracy which that code implied, the connexion between the cause and the consequence was more visibly patent than in the history of other nations. It was, to use an image

which the soul had kept itself free is followed by a recital of the good which it had done. "I have made to the gods the offerings which were their due; I have given food to the hungry, drink to the thirsty, and clothes to the naked."—Le Normant, *ibid.* i. p. 313.

which I owe to Augustus Hare (*Village Sermons*, ii. p. 37), as if in this instance we were allowed to see the works of the clock of the world's history, while elsewhere we saw only the movement of the hands and heard the striking of the hours. But this apparent suppression of a doctrine was, in fact, but the necessary preparation for its reappearance in a clearer light, and as resting on a firmer basis. Men were to begin with belief not in the immortality of the soul, but in the eternity of God, who had revealed Himself by the new name of the I AM THAT I AM. They were to be made to feel as in the Psalm that at least represents the thoughts of Moses, the man of God, that a thousand years were with Him as a watch in the night; that He is God from everlasting and world without end (Psalm xc. 1—4). But the thought of that eternity ennobled rather than depressed man's life. In some way or other he felt that he was called upon to share it. It stirred him to "apply his heart" unto a wisdom which was not of earth, to believe in a love which endured to a thousand generations, to pray that the glorious Majesty of the Eternal might be with him and with his children (Psalm xc. 12—17). And unless we are to say that our Lord was reading into the teaching of the older Scriptures what was not really to be found there, there was in that other revelation, "I am the God of Abraham, of Isaac, and of Jacob," the proclamation, or at least the suggestion, of a yet higher truth (Matt. xxii. 32; Exod. iii. 6—16). He is not the "God of the dead, but of the living," and would not have described Himself by a name which seemed to speak only of the past, unless that past had been perpetuated in the present, and was to be continued in the future. To Him all that ever lived are living still. He is their God for ever and ever.

It was, perhaps, natural that the Israelites who had to be brought under the pædagogic discipline of the law should be slow to read what was thus latent, if not patent, in the central article of their creed. The first distinct utterances of a hope stretching beyond the grave are found outside the range of the covenant of Israel. The prayer of Balaam (Num. xxiii. 10) that he might "die the death of the righteous," could hardly have been only for the *euthanasia* of a happy end of life—

> "With all that should accompany old age,
> As honour, love, obedience, troops of friends."

Whatever historical interpretation we may give to his prophetic utterance, when he spoke of the Star and the Sceptre which were the symbols of the future deliverer; the words, "I shall see Him, but not now: I shall behold Him, but not nigh" (Num. xxiv. 17),[4] implied a belief in a life which survives the existence of the body. They throw light upon those other words, themselves spoken by one who seems to have lived outside the range of the teaching of the

(4) It is right to add that the tenses admit of being taken, and are taken by many commentators, as in the present, "I see him--I behold him," the future thought of as seen in the present.

Mosaic law and ritual, though he shared in the central truth of faith in the Eternal, "I know that my Redeemer" (my *Goel*, my next of kin, my brother and my friend, my avenger and my advocate) "liveth, and shall stand in the latter day upon the earth: though after my skin worms destroy this body" (though decay and corruption may do their worst upon the organism in which I lived on earth) "yet in my flesh," (or "*apart* from my flesh") "shall I see God: whom I shall see for myself, and mine eyes shall behold and not another." (Job xix. 25—27.)[5] What Job thus spoke out we may well believe to have been in the heart of Abraham, Isaac, and Jacob, whose faith he had inherited. It may, at all events, be fairly urged, as confirming the interpretation of the name of God who was *their* God, as implying not continued existence only, but an ultimate resurrection, which had, it would seem, escaped the notice of Pharisees as well as Sadducees, till their eyes were opened by the teaching of the Son of Man, to see what faithful hearts had seen before them.

The after history of Jewish thought in relation to the future life was what might have been expected from this beginning. Popular conceptions were hazy and dim and vague, and there was no dogmatic teaching on the subject. It was better that it should

(5) It may be worth while noting the fact that the interpretation which sees in these words the utterance of a faith in immortality is adopted by Ewald, Canon Cook, Delitzsch, and A. B. Davidson, in their respective commentaries. See especially the *Appendix* of the last-named writer.

be so, than that those conceptions should have been darkened by superstitions, or assume, as they did, in the religion of Egypt, Assyria, Greece, the character of fantastic legends, blended with the dreams of the transmigration of the souls of men into lower forms of life. But to those who had ears to hear there were other witnesses. The ever-recurring sacrifices of the Temple, the solemn ritual of the Day of Atonement, the haunting sense of guilt which uttered itself in confessions like the 51st Psalm, the anticipation of deliverance from it—all this implied the twofold thought that the mischief wrought by sin did not terminate with death, that there was a restoration from it possible even after death, the utterances of that thought varying in their form according to the diversities of character, temperament, illumination. David could look forward to the journey through the valley of the shadow of death without fear, for the Divine Guide would be with him even there (Psalm xxiii. 4).[6] It was a thought of comfort to him that he should go to the child whom he had lost, though that child could not return to him. (2 Sam. xii. 23). He felt, echoing it may be the hope of Job, that his own soul would not be left in

(6) I admit, of course, that the drift of modern commentators (Ewald, Delitzsch, Perowne) is towards the conclusions that the Psalmist's hopes were bounded by the horizon of this life. To me, such a limitation seems as constrained and unwarrantable as that which finds in the words "I will dwell in the house of the Lord for ever" (Psalm xxiii. 6) no higher thought than that of visiting the Tabernacle from time to time as a devout worshipper. Did David stand on a lower level than Job?

Sheol (the Hell or Hades of the Hebrews), because he believed in the coming of the Holy One, who should not see corruption. (Psalm xvi. 10.)[7] Others might fix their hopes on the perishable things of earth. He would be satisfied if, when the time came for him to wake out of the sleep of death, it might be, more than he had been on earth, in the divine likeness. (Psalm xvii. 15).[8] So the maxim of the wise that "the righteous had hope in his death" (Prov. xiv. 32, comp. Psalm xxxi. 6) implies at least, if not a hope full of immortality, yet something more than an expectation of good for his children and children's children in the world. Others, again, whose vision was less clear, like Hezekiah (Isa. xxxviii. 18) and his contemporaries, the sons of Korah (Psalm lxxxviii. 10, 11), or the writers, whether David or another, of Psalms vi. 5, xxx. 9, cxv. 17, pictured to themselves the dim realms of Sheol as peopled with shadowy forms, without the joy or the energies of life. From that world there went up no hymns of praise and thanksgiving. In it there was no scope for wisdom or for counsel. There was for those who thus thought no hope of a restoration to fuller life and energy and joy; no fear of more than the loss of the light of the sun which made life pleasant, and of

(7) Here also Ewald, though he rejects the Davidic authorship, is a witness to the higher meaning no less than the more orthodox commentators. He adopts, it may be noted, the plural, "Thy holy ones," as though the psalmist rested in what was not only a personal assurance but a universal law.

(8) So Ewald once again. Assuming the later date of both Psalms, he traces in both the influence of Job.

the light of the soul which was the presence of the Eternal.

In the prophets, as might be expected, we begin to trace the dawnings of a clearer hope. We read the language of Hosea, in the light thrown upon it by the prayer of Hezekiah, as embodying the feelings even of devout and God-fearing souls, and we enter into the sense of triumph with which he proclaimed (Hos. xiii. 14), as St. Paul (1 Cor. xv. 55) and St. John (Rev. xx. 14) proclaimed after him, the destruction of Hades and of death, as the two powers which had seemed the destined devourers of all human capacities and hopes. Joel brings before us a vision of judgment which, though localised in its symbolic form, must have suggested then, as it did to patristic interpreters and the great mediæval poet (Dante, *Inferno*, x. 11), a wider gathering of the nations than that which was to assemble in the valley of Jehoshaphat (Joel iii. 2). It was given to Isaiah, or to the later prophet whose writings pass as his, to see more clearly on the one hand the terrors of the worm and of the fire, as images of a future judgment (Isa, lxvi. 24), and on the other the redemption from that judgment, or by means of it, which should be wrought by the Servant of the Lord, who should "make his soul an offering to sin," and should "see of the travail of his soul and be satisfied therewith" (Isa. liii. 11). If that vision of a "new heaven and a new earth" (Isa. lxvi. 22), which was the counterpart of the worm and of the fire, did not in terms involve a resurrection, it yet required that hope to be read between the lines in order that it might be a message of comfort to the prophet himself and to his readers. It was given, however, to the prophets of the exile to be the heralds of a more definite hope. Ezekiel's vision of the valley of dry bones, clothed with skin and flesh, and quickened to a new life (Ezek. xxxvii. 1—14), though it was primarily the symbol of a national revival, implied in its imagery the possibility of a personal resurrection. And that possibility was attested by the more definite prediction, probably of a somewhat later date (I purposely avoid discussing questions of authorship) that at the great day of redemption "many that slept in the dust of the earth should awake, some to æonian life (literally *life of the ages*) and some to shame and æonian contempt," and that "those who had been wise should shine as the brightness of the firmament, and those that had turned many to righteousness as the stars for ever and ever" (Dan. xiii. 2, 3). And in Ezekiel himself we find a teaching that throws light at once on the punishment and the restoration, when in contrast with the traditional doctrine of a transmitted hereditary doom, embodied in the proverb that the "fathers had eaten sour grapes and that the children's teeth were set on edge," he asserted the truth of individual responsibility. It is clear that the sentence that "the soul that sinneth it shall die," and the promise that "he who repented and turned to righteousness should live" must have involved a life and a death beyond the limits of man's earthly existence (Ezek. xviii. 1—32). And the significance of those words must have thrown light on others. He painted the restoration, not of Jerusalem and Judah only, but of Sodom and Samaria and their daughters, in words which all but absolutely exclude the possibility of any historical fulfilment. They also should be restored to their former estate. Jerusalem, penitent and ashamed, should receive them as her sisters and her daughters, and Jehovah would remember the covenant which He had made with her in the days of her youth. And the process by which that restoration of the covenant was to be brought about was to be one in which pardon and penitence were to work together, each doing its appointed work. The Lord God would be "pacified" with His people, and yet the daughter of Zion, the Israel of God, whom He pardons, should "remember and be confounded, and never open her mouth by reason of her shame" (Ezek. xvi. 55—63). They "should lothe themselves in their own sight for all their evils which they had committed," and yet should know that the Lord God had "wrought with them for His name's sake, and not according to their wicked ways nor according to their corrupt doings" (Ezek. xx. 43, 44). An æonian blessedness and an æonian punishment were thus strangely blended, and the one was thought of as the condition and the safeguard of the other, and so those who had murmured at the seeming anomalies of the divine government should be taught how to answer the question which the prophet asked in the name of the Lord, "O, house of Israel, are not my ways equal? are not your ways unequal?" (Ezek. xviii. 25), and should understand that the Lord had no pleasure in the death of him that dieth, but was evermore seeking to bring him back to life. Of all the passages of the Old Testament that bear upon the problems of eschatology, few, I venture to think, can compare with these utterances of Ezekiel's in their pregnant significance.

And that significance is not limited to Ezekiel's own teaching. What had been spoken by him must have left its impress on the minds of later prophets, even when their language seemed limited, as his, to some at least, has seemed, to judgments and blessings that were to find their scene of action on the visible stage of the world's history. The King who was to come to Zion, just and having salvation, who was to speak peace unto the heathen, was also He who by the blood of His covenant with Israel should "send forth the prisoners out of the pit wherein was no water." Those "prisoners of hope" should turn from the mire and clay into which they had fallen to the stronghold in which they should find safety and protection (Zech. ix. 11, 12) and that stronghold, as interpreted by the language of earlier writers, could be nothing else than the eternal compassion of the God who was to be a strong tower for them against the enemy.[9] The language of the last of the prophets

(9) The choice of Zech. ix. as the lesson for Easter Eve, both in the

as to the day of the Lord that should "burn as an oven, for which the proud and they that do wickedly shall be as stubble," while "to those who feared the Lord the Sun of righteousness should arise with healing in his wings," the day in which the Lord should "sit as a refiner and purifier of silver," a swift witness against all doers of evil, in whose unchanging love the sons of Jacob should find an assurance that they "should not be utterly consumed," who should "make up his jewels and spare them, as a man spareth his own son that serveth him" (Mal. iii. 1—6, 17; iv. 1, 2), passes naturally, even if not necessarily, beyond the horizon of any earthly discipline or restoration.

To pass from these glowing utterances of the later prophets of Israel to the cold moralisings of Ecclesiastes is to enter upon a different and probably a later stage of Jewish thought. The writer of that book (I again avoid discussions as to date and authorship[10]) was one who had either come under the influence of Greek thought or had anticipated its workings, and the teaching of the law and the prophets of Israel is simply "conspicuous by its absence." At one time, in the wanderings of thought through which he had been led, it had seemed to him that man could not know whether the spirit of the beast went downward to the

old and the revised Lectionary, shows how readily the words of Zechariah adapted themselves, in the minds of the compilers, as they had done in those of a long *catena* of patristic interpreters, to the thoughts of Christendom as to the descent into Hades.

(10) I may perhaps venture to refer to my own *Commentary on Ecclesiastes* for what seems to me the true solution of the problems presented by that marvellous book.

earth and the spirit of the man went upwards (Eccles. iii. 21). Life appeared to him so full of misery, of "vanity and feeding upon wind,"[1] with so little of hope beyond it, that he thought it would have been better to have been as "an untimely birth," never to have been at all, or to have passed back into nothingness without tasting of the experiences of life (Eccles. iv. 1—3; vi. 3). At last it would seem that experience taught him a truer lesson which was worth living for. The spirit should "return to God who gave it," and He would bring "every secret work to judgment, whether it were good or evil" (Eccles. xii. 7, 14). To "fear Him and keep His commandments" was after all the whole duty, the whole work and wisdom, of man in his sojourn upon earth (Eccles. xii. 13).

The development of the germs of truth which had been thus scattered upon the field of Jewish thought is to be traced partly in the books of the Apocrypha, which represent in the nature of the case, as being written in Greek, the belief of the Hellenistic Jews in Alexandria and elsewhere, and partly in the traditions of the Mishna and the Gemara, which represent that of the Jews of Palestine and Babylon. Beginning with the former, we note in the Wisdom of Solomon, probably written within half a century of the Christian era, possibly the work of Apollos[2] in the earlier

(1) I adopt this as the right rendering of what the A. V. gives as "vanity and vexation of spirit."

(2) See Deane's *Book of Wisdom*, *Introduction*, and two papers on

stages of his spiritual growth, we note a vehement protest against the scepticism which taught that man's life was limited to the years which he passed on earth, that it was a vapour that melted into air, or as the flight of a bird that leaves no trace behind it (Wisd. i. 1—5; v. 9—14). The writer has no doubt that the ungodly who thus reason not aright (Wisd. ii. 1) shall one day look upon the righteous whom they had mocked and scorned, and see that they were in the hand of God, and that no torment should touch them, crowned with a diadem of glory, at rest for evermore (Wisd. iii. 1—9). The teaching of the son of Sirach, on the other hand, seems to ignore that future judgment and to confine its appeal to men's hopes and fears, to the consequences of their conduct as affecting their happiness on earth. With the exception of one obscure passage (Ecclus. xlviii. 11), the whole tone is that of one who sees in death the limit of man's existence. The dead cannot give thanks (Ecclus. xvii. 21—28); the perpetuity of fame takes the place of personal immortality (Ecclus. xliv. 14, 15). Death is said to be bitter to the prosperous, acceptable to the needy (Ecclus. xli. 1, 2), without a word as to that which comes after death. The struggle with the idolatry of Syria, recorded in the books of the Maccabees, and the readiness of men to face tortures and death rather than apostatise, called forth the belief in an eternal

"The Writings of Apollos" by the present writer in the *Expositor*, vol. i., 1875.

blessedness which is almost the condition, and is certainly the natural concomitant, of the martyr spirit.[3] And with this we have the first recognition of a liturgical act which would have been impossible had not the belief in a continued life after death been firmly rooted in the minds both of priests and people. It was counted a "godly and righteous thing" to pray for the dead, and to offer sacrifices for their pardon and peace (2 Macc. xii. 41—45). They, or some of them at least, were thought of as being in a state of imperfect blessedness, in which their growth in holiness could be helped, as it had been helped on earth, by the prayers of those who loved or pitied them.[4] Not without significance also, as showing the thoughts that were working in men's minds, though clearly of post-Christian date, is the strange rhapsody that we know as the Second Book of Esdras, with its desponding pessimism as to the failure of God's purposes in the history of mankind, its lamentations over the few that should be saved, its feeling that the curse of Adam was resting on all his descendants, condemning all but an infinitely small fraction of them to an everlasting woe (2 Esdr. vii., viii.).

The question what beliefs were current among the Jews of Palestine at or about the time of our Lord's ministry is obviously not without its bearing on His

(3) See Pusey's *What is of Faith as to Everlasting Punishment*, pp. 150—167.

(4) See the fuller discussions of the passage in Study IX. on *Prayers for the Dead.*

teaching as recorded in the Gospels. We ask, Did He sanction those beliefs wholly or in part? Did He protest against denials or errors on either side? Did He recognise popular opinions as far as they were true, and yet seek to lead those who heard Him to clearer and higher thoughts? These questions will claim an answer when we come to examine the teaching of the New Testament as to the life after death. In the meantime we can summarise what is known or inferred as to the popular eschatology.

Putting aside the Sadducees, as altogether rejecting the belief in the immortality of the soul, or removing it by their denial of the resurrection into a region of thought in which it ceased to act on the minds of men, we have to ask what was the dominant belief of the Pharisees, and of the great mass of the people who thought with them. On this point the judgment of experts differs widely. Dr. Pusey (*What is of Faith*, &c., pp. 46—102) relies chiefly on the authority of Josephus, who, himself a Pharisee, states (1) that they held that all souls were incorruptible, that the souls of good men are only removed into other bodies, but that the souls of bad men are subject to eternal punishment (*Wars*, II. viii. 14); or (2) as he puts it elsewhere, that "souls have an immortal vigour in them, and that under the earth there will be rewards and punishments according as they have lived virtuously or viciously in this life, and the latter are to be detained in an everlasting prison, but that the former shall have power to revive and live again" (*Ant.* XVIII. i. 3).

On the other hand, it has been urged by Dr. Farrar (*Mercy and Judgment,* ch. viii.) and others that the Hellenising tendencies of Josephus led him to give a classical colouring to the teaching which he had inherited from his Jewish masters; that in the spirit of a weak eclecticism he mingles with the belief of the Pharisees some elements of what he had read or heard of in the popular Platonism or Stoicism of his own time; and therefore that if we wish to ascertain what Jewish belief actually was from sources outside the writings of the New Testament, we must look not to him, but to the sayings of the great representative Rabbis which are embodied in the Talmud.

On this point the language of Dr. Deutsch, conspicuous among the Talmudic scholars of our time, is clear and strong.

"There is no everlasting damnation according to the Talmud. There is only a temporary punishment even for the worst sinners. 'Generations upon generations' shall last the damnation of idolaters, apostates, and traitors. But there is a space of 'only two fingers' breadth between hell and heaven.' The sinner has but to repent sincerely and the gates to everlasting bliss will spring open. No human being is excluded from the world to come. Every man, of whatever creed or nation, provided he be of the righteous, shall be admitted into it." (Deutsch, *Lit. Remains, Talmud,* p. 53.)

It may be questioned, however, whether this unqualified statement can be accepted in all its fulness. The classical passage of the Talmud bearing on this question is given by Dr. McCaul, from the *Rosh Hashanah,* fol. 17, 1, and is quoted also by Dr. Farrar (*Mercy and Judgment,* p. 201). "Israelites who sin with their body, and also Gentiles, descend into hell (Gehenna), and are judged there for twelve months. After the twelve months their body is consumed, and their soul is burnt, and the wind scatters them under the soles of the feet of the righteous, as it is said, 'Ye shall tread down the wicked, for they shall be ashes under the soles of your feet' (Mal. iv. 1). But heretics" (probably, *i.e.*, Christians) "and informers and Epicureans, who have denied the law or the resurrection of the dead, or who have separated from the customs of the congregation, or who have caused their fear in the land of the living, who have sinned, or caused many to sin, as Jeroboam the son of Nebat, all such go down to hell and are judged *for ever.*" (McCaul, *Old Paths,* p. 410.)

The last two words of the extract are, however, literally "for generations of generations," a phrase which Dr. McCaul takes as equivalent to endlessness, while Dr. Deutsch, with a manifest leaning to the wider hope, understands by it an undefined but still terminable duration.

It would appear from this that at least one form of

popular Rabbinic teaching taught (1) that the righteous Israelites passed into Paradise or Abraham's bosom; (2) that imperfectly righteous Israelites and Gentiles suffered for twelve months and were then annihilated; (3) that the incurably evil were punished for a period which was described by a phrase that was popularly, if not strictly, synonymous with "everlasting." As far as the Israelite was concerned, "there was for the second class the hope both of alleviation and deliverance through the *kaddisch*, or prayer for the dead, which was to be said by the son or other relative of the deceased for eleven months after his death." (McCaul, *Old Paths*, pp. 409, 411). The general tendency of modern Jewish thought, as shown in the numerous extracts given by Dr. Farrar (*Mercy and Judgment*, pp. 203—212), shows something like a *consensus* against the doctrine of endless punishments, some writers accepting the theory of annihilation and others that of restoration after punishment has done its purifying work. On the other hand, Dr. Pusey contends that the view as to the limit of twelve months' Gehenna for the intermediate class of sinful Israelites and Gentiles was a new speculation, originating circ. A.D. 90 in the teaching of Rabbi Akiba (*What is of Faith*, pp. 76, 83), but fails, as it seems to me, to show that it actually was so. (See Farrar's *Mercy and Judgment*, pp. 212, 213.) The most recent writer on the subject, Dr. A. Edersheim (*Life and Times of Jesus*, ii., App. xix. pp. 788—793), occupies an intermediate position between the two theologians just named. He holds that the teaching of the passage of the *Rosh Hashanah* given above represents, not the new speculations of Akiba at the close of the first century, but the traditional belief of the schools of Shammai and Hillel before the time of our Lord; the former inclining more to a purgatorial theory for the not incurable wicked, who are not "written and sealed for Gehenna, but go down and moan, and come up again," the latter to annihilation. Dr. Edersheim (ii. p. 789) inclines accordingly to the conclusion "that the doctrine of the eternity of punishments" (in the case of *some*) "seems to have been held by the synagogue during the whole of the first century of our era." In proof of this, in addition to the passage just referred to, he quotes a passage of singular and sad pathos from the treatise *Beracoth*, fol. 82, &c., which I give in a somewhat fuller form than he gives it, from Lightfoot. (*Cent. Chorogr.* chap. xv.). Johanan ben Zaccai, one of the masters of Israel in the first century of the Christian era, president of the Great Synagogue after its removal to Jamnia, was, it is there stated, on his death-bed, surrounded by his disciples, and they noticed that he wept bitterly. They asked him, "Whence these tears?" and he made answer, "If I were going to appear before a king of flesh and blood, he is one who to-day is and to-morrow is in the grave; if he were wroth with me, his wrath is not eternal; if he were to cast me into chains, those chains are not for ever; if he slay me, that death is not eternal. I might soothe him with words or appease him with a gift. But they are about to bring me before the King of kings, the Lord, the Holy and Blessed One, who liveth and abideth for ever. And if He is wroth with me, His wrath is eternal; and if He bind, His bonds are eternal; if He slay, it is eternal death; and Him I cannot soothe with words or appease with gifts. And beside all this there are before me two paths, one to Paradise and the other to Gehenna, and I know not in which they are about to lead me. How can I do aught else but weep?" Whatever questions may be raised as to the precise force of the Hebrew words here translated "eternal," the whole tone of the passage seems to me to confirm Dr. Edersheim's conclusions, that the dying man who thus spoke was contemplating as possible a punishment to which he saw no end. I am unable accordingly to accept the doctrine of Dr. Deutsch, or of the minimising, liberalising school of modern Jewish scholars whom Dr. Farrar cites, and think that the evidence points to the conclusions that then, in the time of our Lord, as in earlier and later periods, among heathen and Christian thinkers, there were current among men opinions of very varied character, that those who listened to His teaching were familiar with the thoughts of a blessedness which endured for ever, of a penalty to which there might be an end for some and not for others, of a process of suffering which might end in annihilation or in the restoration of the soul that suffered, and in which it might be helped by the prayers of those that yet remained on earth.

It remains for us to see how the teaching of our Lord bore on the thoughts that were thus floating in men's minds, what developments of that teaching belong to the period in which the Church was still under the guidance of the apostles, what, in other words, is the eschatology of the New Testament.

II.

THE TEACHING OF THE NEW TESTAMENT AS TO THE LIFE AFTER DEATH.

WE have seen that the beliefs that were floating in Palestine at the time when our Lord began His ministry included well-nigh every variety of speculation. There was the denial or the scepticism of the Sadducee; there were the thoughts of a temporary or an indefinitely permanent Gehenna; of a Paradise to which there was absolutely no end; of the ultimate destruction of the evil-doer. We can easily understand how men would tend to choose the view which most fell in with their indolence or their pride, or tolerance of evil, or their love of God and man, how hazy and indistinct and inoperative each and all of the opinions would prove in leading men to holiness. What we note in the teaching of the Christ is that it leads to a Truth which was above them all; that it adopts, for those who were in the earlier stages of spiritual education, the familiar imagery and the well-known phrases; that for those who were at last able to bear it, it lifts up a corner of the veil, and shows the eternal realities that lie below the phrases and the imagery. It does not call on men to love virtue and holiness for their own exceeding beauty, to find in doing good its own exceeding great rewards. The history of the Sadducees, who started from the saying of Antigonus of Socho, "Be not like servants who serve their master for the sake of receiving a reward" (*Pirke Aboth*, c. 1), had shown what that attempt to eliminate hope and fear from the motives of righteous action might lead to; how it might stiffen into intellectual haughtiness, and become the creed of a rich and luxurious aristocracy (Joseph. *Ant.* xiii. 10, 6), and issue in the denial of immortality, and have as its practical outcome a ruthless severity of judgment (Joseph. *Wars*, v. 8, 14), substituting the terrors of immediate punishment at the hands of men for the fear that went beyond this life into the world to come. The ever-recurring assurance of the teaching of the Christ is that there is a "great reward" for those who continue patient and persevering in well-doing (Matt. v. 12); that the least act of loving-kindness shall not lose its "reward" (Matt. x. 41, 42; Mark ix. 41). The labourers in the vineyard receive their appointed wage (Matt. xx. 1—16). The servant who is faithful in a very little shall be made ruler over ten cities (Luke xix. 17). The twelve apostles are to sit on thrones judging the twelve tribes of Israel (Matt. xix. 28). And, on the other hand, the punishments of the future are held forth to men with a new and awful emphasis. There is the Gehenna of the fire which is not quenched, and the worm that dieth not (Matt. v. 22; Mark ix. 43—48). The æonian life had, as its counterpart, the æonian punishment (Matt. xxv. 41—46). For those who are counted unworthy of the wedding feast of the great King, there is the "outer darkness, where there is wailing and gnashing of teeth" (Matt. xxii. 13). There is a sin which hath never forgiveness, neither in this world nor in the world to come (Matt. xii. 31). All that men had heard of the terrors of the Lord from the schools of Shammai or of Hillel is reiterated with a new authority. It must be admitted that the teaching of the gospel sanctions the appeal to the fear of hell, even in the form from which we often shrink as too strong and coarse for the refinements of a later age. It was true then, as it has been since, that that fear might be the first step to the eternal life; that the baser elements of the fear that "brings with it chastisement." (1 John iv. 18) might be left to do their work, and pass, as the man advanced in holiness, to the love that casteth out fear.[1] The preaching of Mendicant Friars, of Jesuit Missioners, of Anglican Revivalists, of Wesley and Whitfield, of the Salvation Army, so far as it is addressed to those who are in the same spiritual state as those who listened to our Lord, may legitimately appeal to the sanction of His authority. They cannot be altogether wrong if they speak now as He spake of old.

(1) See Pusey, *Sermon on Everlasting Punishment*; and A Kempis, *Imitation of Christ.*

But then it must be remembered, also, that He recognised another of the beliefs which were, as we have seen, accepted by those to whom He spoke. When He told them of the prison from which a man should not escape till "he had paid the uttermost farthing" (Matt. v. 26; xviii. 34); of the servant who knew not his lord's will, and should be beaten with "few stripes" (Luke xii. 48); of the "more tolerable" penalty for Tyre and Sidon, for Sodom and Gomorrah (Matt. xi. 21; Luke x. 13); of all sin and wickedness but one being forgiven, either in this world or in the world to come (Matt. xii. 31, 32), His words could not fail to seem to those who heard them to be almost an echo of those which taught that some souls might descend into Gehenna, and remain there for a time mourning for their evil deeds, and then rise up again. Even the parable in which the terrors of the unseen world were set forth in the most appalling vividness, represented the sufferer as having at last learnt to care, more than he had done in his lifetime, for the welfare of others, of the father of the faithful still recognising the sufferer in Hades as his son (Luke xvi. 25—28). To those

(2) It would, of course, be an easy task to bring together from Protestant or even Romanist commentaries, interpretations of these texts, which exclude the idea of terminable and corrective punishments. I confess that they seem to me, for the most part, non-natural interpretations, ignoring the historical conditions of a true exegesis, such as no one would adopt except for the sake of maintaining a preconceived hypothesis. The more natural and reasonable interpretation has, I need scarcely say, abundant support in the writings of many of the Fathers and the best among modern Lutheran theologians.

who were familiar with the thought that there was a curable as well as an incurable evil, there must have been something suggestive in the fact that the word which He chose (*kolasis*) even for the æonian punishment was one which carried with it, strictly interpreted, the thought that it was inflicted for the sake of the sufferer, and not merely to work out the retribution, however righteous, awarded by the Avenger.[3]

And with this we must remember there was the fullest setting forth of the mind of the Father as one of absolute love as well as righteousness. It was not His will that one of the little ones should perish (Matt. xviii. 14). He had not sent His Son to judge the world primarily or exclusively, though all judgment was committed to him; but that the world —the evil world lying in wickedness, living and moving, as it were, in the sphere of the Evil One— might through Him be saved (John iii. 17). He taught men the truth afterwards proclaimed by St. Peter (Acts x. 34, 35), and St. Paul (Rom. x. 12; iii. 29), that the barriers of race and nationality were broken down. As the Baptist had declared that God was able of the very stones to raise up children unto Abraham (Matt. iii. 9), so He proclaimed that many should come from the east and from the west, and should sit down with Abraham

(3) The definition thus given of the word used in Matt. xxv. 46, is found in Aristotle (*Rhet.* i. 10, 31) and is significantly quoted by Bengel in his note on this passage. It is also used in 1 John iv. 18, where the A.V. has "torment."

and Isaac and Jacob in the Kingdom of God (Matt. viii. 11). In His Father's house there were many "mansions" (John xiv. 2), many dwelling-places for repose and rest; and He was about to go and prepare a place for His disciples. He had come to give His life a "ransom for many" (Mark x. 45); and the "many" was to develop, even if at the time it did not absolutely imply the wider significance, into "all" (1 Tim. ii. 6). Even the abasement of those who came seeking in their pride the chief places in the Kingdom did not, in the feasts of Heaven any more than in the feasts of earth, necessarily imply exclusion from it (Luke xiv. 9). The lowest place, and the shame and humiliation of accepting it, might be for such persons the beginning of better things. The labourers in the vineyard who did their work, and bore the burden and heat of the day, did not altogether lose their reward because they murmured against the larger generosity, the considerate equity, of the lord of the vineyard (Matt. xx. 13, 14). The elder son, who murmured, in like manner, at the welcome given to the repentant prodigal, was not therefore shut out from the father's house, but was reminded, rather, that he was ever with that father, and that he had, and might, if he would, evermore enjoy, his full share of the inheritance (Luke xv. 31). It is not said even of the foolish virgins, or of the man that had not on a wedding garment, that the door which was shut upon them would never again be opened, and that they were to be left for ever in the outer darkness.

The terms of the parable would be satisfied by their exclusion from the joy and triumph symbolised by the first resurrection of Rev. xx. 6. If admitted at all, it must be after a long discipline of suffering, and under the eternal conditions that there must be the wedding garment and the burning lamp; that there is no Heaven possible without holiness. We may admit that the drift of the whole teaching is to lead men to contemplate the exclusion as something infinitely terrible, but the glimpses given elsewhere of the miracles of the divine mercy lead us to think it at least possible that the sentence may not be irrevocable. If it be so, it must be because the absence of the wedding garment, the failure to keep the lamp burning, is, though different in form, yet identical in essence with the blasphemy against the Holy Spirit, which has never forgiveness, and implies the induration of heart which makes repentance impossible, and therefore excludes forgiveness. And of that conclusion it is at least true to say that it is not the inference which naturally suggests itself to the interpreter of either of the parables.

But there came a time in our Lord's teaching when He spoke to men no more in parables and proverbs, but began at least—for even then they were not able to bear more than the beginning—to show them plainly of the Father (John xvi. 12, 25). Now for the first time they heard what that eternal life was which had been shadowed forth under such varied imagery, and learnt that "this was life eternal, to know the only true God, and Jesus Christ, whom He had sent" (John xvii. 3). It was at least the natural inference from this that the eternal punishment, the Gehenna, the fire, the worm, the darkness, were all of them figures of the truth, symbols of the state in which the soul knows not God, or knows Him only as one with whom it has no element of life in common. At the same period the universality of His work assumes a new prominence in His teaching, and He tells His disciples that "if He be lifted up He will draw all men unto Him" (John xii. 32). It is true that to this period there also belongs, with a new prominence, the idea of an election which gives a special priority of privilege to those on whom the choice of the divine good-pleasure rests, and who, if they are faithful to that election, stand out as the "few" in contrast with the "many" that are "called" (Matt. xx. 16; xxii. 14). The fall of Judas showed that that election did not in itself insure the certainty of salvation (John vi. 70; Matt. xix. 2, 8). It would have been good for him by whom the Son of Man was betrayed if he had never been born (Matt. xxvi. 24). But the very form of that condemnation suggests the thought that such a case stood out as in a solitary horror of great darkness, that for others who were not among the elect, existence might still be better than annihilation. In any case speculations as to the number of the saved were deliberately discouraged, and men were told to concentrate their efforts on bringing themselves within the number (Luke xiii. 23). Those who had no the blessing of that prerogative might yet be brought within the covenant of grace at some later date, and though they seemed to be, or actually were, among the sheep that were lost, might be brought, through the instrumentality of the elect, and, as it were, for the elect's sake, within the one flock, under the one great Shepherd, who came to seek and to save that which was lost (John x. 16; Matt. xviii. 11). It is at all times true that the number of those who are in the way of salvation are few as compared with that of those who are lost out of that way; but each member of the latter company may at any moment transfer himself from the one company to the other, and the whole work of Christ and His Church is to bring about that transfer.

There remains further the element of negative evidence. Prayers for the dead were at the time of our Lord's ministry offered in every synagogue.[4] Sacrifices were offered in the Temple for those who had departed in an imperfect state of preparation. Not one word of protest is recorded as uttered by our Lord against that practice or the belief which it implied. His teaching, as we have seen, from time to time, at least falls in with that belief. He condemns other traditions of the Scribes and Pharisees, but not this. Are we to assume, looking both to the earlier and the later history of the practice, that such prayers lay altogether outside the range of His sympathy and approval?

(4) See Study IX., on *Prayers for the Dead.*

The preaching of the Apostles was naturally after the pattern of their Master's; but from the nature of the case it took a wider range, for they had to proclaim a work completed, which was before only a purpose, the manifestation of the love of the Father in the death and resurrection of the Son. They, too, call on men to flee from the wrath to come (Rom. i. 18, ii. 5; 1 Thess. i. 10; Rev. vi. 16, 17), and proclaim the dread realities of judgment (Acts xvii. 31; Rom. ii. 16; 1 Cor. iv. 5; 2 Tim. iv. 1). They persuade men, knowing all that was wrapt up in that fear of the Lord ("terror" seems a needless change from the usual rendering) which was the beginning of wisdom (2 Cor. v. 11). But side by side with this they proclaim the love of God, and call on men to love Him because He has first loved us (John iv. 10, 19). The love of Christ is to them a new constraining power (2 Cor. v. 14), and in proportion as they feel it, the mere fear of hell, though it may have done the work that it was meant to do, of startling men from the sleep of sin and leading them to repentance, drops into the background. They aim at making men perfect in the love of God that casts out fear (1 John iv. 18). The fire and the worm, the darkness and the scourge, are less prominent in their teaching,—not, however, absent (comp. 1 Cor. iii. 13; 2 Thess. i. 8)—than in that of their Master, for they have the Master Himself to make known to men, and to lift Him up, so that He may draw all men under Him; and the wrath of God against all unrighteousness is for them more terrible than all symbols of that wrath. And the Spirit, who was guiding them into all truth, led them to face the wider problems which lay, almost or altogether, outside the range of their Master's teaching during His ministry on earth. St. Paul, at least, sought, as in the Epistle to the Romans, to vindicate the ways of God to man, and to show, as prophets of old had shown as regards the history of Israel, that He had not done without cause all that He had done in the history of mankind (Ezek. xiv. 23, xviii. 25). The result of that vindication tends, to say the least, to something wider and better than the limitations of mediæval or Calvinistic theology. Of the purpose of God they have no more doubt than Ezekiel had, or than the Master had proclaimed. God willeth all men to be saved (1 Tim. ii. 4), and to come to the full knowledge of the truth (2 Tim. ii. 25, iii. 7). He is not willing that any should perish, but that all should come to repentance (2 Peter iii. 9). He is the Saviour of all men, "specially," it is added, with a significance that throws light on the whole doctrine of election, "of them that believe," of the faithful, of the baptized members of the Church of Christ (1 Tim. iv. 10). Baptism is a witness to all who receive it that they are children of light (Eph. v. 8), heirs of God and joint heirs with Christ (Rom. viii. 17), a witness of that calling (Heb. iii. 1) and election, while they on their parts are made sure and steadfast unto the end by their faith, their loyalty, their obedience (2 Peter i. 10). Men might frustrate that grace of God (2 Cor. vi. 1; Gal. ii. 21). The Apostle still reminds men, as Isaiah had done before him (Isaiah xlix. 7, 8), that now is the accepted time, now is the day of salvation (2 Cor. vi. 2). Are there any limits to that power of frustration? Is there any prospect of an ultimate triumph of light over darkness, of good over evil, of God's loving purpose over man's rebellious will? That is the question with which St. Paul grapples in the Epistle to the Romans. And the result is found in two lines of thought which we commonly associate with theological systems separated widely from each other. On the one hand, the Calvinist turns to that Epistle as giving the clearest witness to the predestinating purpose of God as the source of all salvation, of all holiness. He finds in the parable of the potter and the clay (Rom. ix. 21), that which accounts sufficiently for the vessels of honour and of dishonour being what they are. All objections on the grounds of equity are silenced by the words, "Who art thou that repliest against God? Shall the thing formed say to him that formed it, Why hast thou made me thus?" (Rom. ix. 20.) On the other hand, there are passages in the same Epistle which have appeared to many to strike the keynote of universalism, and seem to lead logically to its conclusions. The argument of the fifth chapter halts, unless we give to the assertion that "where sin abounded grace did much more abound,"—that "as by one man's disobedience many were made sinners, so by the obedience of one shall many be made righteous," a wider range of meaning than we find recognised in most commentaries (Rom. v. 15—21). The reign of sin unto death, death physical and spiritual (the latter, not the former, is prominent in the Apostle's thoughts), has been universal over the whole human race. Is the reign of grace through righteousness unto eternal life to be narrowed, as it has been narrowed in our theological systems, to an infinitesimally small fraction of it?

And so with the argument of chaps. ix.—xi. on the apparent failure of God's purpose in the election of Israel. The sovereign mastery of the potter over the clay might serve to stop the mouth of the objector, but St. Paul, following in the footsteps of Jeremiah, rests ultimately on the mind and purpose of the potter, who can remould the vessel that was marred, as it seems good to him (Jer. xviii. 4). And so he can reconcile himself to the fact of the unbelief and rejection of Israel, by the assurance that though they have stumbled, they have not fallen (Rom. xi. 11), that that, at any rate, was not the end contemplated when the stumbling-block was placed in their way. He believes that the severity of God will but prepare the way for the manifestation of His goodness (Rom. xi. 22); that the gifts and calling of God are without repentance, that God hath shut up all men in unbelief that He might have mercy upon all (Rom. xi. 32). Translated into another phraseology than that with which St. Paul was familiar, his thought seems to be that God could not manifest His perfections except through the instrumentality of free agents, such as men; that that freedom brought with it the possibility of an evil choice, that that choice being foreseen was permitted (or even pre-determined), that men might, through their knowledge of the wretchedness of alienation from God, be taught to know the blessedness of fellowship with Him; that all the miseries of the world, moral and material, visible and invisible, past, present, and to come, would be found to have subserved to that great result. In that thought he rests as in the ecstasy of doxology. ‘O the depth of the riches both of the wisdom and knowledge of God! how unsearchable are His judgments and His ways past finding out!" (Rom. xi. 33—36.) That glorious vision seems at times, as it has done with later thinkers, to absorb and monopolise the Apostle's thoughts. He sees in the reign of Christ, a reign begun with His resurrection, a work of continued victory, till all things are made subject unto Him, and beyond that, the cessation of conflict, and therefore of mediatorial sovereignty, and the time when God shall be "all in all" (1 Cor. xv. 24—28); and it is at least hard to reconcile the idea which those words suggest with the continued antagonism of rebellious wills, and the frustration of the Divine purpose. So the "mystery" or revealed secret on which he loved to dwell was that in the dispensation of the fulness of the times God would "gather together in one all things in Christ, both which are in heaven and in earth" (Eph. i. 10), that by Christ He had reconciled all things to Himself, and these "all things" are emphatically described—as before—as including the visible and the invisible universe, "whether they be things in earth or things in heaven" (Col. i. 20). That is the gospel which St. Paul has to preach to every creature under heaven, to the Gentiles whose only hope lay in the fact that they had already thus been reconciled by the finished work of Christ.

And words tending to the same conclusion are found in the writings of others. Christ had come that He might destroy (better "annul," or "bring to nought") "him that had the power of death, that is, the devil" (Heb. ii. 14). "For this purpose the Son of God was manifested that He might destroy the works of the devil" (1 John iii. 8). In the apocalyptic visions which were given to the writer of the last-cited words, he saw that, "death and hell" (Hades, not Gehenna, but the personified power of death, physical and spiritual), "were cast into the lake of fire" (Rev. xx. 14). The words of 1 Pet. iii. 18, iv. 6, which are dealt with separately in the sermon that gives its title to this volume, open a wide field of hope as to the extent and *modus operandi* of the mediatorial work of Christ. We cannot wonder that words like these should have led not a few earnest minds in every age of the Church, from Origen and Gregory of Nyssa downwards,[5] to cherish, openly or secretly,

(5) See Studies IV. and VII., on *Eschatology* and the *History of the Wider Hope.*

the belief in a universal restoration of all fallen intelligences, in the utter expurgation of every stain of evil, the silencing of every discord in the great harmony of the universe of God. But it remains true, whatever explanation may be given of the fact, that the Apostles who thus wrote, wrote also, sometimes in the closest juxtaposition with such language, words that tended to modify that hope. I do not speak only or chiefly of their language when they dwell on the judgment to come, of men giving an account of the things done in the body (2 Cor. v. 10), of tribulation and anguish coming upon every soul of man that doeth evil (Rom. ii. 5—9), of the day of judgment and perdition of ungodly men (2 Pet. iii. 7), of the flaming fire, and the æonian destruction from the presence of the Lord (2 Thess. i. 9). These are compatible with the thought of a restoration after punishment shall have done its work; or the punishment, as lying in the memory of past evil, and the shame and self-reproach which it involves, may be thought of as compatible with pardon, peace, and blessedness (Ezek. xx. 41—44). That which is more terrible than all punishment is the possibility that it may work no change for good. The natural law, to which the experience of all history bears its witness, however it may be modified by the recuperative power of the will, or spiritual renovation from without, that acts ripen into habits, and that habits mould character, and that character determines destiny, is reproclaimed as the ultimate sentence of the eternal Judge. It is not only death and hell that are cast into the lake of fire, but also with them whosoever was not found written in the book of life, in whom, *i.e.*, all capacity for spiritual life was at last extinct. From the "fearful" to the "liars" they have their portion in the lake of fire which is the second death. And for them there is the doom, terrible beyond all other terrors, that the law of continuity must be left to do its work unchecked. "He that is unjust, let him be unjust still: and he that is filthy, let him be filthy still" (Rev. xxii. 11).

I do not attempt to formulate a reconciliation of the two contrasted views which I have endeavoured to set forth faithfully, as each of them finding an adequate, or at least an apparent, support in the teaching of the New Testament. We seem landed, as in other questions, God's fore-knowledge and man's free-will, God's predestination and man's responsibility, in the paradox of seemingly contradictory conclusions. I do not say that any such reconciliation is for our faculties and under our conditions of thought, possible. We must, it may be, be content to rest in the belief that each presents a partial aspect of the truth which may one day be revealed in its completeness. We may at least tolerate, as the Church of the third and fourth centuries tolerated, those who hold either to the exclusion of the other. We may endeavour to appropriate to ourselves whatever is profitable in the way of encouragement or warning, of hope or fear, in each.

If we find ourselves face to face with two widely contrasted solutions of the great problems of God's government of the universe, for each of which there seems so strong a show of proof that it has commanded the assent of thoughtful and wise and devout students, of those who rank high among the saints of past ages or the present, while yet we find it impossible to reconcile them, we may, without blame, fall back on the thought that "the things which are impossible with men are yet possible with God" (Luke xviii. 27).[6]

(6) I gladly supplement what I have said by a reference to the sermon on *Sin and Judgment* in the volume *Human Life and its Condition*, by Dean Church, to which my attention has been called since the above was written. The whole of that sermon deserves a careful study, and it is a supreme satisfaction to me to find that the lines of thought are so closely parallel with those which I have myself been led to follow. I cannot refrain from quoting from its concluding paragraph, "We cannot tell what is between the grave and the judgment, but we know that the living God is there, very terrible, very pitiful, very just, who leads his creatures by ways they know not to the end which only He knows. We may be sure that He will set right in His own way all the inequalities of this world. We may be sure that all who seek Him in truth shall one day find Him, for He has said so. We may be sure that every one in every nation who feareth Him and worketh righteousness is accepted with Him, for His accredited Apostle has said so. Is the righteousness of God too small a thing to trust to unless we can say in detail how it is to be carried out? Are the 'multitude of His mercies,' to use a favourite phrase of the Psalms, the multitude of His mercies, to which saint and penitent must alike appeal, are they too stinted, too straitened, that we cannot commit to them all the infinite issues of human life, which move our fellow-feeling, our pity, our sympathy? Can we be so compassionate and so just, and cannot we trust Him to be so, unless He shows us how?" —Pp. 123—4.

III.

THE DESCENT INTO HELL.

I.—Historical Tradition.

THE history of the insertion of this article of the Creed presents many curious features. On the assumption that the rule of Vincent of Lerins, *Quod semper, quod ubique, quod ab omnibus,* is the measure and test of truth, it would not be difficult to construct a tolerably strong case against it. It does not appear in any of the earlier forms of the Apostle's Creed. It is not recognised in that of Nicæa either as at first drawn up in A.D. 325, or as expounded at Constantinople, or as re-affirmed at Ephesus or Chalcedon. It is wanting so far in the authority which the consent of the first four Œcumenical Councils has given to other dogmas. It was not found, in the time of Ruffinus, in the creeds either of Rome or of the Churches of the East, probably only in that of the Church of Aquileia.[1] It might even seem at first to be tainted with an heretical origin, as having made its first appearance, as part of any dogmatic formula,

(1) Ruffin., *in Symbol.*

in the Creed which was put forward by the Arian party at the Council of Ariminum.[2] (A.D. 359). For nearly three centuries more it was still in the background, not appearing in the creeds of the East, sometimes found, sometimes not found, in those of the West. When it next meets us it is in the Confessions of Faith which serve as transition steps towards the so-called Athanasian Creed, and which were published at the Fourth (A.D. 633)[3] and Seventh (A.D. 693) of the Councils of Toledo. It occurs, without an explanation, in the pseudo-Athanasian Creed. I have not shrunk from stating the facts of the case thus clearly, even though they may seem to make against the claims of this doctrine on our assent. They are instructive as reminding us that those claims do not rest on the decrees of Councils, nor even on the most ancient formularies of Christian antiquity. Members of the Church of England might view even a much stronger case with comparative equanimity. It will be enough for them to remember that they have given their assent to this as to other articles of the Faith expressly on the ground that it "may be proved by most certain warrant of Holy Writ" (*Art.* viii.).

I reserve that proof for a later stage of our inquiry.

(2) Socrates, *Hist. Eccl.* ii. 37. The words may be quoted as showing the thoughts then connected with the Article . . . . Christ is spoken of thus: "He (Christ) was crucified and died, and descended to the parts below the earth, and there fulfilled His ministry, before whom the keepers of the gates of Hades trembled."

(3) Conc. Tolet. iv. 1. Here also the same explanation is given as at Ariminum. "Descendit ad inferos, ut sanctos qui ibidem tenebantur erueret."

It may be well, meanwhile, while admitting the comparative absence of formal ecclesiastical authority for the dogma now under discussion, to collect the evidence which shows that, in spite of that absence, it yet entered into the creed of Christendom almost from the first, and was associated with the belief that it represented the continuance in the unseen world of the redeeming work that had been completed on the cross. The *consensus* of writers of different schools of thought or belonging to different Churches is in some respects even more weighty, because it represents a widely diffused belief, standing in some sense by itself, aloof from the dogmas which became matters of controversy, and were therefore formulated in more definite and authoritative statements.

The earliest distinct statement of the Descent into Hades is probably that given by Eusebius, as found by him in the public archives of Edessa, in connection with the apocryphal correspondence between Abgarus, the toparch of that city, and our Lord. Thaddæus is related to have come to that city after the Ascension, and to have preached the Gospel there. In the summary of the faith thus given we read that he told how Jesus "humbled himself, and died, and set limits to (literally *minimised*) His Godhead; and was crucified, and descended into Hades, and burst asunder the barrier that from the beginning of the world had not been burst, and brought up the dead with Him. For having descended by Himself alone, He raised up many with Him, and brought them to His Father, and then He ascended into heaven."[4]

It need hardly be said that these documents have not the slightest claim to be looked on as historical; but they were old enough at the beginning of the fourth century to be received by Eusebius, a diligent and not altogether uncritical collector of ancient documents; and we cannot assign to them a later date than the middle, perhaps the beginning, of the third century. They may therefore be received as evidence that at that period the Descent into Hades was received in the Churches of the East as a thing of course, part and parcel of the Church's creed. The letters may have been written by some over-zealous citizen of Edessa in order to exalt the glory of his native city. They were clearly not written for the purpose of introducing the Descent as a new dogma. They do not even lay special stress on it. It is simply taken for granted, mentioned because every one would expect it in what purported to be a summary of apostolic preaching.

What was thus given in meagre outline is found developed with a strange fantastic elaboration in the apocryphal Gospel of Nicodemus. As partly embodying the beliefs of an earlier time, partly impressing its own legends on the imagination and art and poetry of Christendom, it will be worth while to give a fairly full account of it. The starting point of the narrative is that two sons of Simeon (the Simeon of Luke ii.),

(4) Euseb., *Hist. Eccles.* i. 13.

Karinus and Leucius, were among those who had risen from their graves at the time of the Resurrection, and had appeared to many.[5] They tell the tale of what they had seen and heard in the world of the dead. They were with their fathers in the thick darkness, when suddenly there shone upon them a bright light as of the sun. Adam and the patriarchs and prophets exulted at its coming. Isaiah knew it to be the light that should shine upon those who sat in the region of the shadow of death. Simeon saw that it was the light to lighten the Gentiles, over which he had rejoiced in his *Nunc dimittis.* The Baptist, doing there also the work of a forerunner, came to prepare the way and to announce the coming of the Son of God. Seth narrated how Michael the Archangel had told him, as he prayed at the gates of Paradise, that one day, after five thousand five hundred years, the Son of God would come to lead his father Adam into Paradise and to the tree of mercy.

Meantime Hades (here personified as an actor in the drama) and Satan held counsel with each other, and were full of fear. He who had rescued so many of their victims upon earth, who had raised Lazarus from the grave, was now about to invade their kingdom, and to set free all who were shut up in prison, bound with the chain of their sins. And, as they spoke, there was a cry like as of thunder: "Lift up your heads, O ye gates, and be ye lift up, ye everlasting doors, and the King of Glory shall come in."

(5) Matt. xxvii. 57.

Hades sought in vain to close the gates and to set fast the bars. David and Isaiah uttered aloud the prophecies in which they had foretold this victory. Death and Hades trembled, and owned themselves conquered. They saw that One had come to set free those who were fast bound with the evil of their nature, to shed light on those who were blinded with the thick darkness of their sins. Hades and Satan wearied themselves in vain murmurs and recriminations. Adam and his children were rescued from the power of Hades; Satan and his hosts were left to take their place. Then the Lord stretched forth His hand and said, "Come unto me, all my saints who have my image and similitude." Adam and the saints rose up from Hades with psalms of jubilant thanksgiving; prophets burst out into cries of joy. Michael the Archangel led them all within the gates of Paradise. There they were met by Enoch and Elijah, who had not tasted death, and were kept there till they should return to earth before the coming of Antichrist. There, too, was the repentant robber, bearing on his shoulders the cross to which he owed his entrance within the gates. The cross on which the redemption of mankind had been achieved was left, according to another version of the legend, in Hades itself, as a perpetual witness of the victory thus gained, that the ministers of Death and Hades might not have power to retain any one whom the Lord had pardoned. (*Evang. Nicod.* Part II.)

All this is, of course, wildly fantastic; the play of an over-luxuriant imagination seeking to penetrate into the things behind the veil. But a *mythus* of this kind pre-supposes the existence of the belief of which it is the development, and is, therefore, so far as its date can be ascertained, an evidence as to its antiquity. In this instance the critics who have gone most deeply into the questions connected with the Apocryphal Gospels are not agreed. Thilo, who hardly discusses the origin of the Gospel in question, indicates in a single sentence his belief that it was not earlier than the fifth century.[6] M. Nicolas, in his *Etudes sur les Evangiles Apocryphes*, p. 377, pronounces more dogmatically: "La seconde partie de l'Evangile de Nicodème remonte tout au plus à la seconde moitié du quatrième siècle. Il ne saurait avoir le moindre doute sur ce point." He admits, however, the earlier existence of the belief which it represents, and is led, indeed, to fix the later date on the ground that the book embodies a fuller development of the idea than that recognised by the writers of the second century. M. Maury, in his *Nouvelles Recherches sur l'époque à laquelle a été composé l'ouvrage connu sous le titre d'évangile Nicodème*, takes substantially the same view as to the date, though differing as to the origin of the book. Tischendorf, however, whose authority as an expert must be admitted to stand higher than that of either of the two last named writers, does not hesitate to

(6) "Quo seculo vixerit ille homo, quinto an recentiori . . . . dubitationibus obnoxium est et alibi a nobis disceptabitur."—Thilo, *Cod. Apocryph. N.T.I.* p. cxix.

assign a far earlier date, and believes it to have been "derived or copied from a very ancient apocryphal Gospel of the *second* century."[7] On this assumption the antiquity of the belief which the legend presupposes is carried up to the immediately sub-Apostolic period. It is every way noteworthy that throughout the whole narrative there is no reference to the passages in the 1st Epistle of St. Peter (iii. 18—20; iv. 6), which might have seemed the most natural starting point for it. Whatever may be the right interpretation of those verses, the belief would appear to have had an existence altogether independent of them, to have entered, that is, into the circle of widely diffused dogmas, which were embraced everywhere in East and West. The legend may have given a greater prominence to the belief than it had before, may in some ways have modified men's thoughts about it, may have led to the reception of the article into the Apostles' Creed first in the Church of Aquileia, then in that of Western Africa, afterwards in that of Western Europe; but it did not create the belief. To some extent it even tended to weaken its hold on minds of a higher stamp by connecting it with so much that was puerile or fabulous. And it will be clear, as we advance, that those of this class who refer to the belief do so either in direct reference to the words of Scripture, or as having in view its primitive and more simple form, not as referring to, or quoting from, the Gospel of

(7) Tischendorf, *Evangel. Apocr.* p. lxviii.

Nicodemus. Their evidence, so far, will have the value which attaches to independent as distinct from derived testimony.

That evidence may be given without much abbreviation. It will be seen that it includes all the familiar names which meet us in all inquiries as to the Church's early faith and practice. Whatever weight attaches to the witness they bear to the truth of the Incarnation, or to the primitive doctrine of Baptism, or the Eucharist, or the authenticity of the Gospels, attaches also to this. (1) Justin accuses the Jews of having[8] mutilated a prophecy of Jeremiah's, in which the words had once stood, "The Lord God, the Holy One of Israel, remembered those His dead who slept in the dust of the grave, and descended to them to proclaim to them His salvation." (2) Irenæus twice quotes the same passage, once as from Isaiah (iii. 20, § 4), once as from Jeremiah (iv. 22, § 1), in the latter instance in direct connexion with the descent of Christ into Hades "to behold with His eyes the state of those who were resting from their labours." Elsewhere (iv. 27, § 2) he says more explicitly that the Lord "descended into the regions beneath the earth, preaching His advent there also, and the remission of sins ready for (*existentem*) those who believe in Him," and enumerates "all who had hopes towards Him, who proclaimed His advent and submitted to His dispensations" as so receiving it.

(8) *Dial. c. Tryph*, c. 72.

The chain of testimony is carried on by Clement of Alexandria with the enlargement of thought characteristic of the school of which he was the great master. Hitherto those to whom the Gospel had been preached in Hades had been the chosen people, chiefly the saints, martyrs, prophets of the Old Testament. The words of St. Peter had not been quoted by earlier writers in connexion with the traditional belief. From Clement's point of view Heathens as well as Jews were sharers in the benefits of that revelation of Christ to the souls in Hades. If the former were as "those in bonds" to the burden of the law, the latter were as "those in darkness," and to both alike, as in Isaiah (xlix. 9), had the call been given to come forth and show themselves. They, too, repented when the truth was revealed to them, as did the "spirits in prison" to whom the Lord preached His Gospel. His own belief is that they heard the voice of the Redeemer; but if it were otherwise and He had preached to the Hebrews only, then he follows Hermas in believing that the Apostles, when they fell asleep, became fellow-workers with their Master in the unseen world and proclaimed their glad tidings to the Heathen.[9] That proclamation involved the offer of salvation, the possibility of repentance, the forgiveness of all sins that a man had committed in ignorance, not clearly knowing God.

(9) The passage from the *Shepherd* of Hermas was clearly a favourite one with Clement. He had already quoted it *in extenso* in *Strom.* ii. 9, p. 452, Pott., as showing that the goodness of God was extended to Jew and Gentile alike.

The instance referred to by St. Peter was but an example of a wide, far reaching law.[10] He draws from it inferences as to the purpose and nature of the punishments of the world to come which will meet us at a later stage of our inquiry.

Origen follows, as might be expected, in the footsteps of his master. Here, as in regard to other doctrines, Celsus becomes a witness to the antiquity and catholicity of the belief which he attacks. "You will not surely say," he asks scoffingly, "that Christ when He failed to persuade the living went down to Hades to persuade those who dwell there?" Origen meets the question without hesitation: "We say, whether it pleases him or no, that His . . . . soul, stript of the body, did there hold converse with other souls that were in like manner stript, that He might there convert those who were capable of instruction, or were otherwise in ways known to Him fit for it."[1]

We should not expect to find the wisdom and largeness of the heart of the Alexandrian fathers in a writer like Tertullian, but for that very reason his testimony to the belief as having been held in the Church since the days of the Apostles is of greater value. Had it been a new belief it would have fallen under the censure of one who was, above all things, in the earlier stage of his mental history, the antagonist of innovation. What we find in him, as representing

(10) Clem. Alex., *Strom.* vi. 6, pp. 762—792. Pott.
(1) Origen *c. Celsum*, ii. 43.

the Christianity of Western Africa, is identical in substance with the legend of the Gospel of Nicodemus. "Christ," he says, "satisfied the law in this point also, and in Hades (*apud inferos*) underwent the law of human death, nor did He ascend to the heights of heaven until He descended to the lower parts of the earth, that there He might make patriarchs and prophets sharers in His life (*compotes sui*)" (*de Animâ*, c. 55). On the strength of that belief he resists the teaching of those who held that the souls of the faithful were admitted at once to the kingdom of heaven, and had written a book, *De paradiso* (not extant), to prove that all souls were kept in Hades (*apud inferos*) to the day of the Lord.

The witness of Cyril of Jerusalem has a special value as coming from one who lived in the period of the great creeds in which the article of the Descent into Hell does not appear, and who was actually present at the Second General Council, in which the Nicene Confession assumed its present form.[2] It shows that its absence was due to the fact that it was received everywhere by both parties in the great Arian struggle (as, indeed, its presence in the creed of Ariminum sufficiently shows), was in no sense touched by the controversy, and was left, therefore, to be taught

(2) It is noteworthy, in connexion with this fact, that though the article, "He descended into hell," does not appear in the Nicæno-Constantinopolitan Confession, it is distinctly mentioned in an anathema of that Council directed against those who denied that the Logos in his "reasonable soul" (ψυχῇ λογικῇ καὶ νοερᾷ) had descended into Hades (Mansi. iii. p. 565).

as resting on the oral traditions which all acknowledged. The form in which he teaches it, as part of the doctrine which all catechumens were to learn, is sufficiently interesting to be worth quoting in full :—"He (Christ) was laid truly as man in a tomb of rock, but the rocks burst asunder through fear because of Him. He descended to the regions beneath the earth, that from thence also He might redeem the just. For wouldest thou, I pray, that the living should enjoy His grace, and that, being most of them unholy; and that those who from Adam had been imprisoned longwhile should not now obtain deliverance? The prophet Esaias heralded with a loud voice so many things concerning Him, and wouldest thou not that the King should descend and rescue his herald? David was there, and Samuel, and all the Prophets, and John himself, who said by his messenger, Art thou He that should come, or do we look for another? Wouldest thou not that He should descend and rescue such as these?" [3]

He returns to the doctrine in a later lecture, in words in which we trace more distinctly the influence of the tradition embodied in the *Gospel of Nicodemus.*

"He (Christ) descended into hell alone, but ascended thence with a great company; for He went down to death, and many bodies of the saints which slept arose through Him. Death was struck with dismay on beholding a new visitant descending into Hades, not bound by the chains of that place. Wherefore.

(3) Cyril Hieros., *Catech.* iv. 8.

O ye porters of Hades, when ye saw Him, were ye scared? What unwonted fear seized you? Death fled, and his flight betrayed his cowardice. The holy prophets ran unto Him, and Moses the lawgiver, and Abraham and Isaac and Jacob; David also and Samuel, and Esaias and John the Baptist, who bore witness when he asked, Art thou He that should come, or do we look for another? All the just were ransomed whom death had devoured, for it behoved the King who had been heralded to become the redeemer of His noble heralds. Then each of the just said, O death, where is thy sting? O grave, where is thy victory? For the Conqueror hath redeemed us."[4]

I have reserved, at the cost of a deviation from a strictly chronological order, the great name of Athanasius as the last of the witnesses whom it seems necessary to quote in proof of the primitive, Catholic character of the interpretation of the words of the Creed which I am seeking to maintain. Here, too, it will be remembered the circumstances of the case are peculiar. The Arians had given a new prominence to that interpretation in the Confession at Ariminum. Had it been in any sense a novelty, had it seemed to him in any degree doubtful, it would have been natural for him to have entered a protest against it. How does he actually treat it? He, too, thinks of the warders of the gates of Hell, as having "cowered in fear at the pre-

(4) Cyril Hieros., *Catech.* xiv. 9, 10.

sence of the Lord."[5] He quotes the words, "He descended into Hades," as though it were a truth familiar to all Christians.[6] He speaks of the soul of Christ as having travelled the path which we travel, and so loosened the bonds that held us fast, and calls this the great wonder of His death.[7] With a true Alexandrian width of thought he stretches the circle of those whom Christ thus delivered beyond the narrow circle of patriarchs and prophets named in the Gospel of Nicodemus, and thinks of "the soul of Adam" as held fast under sentence of death, and crying to his Lord evermore, and of those who had pleased God, and had been justified by the law of nature, as mourning and crying with him" till the mercy of God revealed to them the mystery of redemption.[8] With as distinct a reference to the earlier tradition as we have seen in Cyril, he urges that the soul of Christ was thought by Death to be a human soul, that He had come with a soul which could not be kept in bonds, to burst the bonds of those who were so kept, and give them a perfect freedom.[9] And he connects it, lastly, without any hesitation, with the "spirits in prison" of 1 Peter iii. 19.[10] So Synesius (*Hymn* ix.) speaks of Christ descending to Tartarus, where Death ruled over the myriad tribes of souls, and of Hades as shuddering at His presence.

It may fairly be contended that this aggregate of

(5) *Orat. c. Arian*, iii. p. 505. (6) *De Incarn. Christi.*
(7) *De Salutari Advent.*, i. 643. (8) *De Salut. Advent.*, c. 9.
(9) *De Incarnat.*, i. p. 626. (10) *Epist. ad Epict.*, i. 586.

evidence more than outweighs the admitted absence of the Article under discussion from any of the earlier writings of individual Fathers, or from the earlier forms of the Apostles' Creed itself. That absence gives, indeed, a new significance to its appearance when it was at last inserted. Had it been there from the first in the simple unexpanded form in which we now find it, it might have been said with some plausibility that the popular tradition was a development and after-growth, a corruption of the original dogma. As it is, the tradition is full-grown almost from the very first. When the Article appears in the Creed it comes with the well-defined significance which the tradition gives it, and is accepted on the strength of that significance.

We come now to the first serious break in the continuity of testimony, and that break is connected with the teaching of Augustine. In the earlier stages of his growth as a theologian he is, indeed, content to accept what he had received. He bears witness, at any rate, to the fact that it was received. He does not see with the clearness of the Greek fathers the distinction between Hades and Gehenna, and assumes a ludicrously false etymology of the former word (apparently from *α* privative, and ἡδὺς) "ex eo quod nihil suave habeat," identifying it with the latter.[1] But taking this view, doubting whether Hades is ever taken for anything but the place of torment, he yet admits with a "*non immerito creditur*" that the soul of Christ descended there to do a work of redemp-

(1) August., *De Genes. ad litt.* xii. 68.

tion.[2] A more elaborate discussion meets us, however, in a letter to Evodius, Bishop of Uzala, written some years after he himself became Bishop of Hippo. Evodius had written to ask his judgment as to the right interpretation of 1 Peter iii. 19, and Augustine enters elaborately into the difficulties which that passage presented.[3] "Why," he asks, "out of all the tens of thousands who had died before the coming of Christ, some at least, though heathens, penitent and believing, did He bestow the knowledge of His Gospel on those only who had perished in the flood?" He admits, however, in accordance with the Church's belief, that Christ descended into hell, and that He might have loosed the pains of some who were there bound.[4] But who were there? With a perceptible sneer at the admirers of the heathen virtues which to him were but "splendid vices," he says that he would be glad if he could think that those in whom such virtues had been found had thus been admitted to any degree of blessedness. He starts, therefore, with the idea of limitation. That Adam had been released almost the whole Church with one consent believed, and he could not bring himself to reject that belief,[5]

(2) "Et Christi quidem animam venisse usque ad ea loca, in quibus peccatores cruciantur, ut eos solveret a tormentis, quos esse solvendos occultâ nobis suâ justitiâ, non immerito creditur."—August., *De Gen. ad litt.* xii. 63.

(3) August., *Epist. ad Evod.*

(4) "Potest et sic, ut eos dolores eum solvisse credamus, quibus teneri ipse non poterat, sed quibus alii tenebantur, quos ille noverat liberandos."—*Ibid.* c. 3.

(5) "Et de illo quidem patre generis humanis, quod eum inde solverit. Ecclesia fere tota consentit, quod eam non inaniter credidisse cre-

in spite of the absence of any scriptural authority. Some, he says, added to the lists Abel, Seth, Noah, and the Patriarchs. His old difficulty about Hades returned upon him. If that were the place of torment, how could Abraham's bosom be a synonym for Paradise? If Abraham were thus blessed, how could patriarchs and prophets be worse off than he? How could those and other righteous men then receive any benefit from Christ's descent into Hades if they were already in a place of rest? Entering more directly upon the words of St. Peter, he cannot see why what was commonly believed to have been done for those of whom we speak, "who sometimes were disobedient," in the days of Noah, should not, in logical consistency, apply to all others before and after the coming of Christ, who had lived and died in a like ignorance? But then it would follow that those who had not heard, or who, hearing, had not believed, while they lived, might believe after their death, and this would, in the case of the former, weaken the appeal of the Christian preachers to the terrors of the Lord, and in that of the latter make the condition of the heathen preferable to that of Christians. It would involve, *e.g.*, the possibility of salvation without baptism, without the knowledge of what Christ had done, and this would clash with the dogma which Augustine maintained so tenaciously. He cuts the knot accordingly, which he is unable to disentangle, and pro-

dendum est; undecunque hoc credendum sit, etiamsi canonicarum scripturarum hinc expressa non proferatur auctoritas."—*Ibid.* c. 6.

pounds the theory that the words of St. Peter had nothing whatever to do with the descent of Christ into Hades, but referred to His preaching in the spirit in the days of Noah as He preached afterwards in the flesh in Galilee. Coming to this conclusion he leaves all the questions which he had started as to the descent itself unanswered. He had done his best to deprive it of its scriptural foundation, to rob it of its power to comfort, to reduce it to a formula of little meaning, and so, as Pearson has done after him, he leaves it.[6] To him the Article itself, and the thoughts which it suggested, were manifestly distasteful. Once more only (with the exception of a passing allusion in the *De Civitate Dei*, xviii. 11) does he refer to it, and then it is to place the opinion that those believed through the preaching of Christ then, who had not believed before, in his list of heresies.[7]

The general belief of Christendom, however, was but little affected by Augustine's teaching in this matter. It did not hinder his contemporary and correspondent Jerome from reproducing the old tradition in its completeness,[8] as indeed had been done by

(6) The question whether the exegesis thus given is tenable will be discussed afterwards. Here, it may be enough to note Theophylact's judgment on it as "being manifestly forced and unnatural, doing violence to the whole context."—*Comm.* in 1 Pet. *ad loc.*

(7) August., *de Hæres.* lxxix

(8) "Dominum nostrum Jesum Christum qui ad fornacem descendit inferni, in quo clausæ et peccatorum et justorum animæ tenebantur, ut absque exustione et noxa sui, qui tenebantur inclusi, mortis vinculis liberaret."—Hieron. *in Dan.* i. 3. Comp. also *in Lament.* ii. 3 (this book is, however, of doubtful authenticity); *in Ezek.* c. 12; *in Oseam*, c. 13.

Augustine's master, Ambrose.[9] Cyril of Alexandria, true in this respect to the traditions of his Church, in spite of his general antagonism to the school of Origen, commits himself to the view which Augustine condemned as heretical, and speaks of Christ as having by His descent "spoiled Hades utterly, and thrown open to the spirits of those that slept the gates that none may escape from, and leaving the devil there in his solitude and desolation rose again."[10] To him this "preaching to the spirits in prison" appeared (he quotes the very words of St. Peter) as the fullest of all proofs of Christ's love for mankind at large (φιλανθρωπία); that He not only delivered those that were still living upon the earth, but, "as it is written, proclaimed forgiveness to those who had already passed away and were dwelling in the depths of the earth in darkness."[1] The Article of the Creed which came into it, as we have seen, weighted, so to speak, with the tradition in its fullest form, was received more and more universally. The great Creed-hymn of Western Christendom reproduced it when it spoke of Christ as having "overcome the sharpness of death and opened the kingdom of Heaven to all believers." It appeared among the earliest subjects of Christian art, and fur-

(9) "Expers peccati Christus, cum ad Tartari ima descendens seras inferni januasque confringens, vinctas peccato animas, mortis dominatione destructâ, e diaboli faucibus revocavit ad vitam."—Ambros., *de Mysterio Paschæ*, c. 4.

(10) Cyril Alex., *Hom. Pasch.* 7.

(1) Cyril Alex., *in Joann.* xv . 16.

nished subjects for the pencil of Fra Angelico and Sodoma and Simon Memmi. Under the title of the Harrowing of Hell, it was the favourite theme of the writers of Mysteries in the mediæval period of the literature of our country. It appeared, as might be expected, in the great *Divina Commedia*[2] that embodied all the traditional beliefs of Christendom. It was the dominant theory of the great scholastic writers,[3] modified in some respects by the limitations which were mainly traceable to the influence of Augustine on the one hand, and by the fully-developed theory of purgatory on the other.

The intellectual movement which we speak of as the Reformation affected the thoughts of men on this subject as on others. They looked on the popular belief as traditional, not scriptural, they wished to wrest out of the hands of their opponents a belief which seemed to them to give some support to the Romish theory of purgatory, and to the practices which grew out of it. They did not dare to reject an article of the Creed. Those who did not like the associations with which it came to them had to find

(2) *Inferno*, iv. 52—63.

(3) The conclusions of Aquinas (*Summ. Theol.* P. III. *qu.* lii.) are that Christ descended to the place of torments (*ad infernum damnatorum*) as well as to Hades. It was not, however, a local descent, but that of a presence by energy and effect; "hoc modo Christus in quemlibet inferorum descendit; aliter tamen et aliter; nam in infernum damnatorum habuit hunc effectum quod descendens ad inferos, eos de suâ incredulitate et malitiâ confutavit; illis vero qui detinebantur in purgatorio spem gloriæ consequendæ dedit; sanctis autem patribus, qui pro solo peccato originali detinebantur in inferno, lumen æternæ gloriæ infudit."—Art. ii. 9.

an explanation which should be free from them. The catechism of Geneva taught, in defiance of all tradition, that the descent into Hades meant only the "terrible anguish" (*horribiles angustiæ*) with which the soul of Christ was tried.[4] The same view is taken in that of the Church of the Palatinate. The catechumen is taught to say, in answer to the question why has Christ descended into Hell, that it was in order that the Christian, in all his mental and spiritual agonies, might know that there was One who had borne them and could sympathise with him. In most of the Catechisms or Confessions of the Reformed Church the descent is simply ignored. Luther, on the other hand, truer to the historical tradition, holds that the purpose of the descent was "to lay the devil in chains."[5] The history of these conflicting views is written in the dogmatic formularies of the Church of England. In the Forty-two Articles of 1553 the Third Article appeared in the given form on p. 6. The exegesis thus given of the passage upon which, rather than on any other, the doctrine is made to rest is, it may be remarked, more memorable as coming after Calvin's view had become widely known among, and received by many, of the divines of the English Church. As it was, it gave rise to hot discussions, some holding that view, others that of the Early Church, some even dwelling on the fact of its late insertion in the Creeds, as though they would

(4) Niemeyer, *Collect. Confession.* p. 122.
(5) Luther, *Table Talk*, ccvi.

willingly be rid of it, and in consequence of these disputes it was thought wiser to omit the reference in the Thirty-nine Articles of 1563.[6] The controversy continued, however, for some time afterwards, and was fruitful in sermons and treatises on both sides. Since that date it may be admitted freely that the leading theologians of the English Church, in dealing with this, the Article of the Creed, have either adopted the views of Calvin, or have contented themselves with accepting the belief in the Descent without defining anything as to its purpose or result, that the dominant exegesis of 1 Peter iii. 19, among the English theologians of the seventeenth and eighteenth centuries has been that which disconnects it altogether from the descent into Hades.[7] It will be enough, therefore, to show that though in a minority, the patristic view has still had its witnesses among us. Most readers will, I believe, thank me for bringing under their notice one of Taylor's noblest utterances.

"But now it was that in the dark and undiscerned mansions there was a scene of the greatest joy and the greatest honour represented, which yet was known since the first falling of the morning stars. Those holy souls, whom the prophet Zechariah calls 'prisoners of hope, lying in the lake where there is no water,' that is, no constant stream of joy to refresh their present condition (yet supported with certain

(6) Hardwick, *History of the Articles*, p. 137.
(7) So Leighton, Hammond, Whitby.

showers and gracious visitations from God and illuminations of their hope), now that they saw their Redeemer come to change their condition, and to improve it into the neighbourhoods of glory and clearer revelations, must needs have the joy of intelligent and beatified understandings, of redeemed captives, of men forgiven after the sentence of death, of men satisfied after a tedious expectation, enjoying and seeing their Lord whom, for so many ages, they had expected. But the accursed spirits, seeing the darkness of their prison shine with a new light and their empire invaded, and their retirements of horror discovered, wondered how a man durst venture thither, or, if he were a God, how he should come to die."[8]

Not less memorable in its way is Bishop Horsley's well-known sermon on 1 Peter iii. 19 (*Works*, i. p. 410). He adopts without reserve the patristic interpretation, rejects Calvin's view of the descent as utterly unscriptural, identifies the "spirits in prison" with the souls in Hades, regrets the alteration of the Third Article in 1563, finds it very difficult to believe that "of the millions who died in the flood all died impenitent," holds that the beneficial proclamation of the Gospel was limited to those who repented before death, and that Christ "certainly preached neither repentance nor faith, for the preaching of either comes too late for the departed soul," and that, therefore, His purpose was rather to gladden

(8) J. Taylor, *Life and Death of the Holy Jesus*, c. xvi.

the penitent souls and give them fresh gleams of hope. He holds that this is the plain sense of the Apostle's words, "and that it is confirmed by other Scriptures that He went to that place. In that place He could not but find the souls that are in it in safe keeping; and in some way or other, it cannot but be supposed, He would hold conference with them, and a particular conference with one class might be the means, and certainly could be no obstruction to a general communication with all. If the clear assertions of Holy Writ are to be discredited on account of difficulties which may seem to the human mind to rise out of them, little will remain to be believed in revealed, or even in what is called natural, religion; we must immediately part with the doctrine of atonement, of gratuitous redemption, of justification by the influence of the Holy Spirit; we must part at once with the hope of the Resurrection."

It may be noted that Bishop Middleton, though only called on to discuss Horsley's interpretation of the τῷ πνεύματι in 1 Peter iii. 5—18,[9] goes out of his way in connexion with this sermon to speak in the most glowing terms of his various and recondite learning, and the "zeal and intrepidity which enabled him to prosecute a glorious though unpopular career in an heretical and apostate age."[10]

To the present Bishop of Winchester belongs also

(9) "In His spirit," instead of "by the Spirit," as in the Authorized Version. Middleton agrees with Horsley.

(10) Middleton. *On the Greek Article*, in *loc.*, p. 430.

the merit of having dealt with the question frankly and honestly. He gives a prominence to the patristic tradition which had not been given in any previous exposition of the Articles, accepts it as in the main true, agrees entirely with the views expressed by Horsley in his "admirable sermon," repeats and adopts his words, that "it follows not that all who perished in the flood are to perish eternally in the lake of fire;" faces, though he does not solve, the question why St. Peter names these "antediluvian penitents only," while no mention is made of the penitents of later ages, who are equally interested in these tidings. All other explanations of 1 Peter iii. 19 than that which he adopts seem to him "forced glosses," which have been devised in order to avoid, instead of fairly meeting and endeavouring to solve, an acknowledged difficulty. He speaks of Pearson as having treated the whole question "less lucidly than is his wont," and as having "in more passages than one, unless I greatly misunderstand him, contradicted himself."[1]

II. The Scriptural Foundation.

I do not purpose entering into an historical survey of the exegesis of the passages of Scripture which bear on this subject. That has been done sufficiently, though indirectly, in tracing the views which have prevailed at different times or in different schools

(1) *Exposition of the Thirty-nine Articles; Art. III. ad fin.*

within the Church of Christ. What is aimed at is to ascertain as far as possible the precise sense which the words had in the mind of the writer, what impression they must have left upon the mind of the reader. To do this, even approximately, we must endeavour to bring ourselves mentally to their position, to transport ourselves to the circle of thoughts in which they lived and moved. Jew, Heathen, Christian, were all addressed in words to which they attached a distinct meaning. "Hades" spoke to the Jew, who knew it to be the equivalent of the *Sheol* of his older Scriptures, of a state or region in which dwelt the souls of the dead. In that region there were consciousness, memory, sympathy. There was Abraham's bosom, the Paradise of God, for the good; Gehenna, with its quenchless fire, for the evil-doers. To the Greek the word would come with all the associations that had gathered round it from the days of Homer, ripened, developed, purified, as they had been by the teaching of Plato in the myths of the *Republic*, the *Phædo*, and the *Gorgias*. He, too, thought of the dwelling-place of the spirits of the dead, of Tartarus and the Elysian fields, of punishments, partly penal, partly purgatorial, some temporary, and some without end. It might be the work of the preachers of the new doctrine to confirm, correct, discard some of these thoughts, but when the word was chosen which was identified with them, and used, so to speak, without any previous *caveat*, we may be quite sure that they were, as a whole, recognised and adopted, that the word, as the current symbol of ideas, was not, and could not be, stamped with an entirely new connotation. We may be quite sure that no Jew or Greek in the apostolic age would ever have thought that the words "He descended into Hades" meant only that the body of Christ had been laid in the grave, or that His soul had suffered with an exceeding sorrow in Gethsemane and on the cross.

So far our ground is certain. But there seems reason to believe also, as concerns the belief which prevailed among the Jews whom the Apostles addressed, and which, so far as they do not protest against it, it may fairly be supposed they shared, that there was an anticipation, more or less distinct, of the work which the Messiah whom they expected was to carry to completion in that world of the souls of the dead. Thus we read that "the Son of David would pass through Hell, to redeem those who were there under condemnation;"[2] that when the condemned saw the light of the Messiah, they, prepared to receive Him, cried out, "Here is one who will redeem us out of the kingdom of darkness, as has been spoken by the prophet, 'I will deliver them from hell and redeem them from death' (Hosea xiii. 14); and as Isaiah foretold, 'The redeemed of the Lord will return, and will come with singing unto Sion.'"[3]

"What mean the words," is asked in the book last quoted, "'We rejoice over thee?'" and the answer is that they refer "to that time when the prisoners that

(2) *Emek Hamelech*, fol. 138, c. 4.
(3) *Bereshith Rabba*, Id. 24, fol 67.

are in hell (Gehenna) shall be freed and shall come forth, and the Shechinah at their head; as it is written, 'Their King shall go before them and their Lord in front of them.'"[4] We may think of these as Rabbinic dreams, the spurious aftergrowth of the later days of Judaism, but they belong to the same class of thoughts as those which are often appealed to, legitimately enough, by apologists and theologians when they show that there was a pre-existent belief in the Divine nature of the Messiah, which His own words and those of His Apostles presupposed. Whatever was said by them as to Hades or Gehenna was addressed in like manner to men in whom there was this floating, undefined expectation as to the extent of the Messiah's redeeming work. The Apostles themselves were, it is true, under a higher guidance. Partly from their Lord's lips, when He "expounded to them in all the Scriptures the things concerning Himself;" partly from the teaching of the Spirit, they were led to pass over many passages which were popularly treated as Messianic, and to select those in which, if they were not actually predictive, there was at least an unconscious prophetic foreshadowing of the Christ; but it remains true that those who listened to them or read their writings were sure to interpret them by the

(4) *Beresh. Rabba* on Gen. xliv. 18. This and the two previous quotations are taken from Nork, *Rabbinische Quellen und Parallelen*, pp. 290, 348. Schoettgen. *Hor. Hebr. de Messia*, vi. 5, quotes them, but explains them differently. He confesses, however, that it is the "Gehenna" that perplexes him. Had it been "Sheol" he would have taken the words in their natural meaning. Comp. also Eisenmenger, *Entdecktes Judenthum*, ii. 364.

light of that expectation, that the patristic, Catholic belief in the Descent into Hell was the natural, necessary development of that interpretation, just as the Gospel of Nicodemus was its mythical and fantastic after-growth.

Bearing this in mind, we have to deal (1) with St. Peter's application of the words of Psalm xvi. 8: "Thou wilt not leave my soul in hell (Hades), neither wilt thou suffer thy Holy One to see corruption."[5] The two clauses, after the law of Hebrew poetry, were parallel, but not identical. The soul was not left as a prey for Hades. It was implied that it had passed into that unseen world and sojourned there for a time. Nothing was added by the Apostle as to the purpose of that sojourning; but his words would tend to fix the fact itself in their minds, and the floating belief would suggest the associations that soon came to crystallise round it. They contained the germ of the Article in the Creed which affirmed that Christ descended into hell, though they left the truth in its mysterious simplicity.

(2.) The words spoken on the Cross to the repentant robber must have been heard by some at least of the bystanders, and must soon have become familiar to the disciples generally: "This day thou shalt be with me in Paradise."[6] They also presupposed a whole cycle of traditional associations. The dying man had asked for something which seemed to him in the near, but was actually in the distant, future: "Lord, re-

5) Acts ii. 27. (6) Luke xxiii. 43.

member me when thou comest in Thy kingdom." His prayer is answered, and the answer contains the words which met the simplest, most childlike thoughts that then entered into the religious life of Israel. Paradise, the Garden of Eden in its transfigured and ideal form, was in the mind of every Israelite of that age a part of Sheol or Hades. The vague dimness which had shrouded their thoughts of that unseen world in an earlier time had cleared away, and now they thought of it as including the two regions of Gehenna on the one side and "Abraham's bosom," or Paradise, on the other. The imagery of the parable of the Rich Man and Lazarus reflected, we cannot doubt, the popular belief when it represented the two regions as within sight and hearing of each other. It was, then, of this Hades, including the dwelling-places both of the evil and the good, that all Jewish Christians must have thought when they heard as from St. Peter's lips that their Master had descended into it. When we remember the intimate relations which existed between St. Paul and St. Luke, so that the Gospel of the one was the foundation and the counterpart of the Epistles, and probably still more of the oral teaching, of the other, we shall have little difficulty in believing that it was prominent in his mind when he spoke of or alluded to the truth in question.

(3.) The statement in Matt. xxvii. 52, 53, that at the moment of our Lord's death "the graves were opened, and many bodies of the saints which slept arose, and came out of the graves after His resurrection, and went into the holy city and appeared to many," could not fail to exercise a great influence over the growing belief. If we receive it as historically true (and I am at present addressing myself only or chiefly to believers in the Gospels), it must have done so from the beginning. Whether we think of the "saints" as consisting of the patriarchs and prophets of the Old Testament, or of "saints" in the New Testament sense, and so of disciples of Christ, or those who looked for redemption in Jerusalem, the friends and kindred of the apostles and disciples who survived them, the fact must, on either supposition, have made a deep, indelible impression on men's minds. They must have been led by it to feel that the moment of Christ's death was one of a great change in the unseen world of the dead, and that the change was one of emancipation and deliverance; that what seemed the end of His work on earth was but the beginning of His work there. The fact itself, on this assumption, was the substratum of the legend which we have seen in the Gospel of Nicodemus. And if there should be those who, while holding generally to the historical character of the Gospels, and admitting the supernatural element in them, look on this as a mythical addition,[7] then, on that hypothesis, they must be compelled to admit the absolutely primitive character of the idea out of which the *mythos* grew. A widespread belief that was anterior to the Gospel of

(7) This seems to be the position of Meyer and other German commentators; probably, also, consciously or unconsciously, of many among ourselves.

St. Matthew, and was then embodied in it, may well claim to belong to the cycle of apostolic doctrines.

(4.) These *data* will help us in determining the fragmentary notices of the Descent into Hades which meet us in the Epistles of the New Testament. More than fragmentary notices we should not expect to find there, for those Epistles are above all things not sermons, nor systematic expositions of doctrine, nor codes of laws and rubrics, but polemical and pastoral treatises, laying stress on truths which had been attacked, on duties which were most neglected. They presuppose, accordingly, throughout, a whole cycle of familiar thoughts in doctrine, of traditional rules in practice. And it can hardly admit of a doubt that the Descent into Hades takes its place among the former. Look, for example, at the words of Eph. iv. 8, 9: "Now that He ascended, what is it but that He also descended first into the lower parts of the earth. He that descended is the same also that ascended up far above all things." On any other assumption the words are an unaccountable interruption to the train of thought in which they form so startling a parenthesis. We should have looked for a simple discussion, like that of 1 Cor. xii.—xiv., of the relative excellence of the spiritual gifts bestowed upon the Church. What leads the Apostle to the other thought of the descent? Clearly, so clearly that it may well be said to be beyond a doubt, the quotation from Psa. lxviii. 18: "Wherefore He saith, When He ascended up on high, He led captivity captive, and gave gifts unto men."[8] That "leading captivity captive" reminded him, as it would remind others, of the thoughts connected with the Descent into Hades. He pauses, that he may emphasise the fact that the Lord who thus "ascended far above all heavens" is the same also that "descended first into the regions that are below the earth."[9] He might, of course, have said 'Hades,' but the emphasis and rhythm which determine a man's choice of words alike demanded something that should contrast adequately with the words "far above all heavens," which he had in his mind, and was about to use, of the Ascension; and these he found in the words which had been used by the writers of the Old Testament as a synonyme for the unseen world, the equivalent of Sheol and Hades.[10] And he

(8) I am not now concerned with the Apostle's translation of the words, or with their primary historical meaning. It may be sufficient to note that the image which they present is that of a conqueror entering his city in kingly state, and leading the prisoners whom he has subdued as captives in his train.

(9) τὰ κατώτερα τῆς γῆς. The construction of the genitive, as dependent on the comparative, is more natural than that which would make it simply pa titive, as in our version, "the lower parts of the earth;" or simply constituting "the lower parts," *i.e.*, the earth, as contrasted with the heavens. So Meyer, Ellicott, and others.

(10) The following passages furnish a sufficient induction:—

1. Ps. lxiii. 9. "Those that seek after my soul to destroy it shall go into the *lower parts of the earth*"—manifestly equivalent to "the wicked shall be turned into Sheol," of Ps. ix. 17.
2. Isaiah xliv. 23. "Sing, O ye heavens, for the Lord hath done it; shout, ye *lower parts of the earth;* break forth into singing, ye mountains, O forest, and every tree therein;" where the order is clearly (1) the two regions that lie beyond, and (2) that which comes within the ken of human sense.
3. In Ezek. xxvi. 20; xxxi. 14, 16, 18; xxxii. 18, 24. the meaning is still less open to doubt. The phrase is used for that

speaks obviously in the tone of one who is reminding his readers of what they knew already as having formed part of his teaching. He wishes them to remember that in both regions of the unseen world there had been, and there still was, the energetic presence of the glorified Lord. He had descended and had ascended; the first, that He might lead "captivity captive;" the second, that He might "give gifts unto men," that so He might "fill all things."

(5.) Not less decisive, as read by the light thus thrown on them, are the words of Phil. ii. 9, 10: "Wherefore God also hath highly exalted Him, and hath given Him a name which is above every name, that at the name of Jesus every knee should bow, of things in heaven, and things in earth, and *things under the earth.*" Alike to those who came to the words with associations derived from the Hebrew Scriptures, and to those who had thought of Pluto as the Zeus or the Manes as the genii of the lower world,

world of the dead into which the prophet sees the kingdoms of the earth passing as their final home, as they perish and disappear, and is interchangeable with "hell" (= Sheol = Hades). It is merely idle to maintain, as men have maintained, in the face of such evidence, that the words as used by St. Paul would naturally suggest to a Hebrew or Greek reader, the thought of the habitable surface of the earth, and, therefore, that they are rightly to be referred to the "descent" of the Incarnation. It is suggestive, at all events, to note the wide *consensus* of men of different schools of thought in favour of the interpretation: all, or nearly all, the Fathers who notice the passage at all, all the great Roman Catholic, Lutheran and Anglican commentators, modern scholars as widely separated from each other as Meyer, Delitzsch, Ewald among the Germans, Ellicott, Wordsworth, and Alford among ourselves.

they would convey no other thought than that of the dwellers in Hades, the souls of the dead. If we may not say, with Estius and other Roman Catholic commentators, that those of whom the Apostle there speaks are the souls in purgatory, we must at least think of him as declaring that the sovereignty of the Redeemer would be acknowledged in that unseen world where are the souls alike of the righteous and the sinners, each in his appointed place. The only other interpretation which is even plausible, that which identifies "the things under the earth" with demons or evil spirits, is excluded (1) by the fact that the language of St. Paul represents the latter as carrying on their warfare in quite another region (Eph. ii. 2; vi. 12); and (2) that it is altogether inapplicable to the parallel classification in Rev. v. 3: "No one in heaven, nor on the earth, nor *under the earth*, could take the book and look therein."

(6.) We are now in a position to estimate the thoughts which would gather round the startling words which meet us on the threshold of the Apocalypse. The Son of Man in His glory is revealed to the vision of the Seer, and He declares as one element of His sovereignty that He has "the keys of Hades and of Death."[1] Assuming, as we now may, that the descent into Hades was already part of the received teaching of the Church, and that the words stand here in the closest possible connexion with those which speak of Our Lord's death and resurrec-

(1) Rev. i. 18.

tion ("I am He that liveth and was dead"), it is all but impossible not to believe that He speaks here as one who had passed into that world of the shadow of death, and had come forth as a conqueror, who had burst open those "gates of Hades," of which He had said that they should not prevail against His Church. In the vision of judgment which meets us towards the close of the book, the two powers, Hades and Death, half-personified (just as we find them at a later period in the Gospel of Nicodemus), appear as giving up "the dead which were in them," and as being themselves cast, their work being done and their kingdom destroyed, into the "lake of fire," which is "the second death." The interpretation of that vision does not come within the scope of the present inquiry. It will be enough to note that here also the descent into Hades, with much even of the imagery and circumstance of its traditional form, is presupposed throughout.

(7.) I have reserved to the last that which is the *locus classicus* of the inquiry, the memorable passage in 1 Peter iii. 18—20. Were it not for the tendency of superficial interpretations, which seem to avoid difficulties, to re-appear with a strange vitality after they have been again and again refuted, it might seem superfluous, after Horsley's masterly treatment of the subject, to vindicate its intimate connexion with the doctrine of the "descent into Hell." The train of thought which leads the Apostle to refer to it is, it may be admitted, at first sight far from clear; but it is clearer by far, on the assumption that this is what he has in view, than on the supposition that he is thinking of a work done by Christ as preaching in the days of Noah to the spirits that were afterwards in prison. The assignment of such a work to Him as the Christ is at all events entirely foreign to the cycle of Apostolic thought and language. Let us examine the passage on the other assumption, and see how it bears the test.

The analogy of 1 Cor. vii. 34, Col. ii. 5, as regards the use of the case, of Rom. i. 4, 1 Tim. iii. 16, as regards the antithesis between the "flesh" and "spirit" of our Lord's human nature compels us to alter the rendering of the Authorised Version. The dative is not that of the instrument in either clause, but that of "the sphere to which a general predicate is to be limited."[2] To take it as having one force in the first clause, and a different one in the second, is to do violence to the natural structure of the sentence. The authority of all the great uncial MSS., and of all recent editions, is against the insertion of the article before "spirit;" and without it, as the sentence stands, the reference of the second clause to the agency of the Holy Spirit cannot be supported.[3] We have therefore to take the words as meaning that Christ was "put to death in His flesh, but quickened,

(2) Winer's Grammar of the N.T., ed. Moulton, p. 270.

(3) Middleton, *On the Greek Article, in loc.*, p. 430. We may note the agreement of the Vulgate, "*mortificatus quidem carne, vivificatus spiritu*," and of Luther's "getödtet nach dem Fleisch, aber lebendig gemacht nach dem Geist."

endowed with a new power of life, in His spirit." They connect themselves with the death-cry on the cross, "Father, into Thy hands I commend my spirit." That moment of outward death to the body was the entrance of the spirit into a higher life. That thought is what the Apostle is anxious to impress on those who were exposed to persecution, suffering, death. Let men do their worst, if they "armed themselves with the mind of Christ," death would be to them gain, not loss, would bring with it freedom from sin and an increase of spiritual energy.[4]

He goes on to speak of the nature of that new energy. "In (not 'by') which also He went and preached to the spirits in prison." The "flesh" was placed in the tomb, but He, in that other element of His nature, went where go the "spirits" of other men. Almost as if consciously guarding against the distortions of the plain meaning of the words which take their place among the monstrosities of exegesis, St. Peter repeats the word which he uses here ("having gone") when he comes to speak in verse 22 of Christ's ascension ("having gone into heaven"); in both cases there was, as measured by his thoughts, a local motion. As in Eph. iv. 9, 10, the ascent involved a descent. And there he "preached." That word had been familiar to the Apostle's ear during his Lord's ministry on earth. It had become familiar to the Church through the oral or written narratives of the Gospel history. Taken by itself it would suggest, naturally,

(4) 1 Pet. iv. 1.

not to say inevitably, a continuance of the work that had been done on earth, a "preaching" of like nature with that which had been heard in Galilee, "Repent, for the kingdom of Heaven is at hand."[5] And to whom did He thus preach? The answer is, "to the spirits in prison," to human spirits like His own, who were in that Hades which for them was as a prison-house, in which they were in ward, awaiting a yet future judgment. So far his words were general. But he has in his mind one representative class of all those spirits of the dead to which his Lord's teaching had once and again led his thoughts (Matt. xxiv. 37; Luke xvii. 26). Never in the history of the world, as told in the Hebrew records, had there been so vast and terrible a judgment, sweeping off so many myriads, following upon such slighted "long-suffering." That, if any, was a crucial instance of the extent of the redeeming work of Christ. The whole history, as he goes on to show, was as a parable in its inner meaning. The Church of God was as the ark; the water of the flood in which the world was, as it were, born again to a new stage in its life, answered to the baptism which saves men now. Then the disobedient died, and were swept away, but the suffering once for all of Christ for sin, the just for the unjust, availed in its retrospective action to bring to God some, at least, of those who had thus disobeyed. Much more would His resurrection and ascension, after that triumph over "authorities and powers,"

(5) Matt. iv. 17.

avail to save those who suffered as He suffered, and for whom baptism was not merely the "putting away the filth of the flesh, but the *enquiry* of a good conscience after God."

It has been already shown that the traditional form of the Descent into Hades seems to have had its origin and growth entirely independent of this memorable passage, and that there is no exegetical notice of it in the earlier fathers. It is explained, however, of the Descent by Ruffinus, the first writer who gives the doctrine as part of the Apostles' Creed.[6] Augustine, as we have seen, raises the question whether it refers to the Descent at all.[7] Theophylact, the earliest commentator on the whole Epistle, is distinct and unhesitating in giving this meaning to the words, admits that the men who perished in the flood were chosen as a representative example of all who had had the light of truth in any way revealed to them, and had lived well according to their light, and rejects (as we have seen in p. 93), with something like indignation, interpretations like that suggested by Augustine as utterly at variance with the context. He is disposed, however, to recognise a twofold consequence of the "preaching" in Hades. Those who had lived spiritually were saved, those who had lived carnally were judged, at the time of the Descent.

Of later testimonies to what is here given as the

(6) Ruffin., *de Symbol* (Hieron., *Opp.* v. p. 138).
(7) Augustine, *Epist.* 99.

true interpretation of the passage I will quote but two. Others may be seen in commentaries that are in every one's hands.[8] Bishop Horsley's Sermon has already been referred to. The following passage from Luther, however, remarkable as it is, has been for the most part overlooked, and it will be well to quote it. It occurs in his *Commentary on Hosea*, a work which belongs to the latest period of his life, and is remarkable as being much more distinct and outspoken than the explanation given when he was writing of the Epistle itself. He is writing on Hosea vi. 1, and connects the "two days" there mentioned with the Descent into Hades. In this connexion he quotes 1 Peter iii. 19, and adds: "Here Peter clearly teaches not only that Christ appeared to the departed fathers and patriarchs, some of whom, without doubt, Christ, when He rose, raised with Him to eternal life, but also preached to some who in the time of Noah had not believed, and who waited for the long-suffering of God, that is, who hoped that God would not enter into so strict a judgment with all flesh, to the intent that they might acknowledge that their sins were forgiven through the sacrifice of Christ."[9]

Bengel, who quotes Luther, and prints part of the last clause in capitals, as if wishing to give a special emphasis to it, throws out, as is his wont, pregnant

(8) Alford and Wordsworth, it may be noted, are here agreed. The notes in both are admirable, that of the former a masterpiece of bold and truthful exegesis.

(9) Luther, *Opp.*, ed. 1582, vol. iv. p. 624.

hints. While holding, with Theophylact, that the effect of the preaching varied according to the moral state of those who heard it, and assuming a repentance in the last hours of life, when the ark was already built and the waters of the flood rising; he is vehement in his protest against those who wrest these words from their natural meaning, or reject the truth because it is declared here only. "Christ wrought with the living in His flesh, with the spirits in His spirit. He is mighty both among the living and the dead. There are wondrous things in that unseen world.": On 1 Peter iv. 6 he is less satisfying, and assumes, on the ground that the state of the soul is fixed at death, that the "dead" of whom St. Peter speaks are those to whom the Gospel was preached while they yet lived, but who had died. He adds, however, significantly, "As for those to whom that preaching came not in their lifetime, for them the Lord takes heed."

(8.) 1 Peter iv. 6. The connexion between the words "for this cause was the Gospel preached also to them that are dead," and that "preaching to the spirits in prison," of which the force has just been determined, is apparently so close that it is difficult to understand how any interpreters, as *e.g.* Luther and Bengel, who have seen clearly the true meaning of the one, can have failed to get into a right groove of thought in dealing with the other. We have to follow the thoughts of the Apostle, as, with that aspect of the descent into Hades present to his mind, he was led on to speak of Christ as of Him that "is ready to judge the quick and the dead." Both nouns are, as in Acts x. 42, without the article. But the thought occurs to him that there can be no judgment in harmony with the Divine justice unless there has been some knowledge, not only of the law, which is the standard by which the Judge governs his decisions, but of His mind and character. In harmony with his own teaching, he believes that there is none other name given among men whereby they must be saved, but only the name of Jesus (Acts iv. 12). Faith in the Gospel, the acceptance of the glad tidings of salvation, was for him the one condition of blessedness; the rejection of that offer of eternal life, the one ground of forfeiture. The history of Cornelius had led him to see that in every nation "he that feareth God and worketh righteousness is accepted with Him" (Acts x. 35). But the proof of that acceptance was found in the man who had thus lived according to the light within him, the Light that lighteth every man, being led on to see that the light of the world was none other than Christ Jesus. With this thought present to his mind, he is led to the conclusion that not only to those of whom he had before spoken, the "disobedient" in the days of Noah, but to the "dead" generally,[10] had the Gospel in some way or other been preached. In what way he does not think it necessary to add. He had already spoken of it with sufficient clearness as far as one great repre-

(10) νεκρόις, without the article, as in the two passages already cited.

sentative class of the "dead" were affected by it. If he now uses a more indefinite formula, it was, we may believe, because he could not limit the agencies by which that work of evangelising had been carried on. But to what end, with what intention, was that Gospel so preached to them? He gives the answer in words which remind us of the antithesis between "flesh" and "spirit" in 1 Peter iii. 18. As Christ was there said to have been "put to death in the flesh, but quickened in the spirit," so of these he says that the Gospel was preached to them "that they might be judged after the manner of men, as men, in the flesh, but live according to God, as He wills, in the spirit."[1] They, too, were to have the opportunity of being conformed to the likeness of Christ, dying as He died, and thus bearing, as He bore, the penalty of sin, that so they might be sharers in His life. The Apostle at least does not think of that preaching as being intended only or chiefly to proclaim or intensify their condemnation. For them as for the living the purpose of God was one of love. How far that purpose might there also be thwarted by man's frowardness, as it is on earth, he leaves untold, as still behind the veil.[2]

(9.) The direct evidence from Scripture closes here. It is interesting, however, to note how, as time went

(1) *κατὰ θεόν*, as in Romans viii. 27: 2 Cor. vii. 9; Eph. iv. 24.

(2) I have followed Meyer as being almost the only commentator who is bold and clear-sighted enough to give to every word its natural force, without inserting limitations, or distorting them to a meaning which they do not bear.

on, now one passage and now another seemed to fit into the doctrine thus received, and were quoted accordingly as fulfilled in it. It would be idle to contend that this was in every case the true historical meaning, but the transfer was not more violent than that of many of the texts cited in the Epistle to the Hebrews, or of others which, without that authority, are quoted by the fathers as Messianic, and have become the commonplaces of treatises and sermons. The application proves at least the strength and dominance of the ecclesiastical tradition. Their belief in this, as in other Articles of the Creed, was present with them as they read every part of Scripture, and they found there what they sought. The cry, "Lift up your heads, O ye gates, and be ye lift up, ye everlasting doors," had been spoken to the gates of Hades.[3] Isaiah's prophecy of Cyrus, "I will break in pieces the gates of brass, and cut in sunder the bars of iron: and I will give thee the treasures of darkness and hidden riches of secret places," was fulfilled in the yet greater "Anointed" of the Lord, who had burst those gates of Hades and had rescued the great treasures of the human race. In the cries of the Psalmist, "When wilt thou comfort me?" "Bring my soul out of prison,"[4] they heard the echoes of the prayers of the saints who were resting in Hades. The words of Zechariah, "By the blood of the covenant I have sent forth thy prisoners out of

(3) Ps. xxiv. Epiphan. *in loc.*

(4) Hilar., *Tract. in Ps.* cxix. 82; cxlii. 7.

the pit wherein is no water,"[5] calling on "the prisoners of hope" to "turn to the stronghold," were applied to that proclamation of the Conqueror in the prison-house of Hades.

(5) Zech. ix. 11, 12. The choice of this chapter as the First Lesson for Easter Eve in the Prayer Book is clearly a recognition of the legitimacy of such an application of the words.

NOTE.—I avail myself of the space left in this page to add one more witness from the ranks of Anglican divines, in the person of the saintly and honoured Ken. I quote from a poem, *On the Resurrection* (*Works*, i. pp. 170—172). He is speaking of the hours that followed the death upon the cross.

"Meanwhile his separate Soul to Hades flew,
The Receptacles of the Dead to view;
O'er ghastly Death his Triumph to proclaim,
And make all *Tophet* tremble at his Name."

He pictures the "radiant March" as directed in the first instance to the "infernal Arch," where the evil spirits are "restrained," and the "too late impenitent" are "reserved for judgment." But afterwards—

"Thence He to Paradise ascends direct,
Where holy souls with languors Him expect,
There saints are in the interim at rest,
Till, judgment past, they are supremely bless'd.
* * * * * *
Thither our Lord the Thief benignly brought,
Who to the saints the Crucifixion taught;
The holy souls their gracious Lord rever'd,
And He with sweet supports their languors cheer'd,
Advanced their joys to a more rapt'rous height,
And placed them nearer to the blissful sight."

Like the greater part of Ken's poetry, the lines are somewhat prosaic; but they are, I think, worth quoting, as showing that Ken was faithful in this matter, to the earlier tradition of the Church. Later on, when we come to treat of the salvation of the heathen, we shall find him bearing a witness no less distinct to the charity of the wider hope.

IV.

THE ESCHATOLOGY OF THE EARLY CHURCH.[1]

THE word *Eschatology*, of comparatively late origin in theological language, is applied to that branch of theology which deals with the ultimate destinies of mankind, with the four last things (τὰ ἔσχατα)—death and judgment, heaven and hell. Other subjects, which may be thought of as belonging to the last stage of the great drama of the world's history, presented in the apocalyptic language of Scripture with more or less clearness—such as the coming of the Antichrist, the millennial reign of Christ—are dealt with separately. In closer connexion with eschatology properly so called, lying so closely on the border-land that they naturally come within our view, are the questions as to the intermediate state of souls between death and judgment, which are dealt with under DEATH AND THE DEAD and PURGATORY. Three

(1) I have thought it due to Mr. Murray, the publisher of the *Dictionary of Christian Biography*, by whose kind permission this article is reprinted here, to let it stand in its completeness, even though some of the points on which it touches are dealt with more fully in separate studies.

distinct elements may be noted as working upon the minds of the Christian Church in the period in which their belief as to the future state of the souls of men was taking definite shape. There was (1) the teaching of the New Testament; (2) the belief inherited from Judaism ; (3) the mythical or philosophical speculations of the Greek and Roman world. A full examination of (1) lies outside our present province, but it may be noted, as in part explaining the varying phases of the Church's doctrine, that its language also seems to look in three different directions. On the one hand, stress is laid, in parables, and the interpretation of parables, on the separation between the good and the evil as the last act of the Divine Judge. The angels of judgment "sever the wicked from among the just" (Matt. xiii. 49). "The wicked go into *aeonian* punishment, the righteous into *aeonian* life" (Matt. xxv. 46). Words that express an indefinitely prolonged duration are piled one on the other as representing the result of that separation. The smoke of the torment of the lost ascendeth up for aeons of aeons (Rev. xiv. 11). Even those who hold that the finality of that judgment, or the perpetuity of the sufferings to which it leads, is not asserted in terms, must admit that it is at least a natural inference from the language in which Christ and His apostles speak of it. In reference to the intermediate state, its teaching is less definite. On the one hand, the fact that the day of judgment, when the books shall be opened and men shall be judged according to their works, is thought of as in the near or distant future (Matt. xxv. 31; 2 Cor. v. 10; Rev. xx. 12), seems to preclude the thought that an irrevocable sentence is passed at the moment of death, leaving nothing for the judge to do but to proclaim what had been already, as it were, registered in the books of God; while, on the other hand, the adoption of the Hebrew phraseology which spoke of Abraham's bosom and Paradise for the souls of the righteous, of the language of Greek thinkers as to a punishment retributive or reformatory in Hades, of departing and being with Christ, as better than the continuance of the present life (Luke xvi. 22–23; xxiii. 43; Phil. i. 23), excludes the thought of a long sleep, in which the soul is unconscious, between death and the resurrection; while this again is, in its turn, balanced by the language which speaks of death, as others spoke of it, as a sleep (1 Thess. iv. 13, 14; 1 Cor. xv. 20; Matt. xxvii. 52; John xi. 11). That the sleep was not one of unconsciousness, and that some were capable of rising to a higher stage of knowledge and holiness seemed to be implied in the statements that Christ "went and preached to the spirits in prison," and that the "Gospel was preached to the dead" (1 Pet. iii. 19; iv. 6). It cannot be wondered at that, starting from these *data*, the conclusions of Christian eschatology have, for the most part, affirmed the endlessness alike of the rewards and punishments which shall be awarded by the Judge after the resurrection; that they have looked to the intermediate state with both hope and fear; that there, if anywhere, they have seen the region in which a work of illumination and purification might be carried on behind the veil.

On the other hand, it cannot be denied that the teaching of the New Testament tends, in not a few passages, to the thought of an universal restoration. The very term "restitution of all things" (Acts iii. 21) seems to imply a return to the primeval state in which God looked on the works of His hands, and saw that it was good (Gen. i. 31) before sin and pain, evil, moral or physical, had marred its perfection. If evil in both its aspects was the devil's work, Christ came to destroy the works of the devil (Heb. ii. 14; 1 John iii. 8), and that destruction is hardly accomplished by rescuing here and there, as it were, one soul in a thousand. He is to reign, this reigning apparently being closed by the judgment, and therefore including the whole intermediate state, until He has put all enemies under his feet (1 Cor. xv. 25). And among these enemies are death and Hades (1 Cor. xv. 26, 55), which are to be cast into the lake of fire, which is the second death (Rev. xx. 14). The argument of St. Paul in the great *Theodicy* of the Epistle to the Romans halts in chap. v. if we make the ultimate result of the work of the second head of the human race narrower in its range than that of the first. "The many" who "shall be constituted righteous" are represented as corresponding with "the many" who were constituted sinners (Rom. v.

19), and the language of the previous verse shews that "the many" are equivalent to "all." The hope of St. Paul for his kinsmen that "all Israel shall be saved" (Rom. xi. 26) is not satisfied by the conversion of a few, or even of many, individual Israelites in some far-off future generation. Even those who stumbled at the rock of offence had not so stumbled as to fall irretrievably (Rom. xi. 11). All, Jews and Gentiles alike, have been concluded under unbelief that God might have mercy upon all (Rom. xi. 32). Lastly, there were not a few passages in the apostolic writings which might suggest, and, as a matter of fact, have suggested, rightly or wrongly, the idea of "destruction" in the sense of "annihilation" as the ultimate punishment of the wicked. There is the constant use of the words "destruction," and its equivalent "perdition" (ἀπώλεια); of the various forms of the cognate verbs "destroy" and "perish." There is the prominence given to the thought that life, eternal life, is represented as the gift of God (Rom. vi. 23); that unrepented sin brings the loss of that life; that the King destroys his enemies (Luke xix. 27); that the extremest penalty is described as the second death (Rev. xx. 14; xxi. 8). The language of the New Testament writers, it has been urged, does not assume, on philosophical grounds, as Plato did, the natural immortality of the soul. It speaks of God only as having immortality as belonging to His essential being (1 Tim. vi. 15); of the gospel of Christ as having brought to light, or illumined, that hope of immortality (2 Tim. i. 10). Death, which is, at least, the ever-recurring symbol of the punishment of evil, suggests the thought of the loss of conscious existence rather than of a perpetuated consciousness of misery (Gen. iii. 17; Rom. vi. 23).

It is obvious that as the language of the New Testament was, for the most part, addressed to those who had been trained in the popular beliefs of Judaism, it was likely, so far as it did not protest against them, to be interpreted by those beliefs. We have to ask, accordingly, what they were, what sense was attached in them to such terms as "death," "destruction," "Hades," "Paradise," "Gehenna." As far as one Jewish sect, that of the Sadducees, is concerned, there is no room for doubt (Matt. xxii. 23; Acts xxiii. 26). They denied the resurrection, and did not fall back, as the Greek thinker did, upon a belief in the immortality of the incorporeal souls. They confined the action of the retributive justice of God, following, as they urged, the teaching of Moses, to the rewards and punishments of the present life. With the Pharisees and the great body of the Jews of the dispersion, who attach themselves to no school or sect, the case was otherwise. They believed in a resurrection (Acts xxiii. 8), and, if we accept the statement of Josephus (*Ant.* xviii. 13), in the natural "immortal vigour" (ἴσχυς ἀθάνατος) of the soul. They spoke of the joy of Paradise, of the flames and torments of Gehenna. There is no room for doubt that they looked on the state of the dead as one capable of being influenced for good by the prayers of the living. Prayers for the dead were an established part of the ritual of the synagogue at the time of the Maccabees, and in that of the temple sacrifices were added to the prayers (2 Macc. xii. 43-45). They are apparently implied in St. Paul's prayer for Onesiphorus (2 Tim. i. 16-18). They appear in the earliest inscriptions, probably in the second century after Christ, in Jewish cemeteries (Garucci, *Cimitero degli Ebrei*). How far the Pharisaic, or the popular, belief accepted the endlessness of punishments is, from this point of view, a question of great importance. It has been broadly asserted by those who speak with the authority of experts that the Talmud is altogether silent on that point; that the punishment even of the worst sinners is, in the judgment of the Rabbis, but for a season, and that the sacrifices, or even the prayers, of the day of atonement avail to obtain pardon for those who have deserved condemnation (Deutsch, *Remains*, p. 35, and the authorities cited in Farrar's *Eternal Hope*, *Exc.* v.). It may be questioned, however, whether this is not a somewhat one-sided statement. Josephus, who, at least, represents a widely diffused form of Hellenistic Pharisaism, speaks of the Pharisees not only as holding the natural immortality of the soul, but as thinking that those who have done evil are kept in an everlasting (ἀΐδιος, not αἰώνιος), prison-house (*Ant.* xviii. 1, f. 3), and Schöttgen (*Hor. Hebr.* in Matt. xxv. 46), quotes from the Midrash on Koheleth (fol.

74), "In hoc mundo quae peccata sunt possunt reparari, sed futuro tempore quod peccatum est non potest reparari." "If a man prepares no food before the sabbath, how can he expect to share in the sabbath meal?" Taking, however, the great stream of Rabbinic traditions, as represented, *e.g.*, in Eisenmenger's *Entdecktes Judenthum* (part ii. chap. 6), it may be admitted as true that they surround the idea of Gehenna with well-nigh all imaginable alleviations. They think of the condemned as allowed to rest on sabbaths and new moons; Abraham and Moses and Elias, and the prayers of kindred and of friends have power to deliver from it; the souls that are tormented praise God in the midst of the fire for the mercy that is mingled with His judgments. Some are punished for a few days, or weeks, or years (Ugolini, *Thes.* xxx. p. 177), and when they are purified pass to Paradise. A few only, apostates and "Epicureans" (*i.e.* unbelievers in the resurrection), suffer for "many generations;" but in the end, Gehenna, which even now is separated from Paradise only as by a party-wall two hand-breadths thick, shall be itself purified and be made fit for the habitation of the blessed.

Lastly, there were the beliefs which Gentile converts, who were not deterred by physical or metaphysical difficulties from accepting the doctrine of the resurrection, would bring with them, and which were likely to modify more or less, consciously or unconsciously, their interpretation of the teaching of

Scripture. It is, of course, admitted that the cultivated intellect of the age had engendered a widely-spread scepticism as to the existence of a life after death :—

> "Esse aliquos manes et subterranea regna
> * * * *
> Vix pueri credunt." . . .
>
> Juvenal, *Sat.* ii. 149.

The hopes of Tacitus did not go beyond, "Si quis piorum manibus locus ; si, ut sapientibus placet, non cum corpore extinguuntur magnae animae," holding, as it were, an aristocracy of immortality, while the great mass of mankind slept the "eternal sleep," which is almost the stereotyped formula of Greek and Roman epitaphs (*Agric.* c. 46). Cicero, after an eloquent utterance of his hope, confesses his misgiving, "Quod si in hoc erro, quod animos hominum immortales esse credam, lubenter erro" (*de Senect.* c. 23); and though he speaks much of the glory of the just, is silent as to the punishment of evil-doers. Julius Caesar urged torture and imprisonment rather than death as a punishment for those who were traitors to the republic, on the ground that, as men looked for nothing after death, that penalty had lost its deterring power (Sallust, *Catil.* chap. 50). On the other hand, the old belief was not without its followers. The teaching of Plato in the *Phaedo*, the *Gorgias*, and the *Republic*, had been popularised by Virgil in the sixth book of the *Aeneid*, and those who accepted it thought of the unseen world as a scene partly of retribution, partly of purification. Some pass to the Elysian fields, and some are cleansed in the Stygian lake, and some are sent to Tartarus for a year, and some remain there for ever (*Phaed.* p. 113).

> . . . . "aliis sub gurgite vasto
> Infectum eluitur scelus, aut exuritur igni;
> Quisque suos patimur manes. Exinde per amplum
> Mittimur Elysium et pauci laeta arva tenemus."
> Virg., *Aen.* vi. 743–746.

The Eleusinian and other mysteries, perhaps, helped to diffuse and sustain this belief among those who were initiated, and the language of Lucretius is that of one who sees in the belief in endless punishment not an extinct superstition, but one against which the philosopher has to do vigorous and earnest battle.

> "Nam si certam finem esse viderent
> Aerumnarum homines, aliqua ratione valerent
> Religionibus atque minis obsistere vatum.
> Nunc ratio nulla est restandi, nulla facultas,
> Aeternas quoniam poenas in morte timendum." 2
> *De Nat. R.* i. 107–111.

II. It remains for us now to trace the course of Christian thought working upon these materials. For the most part it will be necessary to notice only those who held some modification of what may be

(2) The passage is not without its importance as bearing on the sense of the word "aeternus," which Latin writers accepted as the nearest equivalent of the Greek *αἰώνιος*, and which was, in fact, derived from the same root. Lucretius uses it, as Augustine does afterwards (*infra*), meaning that there is no "certa finis." Comp.

> "Temporis *aeterni* quoniam, non unius horae
> Ambigitur status."—iii. 1073

and,

> "Mors *aeterna* tamen nilo minus illa manebit."
> —iii. 1091.

recognized as historically the general belief of Christendom, that the punishment assigned to evil-doers after the resurrection will be endless as the blessedness of the righteous, or who taught that a redeeming and purifying work might be carried on in the intermediate state, giving fresh opportunities, and therefore a fresh probation to some, if not to all, who, at the time of their death, were not qualified by their faith or works for the peace and rest of God.

Of the two methods which present themselves,—that of noting chronologically the views maintained by the great fathers and teachers of the Church on the point now before us, or classifying them, still retaining as far as may be, subject to that classification, a chronological arrangement, according as they represented this or that school of thought,—the latter will be adopted, as presenting, on the whole, most advantages.

1. It would not be true to say that the theory of the annihilation of the wicked after they have endured, subsequent to the resurrection, a penalty commensurate with their guilt, is altogether without patristic authority; but Taylor's language (*Christ's Advent to Judgment*, vol. v. p. 45, ed. Heber), that it was what "the primitive doctors were willing to believe," is unduly coloured by his own manifest leaning towards that view, and his shrinking from the popular belief in equal and endless tortures for all the lost. The passages that look in that direction are, indeed, very few, and their main purpose is less

to assert the finite character of punishment than to protest against the Platonic assumption of an inherent immortality, involving, as that seemed to do, an eternal pre-existence, and a perpetual series of transmigrations. Thus Justin speaks: "Our souls are not immortal nor uncreated, yet I say not that all souls die, for that indeed would be a godsend (ἕρμαιον) to the wicked, but that those of the godly abide in a better place, and the unrighteous and evil in a worse, waiting for the time of judgment. And thus some, appearing worthy of God, die no more, and some are punished (κολάζονται) *so long as God wills them to exist and to be punished*" (*Dial. c. Tryph.* chap. 5). The words clearly admit the thought of an ultimate "ceasing to be" in the lost; but they cannot be said to do more. Elsewhere, in the same treatise (*Dial. c. Tryph.* chap. 130), he speaks, in reference to Isa. lxvi. 24, of the very bodies of sinners as consumed by the worm and the ceaseless fire, and yet remaining immortal (ἀθάνατα), and in his *Apology* he speaks freely of *αἰώνιος κόλασις* as contrasted with the thousand years of Plato (*Rep.* p. 615; *Phaedr.* p. 249; *Apol.* i. 12), of the punishment as lasting for a limitless period (ἀπέραντον αἰῶνα), (*Apol.* i. 28). What has been said of Justin holds good also of Irenaeus. He, too, speaks of life as the gift of God: "And he who shall reject life and prove himself ungrateful to his Maker . . . deprives himself of continuance for ever and ever" (ii. 34, § 3). "Good things are eternal, and without end in God, and therefore the loss of them is also eternal and never ending" (v. 27, § 2). Taken by themselves, these words, though they are compatible with, and perhaps even suggest, the thought of the annihilation of the wicked, cannot be said to affirm it. Irenaeus, like Justin, argues against the Platonic theory of the pre-existence and natural immortality of the soul. Eternal life is God's gift to those who are worthy of it, but the privation of that life may mean the loss of the blessedness of being rather than of being in itself, and his language elsewhere shews that this is what he actually did mean. "Those who fly from the eternal light of God . . . are themselves the cause of their inhabiting eternal darkness, destitute of all good things" (iv. § 39, 4). "The word of God prepares a fitting habitation for both those who seek and those who shun the light . . . for those who are in the light that they may rejoice in it, for those in darkness that they may partake in its calamities" (v. 28, § 1). So a passage in the Epistle to Diognetus (chap. 10), which speaks of the eternal fire as punishing *μέχρι τέλους*, admits of being interpreted of ultimate annihilation. Hints of the annihilation of the lost after this period are few and far between. Arnobius, however (*Dispp. adv. Gentes*, ii. 15-54) teaches that the soul has no natural immortality, and that after the resurrection souls and bodies are gradually consumed and annihilated in Gehenna.

2. The belief in a universal restoration is commonly associated with the great name of Origen. It would

be truer to say, and this was afterwards treated as the vulnerable point in his system, that he taught the perpetual freedom of the will, and therefore set no time-limits to the capacity for restoration. The fullest statement of his views is found in the treatise περὶ 'Αρχῶν, noticeable as the first attempt at the systematic and scientific treatment of theology in Christian literature. He is brought face to face with the question, What does the whole scheme of redemption issue in; what is the end and consummation of all things? He opens the subject as if half fearing the charge of heresy from prejudiced hearers, and premises that he speaks with caution, discussing rather than dogmatising. But he openly proclaims his belief that the goodness of God, when each sinner shall have received the penalty of his sins, will, through Christ, lead the whole universe to one end. This seems to him involved in the promise that all enemies shall be put under the feet of Christ (Ps. cx. 1; 1 Cor. xv. 25). The end will be like the beginning, and all shall be very good. The statement in Phil. ii. 10, that "At the name of Jesus every knee shall bow, of things in heaven and things under the earth," seems to him to involve a willing subjection, and therefore the cessation of a rebellious and resistent evil. Even the angels who kept not their first estate may, some of them at least, profit by the help of their unfallen brothers and be capable of restoration. The prayer of Christ for unity (John xvii. 21), which embraces the universe, as also does St. Paul's vision of the "perfect man" in whom all shall be united (Eph. iv. 13) will not be left unanswered. Is this hope to be extended to the devil and his angels, or has inveterate habit hardened in them into a second nature? He, for his part, will not refuse to extend the hope even to them. Aeons may pass, greater punishments may be endured; but if the will is free, any nature endowed with reason may pass from one order of being to another, each act of volition bringing with it its own punishment or reward (*De Princ.* i. chap. 6). The change, as distinct from the destruction, of the heavens or the earth (Ps. cii. 26) so that they become new (2 Peter iii. 13), witnesses for him to a like change, and not destruction, of those who are wending their way to that final blessedness. He is led to examine into the nature of the fire which tries every man's work and is the penalty of evil, and he finds it in the mind itself—in the memory of evil. The sinner's life lies before him as an open scroll, and he looks on it with shame and anguish unspeakable. The Physician of our souls can use His own processes of healing. The "outer darkness" and Paradise are but different stages in the education of the great school of souls, and their upward and onward progress depends on their purity and love of truth (*Princ.* i. 6).

The same wide hope shews itself, though less definitely, in his general method of interpretation. "He who is saved is saved as by fire, that if he has in him any mixture of lead the fire may melt it out, so that all may be made as the pure gold. The more the lead, the greater will be the burning, so that even if there be but little gold that little may be purified. If any one has come to nothing but lead then" (here he seems to tend to the annihilation theory) "there shall come to pass that which is written, and he shall 'sink as lead in the mighty waters'" (*Hom.* vi. *in Exod.*). In the legal purification after childbirth he sees an adumbration of the truth that "even after the resurrection we shall all alike need a sacrament to cleanse and purify us" (*Hom.* xiv. *in Luc.*). The fire of the last day will, it may be, be at once a punishment and a remedy, burning up the wood, hay, stubble, according to each man's merits, yet all working to the destined end of restoring man to the image of God, though, as yet, men must be treated as children, and the terrors of the judgment rather than the final restoration have to be brought before those who can be converted only by fears and threats (*Cont. Cels.* v.). Gehenna stands for the torments that cleanse the soul; but for the many who are scarcely restrained by the fears of eternal torment it is not expedient to go far into that matter, hardly indeed to commit our thoughts to writing, but to dwell on the certain and inevitable retribution for all evil (*Cont. Cels.* vi.). God is indeed a consuming fire, but that which He consumes is the evil that is in the souls of men, not the souls themselves (*ibid*). The hope of Origen colours even his view of the guilt of Judas, and he sees in his suicide the act of one who wished to meet his Master in the world of the dead, and there to implore forgiveness (*Tract.* xxxv. *in Matt.*). It is noticeable, however, that he does not there speak of the final salvation of Judas, and that his doctrine of reserve shews itself in his dwelling on the separation of the evil and good in Matt. xxv. 46 as final, without speaking of the hope of a restoration as lying beyond it in the remote future.

What Origen thus whispered, as it were, to the ear in the secret chamber was proclaimed by Gregory of Nyssa as from the housetop. His universalism is as wide and unlimited as that of Bishop Newton of Bristol. The whole course of this life was for him a discipline leading to virtue. If any one remained uncured by it, the healing process (θεραπεία) is continued in the life that follows. It may take for some sharp and severe forms, the work of the knife and cautery; for others, the work of God, restoring the creature of His hands to its original likeness, will be sufficient (*Orat. Catech.* viii.). Those who are not sharers in the purification by baptism will be purified by fire (*Orat. Catech.* xxxv.). Men are angry often with those who use severe remedies, but afterwards they thank them; and so, in like manner, when the evil now intermingled and implanted in their nature has been, after long periods of time, eradicated, and there shall be a restoration (ἀποκατάστασις) of those who are now lying in evil to their primal state, there shall be an accordant thanksgiving to God from all creation, both of those who needed and those who did not need purification (*Orat. Catech.* xxvi.). The same thought of an ἰατρεία is developed more systematically in the treatise *de Animâ et Resurrectione.* "The process of healing shall be proportioned to the measure of evil in each of us, and when the evil is purged and blotted out, there shall come in its place to each, immortality and life and honour" (vol. iii. pp. 255, 260, ed. 1637). "Now the race of man is by its evil shut out from the divine, but the barriers by which sin excludes us from that within the veil will one day be broken down, and when our nature shall be reconstructed, as in a new tabernacle (σκηνοπηχθῇ), and all the corruption that sin has brought in shall be blotted out from the universe; then shall there be the great feast of God for all whom the resurrection has brought together as His guests" (iii. p. 245). In the end there shall be one common joy for all, and those who are now through sin outside the sanctuary of the divine blessedness will then cling to the horns of the altar, *e.g.*, to the Founder of the world above (*de Animâ et Res. Opp.* ii. p. 677). It is true that he, too, speaks of punishment through aeons to which no limit can be assigned (*de Animâ et Res. Opp.* ii. p. 650), of a chastisement that shall extend through an eternal interval (εἰς αἰώνιον διάστημα); but it is clear, as indeed the last word shews, that he looks forward beyond this to the ultimate extirpation of evil and the restoration of mankind, to a time "when there shall no longer be a sinner in the universe (*in Psalm* iii. vol. ii. p. 289), and the war between good and evil shall be ended (*ibid.*), and the nature of evil shall pass into nothingness, and the divine and unmingled goodness shall embrace all intelligent existence" (vol. i. 844). What is noticeable in Gregory of Nyssa is that, in thus teaching, there is no apparent consciousness that he is deviating into the bye-paths of new and strange opinions. He claims to be taking his stand on the doctrines (*δόγματα*) of the church in thus teaching, with as much confidence as when he is expounding the mysteries of the divine nature as set forth in the creed of Nicaea (ii. p. 663). And the same absence of any sense of being even in danger of heresy is seen in most of those who followed in his footsteps or those of Origen. The *Apologia* for Origen, which was the joint work of Eusebius and Pamphilus, defends him without any hesitation. Theodore of Mopsuestia teaches that in the world to come "those who have done evil all their life long will be made worthy of the sweetness of the divine bounty. For never would Christ have said 'until thou hast paid the uttermost farthing,' unless it were possible for us to be cleansed when we have paid the penalty. Nor would He have spoken of the many stripes and few unless after men had borne the punishment of their sins they might afterwards hope for pardon." (*Fragm.* ed. Fritzche, p. 41). Even Gregory of Nazianzus, when speaking of the fire that is not quenched, throws out the thought, as though it were at least admissible, that there may be a *πῦρ φιλανθρωπότερον καὶ τοῦ κολάζοντος ἐπαξίως* ("a fire that is more beneficent belonging to Him who chastiseth according to men's deserts") (*Orat.* xl. 36). Diodorus of Tarsus taught that the penalty of sin is not perpetual, but issues in the blessedness of immortality, and was followed by Stephanus, bishop of Edessa, and Solomon of Bassora, and Isaac of Nineveh. "Even those who are tortured in Gehenna are under the discipline of the divine charity" (Assemani, *Biblioth. Orient.* iii. p. 323); and they were followed in their turn by Georgius of Arbela and Ebed Jesu of Soba (*ibid.* iv. p. 204). Timotheus II., patriarch of the Nestorians, wrote that "by the prayers of the saints the souls of sinners may pass from Gehenna to Paradise (*ibid.* iv. p. 344). Many of these teachers were, it is true, like the last-named, followers of Nestorius, and were so far not in communion with the orthodox churches of the East, but it is obvious that the special point on which Nestorius was condemned had no direct connexion with this or that form of eschatology, and that it was derived by them from those whose orthodoxy, like that of Gregory of Nyssa, was unquestioned. We have no evidence that the belief in the ἀποκατάστασις ("restitution"), which prevailed in the fourth and fifth centuries, was ever definitely condemned by any council of the church, and so far as Origen was named as coming under the church's censure it was rather as if involved in the general sentence passed upon the leaders of Nestorianism than singled out for special and characteristic errors. So the council of Constantinople, the so-called fifth general council, A.D. 553, condemns Arius, Eunomius,

Macedonius, Apollinaris, Nestorius, Eutyches, and Origen in a lump, but does not specify the errors of the last-named, as though they differed in kind from theirs; and it is not till the council of Constantinople known as *in Trullo* (A.D. 696) that we find an anathema which specifies, somewhat cloudily, the guilt of Theodore of Mopsuestia and Origen and Didymus and Evagrius, as consisting in their "inventing a mythology (*μυθοποΐα*) after the manner of the Greeks, and inventing changes and migrations for our souls and bodies, and impiously uttering drunken ravings (*ἐμπαροινήσαντας*) as to the future life of the dead" (*Conc. Quinis.* can. i.). It deserves to be noted that this ambiguous anathema pronounced by a council of no authority under the weak and vicious emperor Justinian II. is the only approach to a condemnation of the eschatology of Origen which the annals of church councils present.

So even in the West, where the harder nature of the African and the practical character of the Roman section of the Latin church made men indisposed to share in the wider sympathies and hopes of the great Alexandrian thinker, there was no formal sentence on the part of any synod, no tone of horror in the language of individual writers. Jerome, who does not accept Origen's view, speaks of it with a tolerant fairness, as though it were almost or altogether an open question: "Those who think that the punishment of the wicked will one day, after many ages, have an end, rely on these testimonies," *sc.* on Rom. xi. 25

Gal. iii. 22; Mic. vii. 9; Isa. xii. 1; Ps. xxx. 20, which he gives *in extenso.* "And this we ought to leave to the knowledge of God alone, whose torments, no less than His compassion, are in due measure, and who knows how and how long He ought to punish. This only let us say, as suiting our human frailty, 'Lord, rebuke me not in thy fury, nor chasten me in thine anger'" (Hieron. *in Esai.* lxvi. *ad fin.*). So in commenting on Isa. xxiv., "*post multos dies visitabuntur.*" "This," he says, "seems to favour those friends of mine who grant the grace of repentance to the devil and to demons after many ages, that they too shall be visited after a time." He explains the text so as to shew that it does not of necessity involve this, and then, as before, falls back upon man's ignorance. "Human frailty cannot know the judgment of God, nor venture to form an opinion of the greatness and the measure of His punishment" (Hieron. *in Esai.* xxiv.).

The drift of Augustine's mind, with his exclusion of all outside the visible church from the hope of salvation, his *levissima damnatio* for unbaptized infants, his doctrine of the divine decrees, hardly leads us to expect anything at his hands less than an absolute rejection of the Origenistic views. It deserves to be noted, however, that it was Pelagius rather than Augustine who laid stress upon the eternity of future punishment, insisted on Matt. xxv. 46 as involving its endlessness, and taunted his Catholic opponents who held a remedial discipline as applicable at least to Christians dying with an imperfect holiness, as being followers of Origen (*de Gest. Pelag.* chap. 9-11). The taunt apparently had its effect. Augustine shrank from the term "*Origenista,*" as the framers of the forty-second Article of 1552 shrank from being classed with the Anabaptists, or others, who revived Origen's wider hope in the sixteenth century, and was led to disclaim more emphatically any approach to the special view of Origen. On the other hand he continued also to assert even more definitely his own view of a purgatorial punishment for the baptized. Even in him, however, there is at times a strange absence of the horror and alarm with which the assertion of the hope of universal restoration has not unfrequently been met in later times. He admits that that view was held by "*nonnulli, imo quam plurimi,*" who were led by feelings of human pity. He does not accept it, but he allows men to believe, if they like, that there will be a *mitigatio* and *levamen* of the punishment of the lost (see *infra*). When he deals more systematically with the question it is in the same half-supercilious tone as Jerome: "We must now enter on a peaceable discussion with our compassionate friends" . . . . He names Origen as holding that even the devil and his angels would after long ages of punishment be restored to fellowship with the holy angels. On this ground, he says, and for other reasons, especially for the "unceasing alternations" of blessedness and misery which Origen's theory was supposed to have involved, the church had rightly rejected (*reprobavit*) it. He condemns two modified forms of the Origenistic view—(1) that of the universal restoration of all mankind, but not of fallen angels, or even spirits, through the goodness of God, or (2) that of a like restoration obtained by the intercessions of the saints, as inconsistently stopping short of their logical consequence. If the assumption that the divine compassion will include the whole human race be true, why should it stop short there? Those who held the latter view, and Augustine states that he had met many who held it, rested (1) on the belief that the saints in Paradise will not cease in their perfection to pray for those for whom they used to pray on earth; (2) on the words of Ps. lxxvii. 10, as in the Latin version, *Num obliviscetur misereri Deus, aut continebit in irâ suâ miserationes suas?* ("Will God forget to be gracious, and will He in anger shut up His tender mercies?"); and (3) on the fact that the history of Jonah's mission to Nineveh proved that punishments threatened in unconditional language might yet be withdrawn. He notices, further, modified forms of the wider hope which held out the promise of salvation to all who have been baptized, even though it be with heretical baptism, or to all who have received baptism in the Catholic church, even if they have fallen afterwards into heresy, or, at least to all who have kept the Catholic faith, irrespective of holiness of life, or have not failed, what ever other sins they may have committed in works of charity. He urges against all these views that the scriptural word *aeternum*, with its equivalent "*in saecula saeculorum*," can only mean "*quod finem non habet temporis*," and that it must bear the same meaning in Matt. xxv. 46, whether describing the blessedness of the righteous or the punishment of the wicked (*de Civ. Dei*, xxi. 17-27). It may be noted that in this discussion of all the views on this matter that seemed to him at variance with the language of scripture, Augustine does not even name the theory of the annihilation of the impenitent doers of evil. That view, if it had been ever really held in the Christian church, had clearly been thrown altogether into the background, and was practically nowhere. From this period, with the authority of the great African father thrown into the scale against it, the doctrine of universal restoration tended to fall into the same position, as far as the Western church was concerned, and though never formally condemned, may be said to have been virtually rejected. It was, perhaps, partly as a consequence of that rejection that the intermediate view, the history of which now remains to be traced, came into greater prominence.

3. Those who shrank from the consequences, real or supposed, of the teaching of Origen, were able to cherish the hope of an undefined though not an universal restoration, even in the case of those who departed this life in a state so imperfect that it called for punishment. As the greater includes the less, it is obvious that the followers of Origen and

Gregory of Nyssa would admit both the beliefs and the arguments of those who maintained the more moderate and cautious view. The dominant thought in the mind of these latter was that the redeeming work of Christ and the possibility of repentance, and the remedial agency of the church in her prayers and sacraments, and the sanctifying work of the Spirit, are not confined within the narrow limits of this life, but have a wide range of action in the period that lies between death and judgment. Here again it is in the church of Alexandria, as represented by Origen's master, Clement, that we find the earliest and most distinct utterances of the wider hope. He recognises that Christ preached the gospel to those in Hades, and that it brought repentance not to the souls of patriarchs and Jewish saints only, but to heathen seekers after righteousness. Then also the apostles had been fellow-workers with their Master in proportion to their likeness to Him, some working, according to the task assigned to them on earth, among the souls of the Hebrews, some among those of the Gentiles (*Strom.* vi. 44, 45). The punishments (κολάσεις) of God in Hades are remedial and reformatory (σωτήριοι καὶ παιδευτικαὶ), and lead to repentance, and this work is easier for those who are no longer hampered by the temptation of the flesh (*ibid.* chap. 46). God is all-good and all-powerful, and is able to save all who turn to Him, whether it be here or there (*ibid.* chap. 47). He quotes the apocryphal *Preaching of Peter*, as shewing that the moral government (*οἰκονομία*) of God requires that those who have had no opportunity of knowing the truth in this life should have that opportunity elsewhere, since otherwise they would have no adequate probation (*ibid.* chap. 48). He recognises in the "final conflagration" of the Stoics an anticipation of the Christian doctrine of the purification by fire of those who have lived evil lives (*ibid.* v. 9). The souls that are punished (*κολαζόμενοι*) are yet purified by the fire (*Fragm.* 14).

The wide acceptance of the gospel of Nicodemus, with its vivid pictures of the descent into Hades, and the work of deliverance accomplished there—robbing Death and Hades of all their prisoners (*Evang. Nicod.* chap. 24), wiping away these tears from all faces (*ibid.* chap. 23), rescuing those whom Satan had held bound, and placing him in chains in place of Adam and his sons (*ibid.* chap. 23)—testifies to the prevalence of the belief which Clement thus asserts; and we must not forget that when the article "He descended into hell" was received into the Apostles' Creed, in the earlier texts of which it does not appear, it came weighted, so to speak, with all the associations that had thus gathered round it. It was received because it spoke to men of the work of Christ as not limited to this world, but extending to the unseen. Even in Hades the cross had been set up as the symbol and pledge of deliverance. Even there He was drawing all men unto Him. So Athanasius (if the treatise *de Passione et Cruce*

Domini is his) speaks of Satan as cast out of Hades at the time of the descent, and seeing all whom he had kept prisoners set free by the victorious Christ (*Opp.* ii. p. 1017, ed. 1586). So Chrysostom (*de Coemet et Cruce, Expos. in Ps.* xlvi.) speaks of the descent into Hades as binding the devil and bringing his prey, the human race, into the treasury of the eternal King. So Cyril of Jerusalem, almost reproducing the very language of the gospel of Nicodemus, speaks of Christ as descending to Hades that He might ransom the just. He descended alone, but He returned with many following Him. The souls that had been long in prison were set free (*Catech.* iv. xiv.). So Epiphanius describes the descent as made to rescue those who had not fallen away utterly from God, but were kept on account of their frailties in Hades, by giving them, as it were, an amnesty (ἀμνηστίαν) (*adv. Haer.* i. 3). And in this view the Latin fathers are at one with the Greek. Ambrose refers the gospel preached to the dead of 1 Peter iv. to the descent into Hades "that as many as desired it might be set free" (*in Eph.* iv.). He ascended into heaven with the souls that He had rescued (*in Rom.* x.). Some of these were they who appeared to many after His resurrection (*in Eph.* iv.). Comp. also the statements in the *de Myster. Pasch.*

It was natural that men like Origen and his school should interpret the "fire that tries every man's work" of 1 Cor. iii. 13, the "saved so as by fire" of a purifying punishment in the intermediate state, and should extend that idea even to the "aeonian fire" of Matt. xxv. 46, and the "unquenchable fire" of Mark ix. 43. It is more suggestive to note that even those who shrank from that conclusion, did not confine the redeeming or purifying work in Hades to the brief period of the actual descent. So Synesius (*Ep.* 44), though he speaks of the deathless soul paying, if its guilt is incurable, a deathless penalty, teaches that there are δαίμονες, whose work it is to purify souls, as fullers cleanse a soiled garment. Even Tertullian (*de Animâ*, chap. 58) teaches that the last farthing "of the sinner's debt, if it be but a *modicum* delictum," may be paid by sufferings there. Even Cyprian (*Ep.* lv. 17) holds that some of those who are sent, on death, into the prison-house may come forth when they have paid the uttermost farthing, while martyrs receive their crown at once; that it may be necessary for some to be cleansed and purified by fire by long-continued suffering, waiting for the judgment of the great day. Even Jerome, while holding that there are eternal torments for the reprobate and godless, speaks of the works of Christians as "having to be tried and purified by fire" (*in Esai.* lxvi. *ad fin.*); of Christians who have fallen into sin as "to be saved after punishment" (*Dial c. Pelag.* i. 28); and adopts the general (*a plerisque*) explanation of the undying worm and the fire that is not quenched, of the anguish of conscience (*in Esai.*

lvi. 24). Even Augustine admits that between death and judgment there may be punishments that endure for a season only (*de Civ. Dei*, xxi. 13); that some sins not forgiven in this world are forgiven in the world to come, *sc.* in that interval (*de Civ. Dei*, xxi. 24) and are *purgatoriae* in their nature (*ibid.* xxi. 16; *Enchirid. ad Laurent.* c. 18). We pray for those who have not fallen utterly from grace, that after punishments the Divine compassion may be shewn to them, so that they may not go into eternal fire (*ibid.* xxi. 24). The fire which tries and purifies is not eternal, and of this view that each soul will suffer according to its need of suffering, Augustine says: "I do not reject it, because it is, perhaps, true" (*ibid.* xxi. 26). The effect of this earlier doctrine of purgatory on devout souls is well illustrated by the touching prayer at the close of the *Hamartigeneia* of Prudentius quoted in Study IX. Those that are suffering that "*ignis purgatorius*" may be helped in the interval between death and the resurrection, by the prayers and alms of the faithful, and by the "*sacrificium altaris*." The fact that that sacrifice was offered in the liturgies of Augustine's time for *all* souls, and not for the elect only, to whom his theory limited the hope of salvation, presented a difficulty which he meets with a characteristic subtlety. These sacrifices differ in their effect according to their object: "For the very good, they are thanksgivings; for the not very bad, they are propitiations; for the very bad, even though they are of no avail for the dead, they are some consolation for the living. For those for whom they avail, they avail for this, either that they bring full remission, or at any rate that their condemnation becomes more endurable" (*Enchirid.* c. 29). But after the resurrection the door of hope will be closed. Admitting the fact that the belief in a respite or cessation of the "eternal punishment of the damned" was held by "some, even by very many" (a doctrine so held must have been at least regarded by the church as not incompatible with the faith of which she was the keeper) he for his part rejects it. He barely allows ("I do not therefore adopt because I do not reject it," *de Civ. Dei,* xxi. 24) the possibility of a *levamen* of the *cruciatus* or *poena sensûs* of the lost, but the *poena damni,* the "alienation from the life of God" will be the common portion of all (*Enchirid.* c. 29).

And so the dark shadow of Augustine fell on the theology of the Western church, and condemned its thoughts of the love of God to many centuries of disastrous twilight. It started from the assumption that the whole human race was, through the sin of Adam, "one mass of perdition." From this Divine grace elected some to salvation. But none are elected outside the range of those who believe and are baptized. The whole heathen world, therefore, was left to eternal torments: its virtues were but "glittering vices" (*de Civ. Dei,* xix. 25). Even for unbaptized infants dying before they had done good or evil there was but the "levissima damnatio" of the alienation from the life of God, which was the common lot of all the lost, and compared with the eternity of which, any torments enduring for ages and then ceasing, would be a light thing to bear (*Enchirid.* c. 29). And baptism, though indispensable, was yet not sufficient. To hold the true faith, to live a holy life, these he rightly saw were conditions of eternal blessedness, and these were possible only for those who came under the decree of God's electing grace. The narrowness of mediaeval scholasticism, the hardness of Calvinistic Protestantism are each of them traceable to the influence of the great bishop of Hippo. And to that influence also, it must be added, is traceable the whole scholastic and Tridentine doctrine of purgatory with all its practical corruptions. The instincts of mankind led them to turn to the one mitigating feature in the terrible theology that shut out ninety-nine hundredths of mankind from all hope of escaping hell; and the "purgatorial fire for those who are not among the very bad," admitting of mitigation, capable even of being shortened by prayers, alms, the sacrifice of the altar, came into greater and greater prominence. Practically each man thought of his own kindred and friends as "not very bad," and natural affection, or even the conventional decorum which required the show of affection, led men to provide the means of mitigation. They could repeat prayers, give alms, pay for masses. The indulgences of Tetzel were but the natural development of the theology of Augustine. It was reserved for Calvinism and popular Protestantism to reproduce all that was hardest in it without even that element of mitigation. The teaching of the Western church from this period offers hardly any exception to the reproduction of Augustine's leading lines of thought. The language of the next great Latin father, Gregory the Great, is indeed even sterner: "There is a purgatorial fire, but it is only for very small sins." Admitting the natural meaning of Matt. xii. 31, it is only for such sins as "an idle word or immoderate laughter" that remission may be looked for in the other world, and then only by those who have deserved remission by good deeds in this life (*Dialog.* iv. 34). Even the "mitigatio" of Augustine has passed into the background, and he teaches a progressive increase in guilt and therefore in punishment: "ad deteriora quotidie impulsus cadit" (*Hom. in Job*, viii. 8-10). The speculations of the schoolmen as to the punishment of the lost and their development of the purgatorial theory, interesting as they are, do not fall within the scope of the present work.

Note.—On the question whether the teaching of Origen as to the life after death was condemned by the Fifth General Council, the reader may be referred to the exhaustive discussion between Dr. Pusey (*What is of Faith as to Everlasting Punishment*, pp. 125—144), and Mr. F. N. Oxenham (*What is the Truth as to Everlasting Punishment*). The latter seems to me to prove his position that there was no specific condemnation.

V.

THE MUTUAL ANATHEMAS OF ROMANISTS AND PROTESTANTS.

A SUFFICIENT illustration of the statements in p. 10 is found in the language of the Homily, *Against Peril of Idolatry*, Part III. "Laity and clergy, learned and unlearned, all ages, sects, and degrees of men, women, and children of whole Christendom (an horrible and most dreadful thing to think) have been at once drowned in abominable idolatry, of all other vices most detested of God and most damnable to man, and that, by the space of eight hundred years and more." I do not say that this excludes in terms every individual soul involved in the "abominable idolatry" and "most damnable vice" from all hope of salvation; but the drift and *animus* of the whole passage are unmistakeable, and it required no little courage to maintain, as Hooker maintained—in this as in other things the forerunner of the wider thoughts of a later generation—that there was hope even for them. It is a relief to turn from the fierce language of the Homily to the noble words of his second sermon:—

"God, I doubt not, was merciful to save thousands of them, though they lived in popish superstitions." The words which follow might almost seem to be a deliberate protest, if not against the language of the Homily, yet against inferences that had been drawn from it, as by a natural, if not necessary, consequence:—

"Many are partakers of the error which are not of the heresy of the Church of Rome. . . . 'Put a difference,' saith St. Jude, 'have compassion upon some.' Shall we lap up all in one condition? Shall we cast them all headlong? shall we plunge them all in that infernal and ever-flaming lake?—them that have been partakers in the error of Babylon, together with them within the heresy?—them which have been the authors of heresy with them that by error and violence have been forced to receive it?—them which have taught it, with them whose simplicity hath by sleights and conveyances of false teachers been seduced to believe it?—them which have been partakers with them in one, with them which have been partakers in many?—them which in many, with them which in all?"—Hooker, *Works,* III., pp. 495, 499 (*ed.* Keble).

Or again—

"As many as hold the foundation which is precious, though they hold it but weakly, and as it were by a slender thread; although they frame many base and unsuitable things upon it, things which cannot abide the trial of the fire; yet shall they pass the fiery trial and be saved, which indeed have builded themselves upon the rock, which is the foundation of this Church."—*Ibid*, p. 500.

In entire consistency with this thought, Hooker does not shrink from extending the hope of salvation even to the Galatians, whose error St. Paul had condemned, if in other respects they were sincere and sound in faith, and "had ended their lives before they were taught how perilous an opinion they held;" and presses it home upon his Puritan opponents that logically they must hold that the doctrine of the Lutheran Churches was also an "overthrowing the foundations," and so "deny the possibility of their salvation, which have been the chiefest instruments of ours" (*ibid.* p. 503); that they must "give sentence of death inevitable against all those fathers in the Greek Church, which died in the error of free-will" (*ibid.* p. 521). He for his part will say even "to a cardinal or pope, whose heart God hath touched with true sorrow for all his sins, and filled with love towards the Gospel of Christ," even though he hold the opinion of merits, "Be of good comfort, we have to deal with a merciful God, ready to make the best of that little which we hold well, and not with a captious sophister, which gathereth the worst out of everything wherein we err" (*ibid.* p. 541). In glowing and earnest words, which almost remind us of the passionate hope of advocates of the wider hope, like Maurice and Farrar, he finally delivers his soul, "Let me die, if ever it be proved that simply an error doth exclude a pope or cardinal in such a case utterly from hope of life. Surely I must confess unto you, if it be an error to think that God may save men even when they err, my greatest comfort is my error; were it not for the love I bear unto this error, I would neither wish to speak nor to live" (*ibid.* p. 543).

It lies in the nature of the case that one whose mind is thus permeated with the spirit of the love which triumphs over the narrowness of human judgments, which seeks to act in the temper that takes "judge not" for its law, should be led to conclusions that in their turn become premises for further developments which he himself would have shrunk from admitting. Hooker does not see that his plea of involuntary error extends to those who have lived and died in the times of an ignorance more entire than that of the Romanist. Of them he holds that they cannot "hold the foundation" which they never knew (*ibid.* p. 513). "Saracens, Turks, and Painims" are still thought of as under a hopeless and irremediable doom (*ibid.* p. 502).

As it was, however, Hooker had to bear the penalty which has at all times been the lot of those who have been led by the Spirit's teaching out of the narrowness of the generation in which they lived. Travers, his colleague in the preachership of the Temple, addressed a supplication to the Privy Council by way of remonstrance. He would not, need not dwell on the "absurdity" of Hooker's speech. "The like to this, and other such in this sermon and the rest of this matter, hath not been heard in public places within this and since Queen Mary's days" (*ibid.*

p. 567). Penry, another Puritan, asserted the dogma which Hooker had attacked in all its nakedness: "We hold that to him which dieth a papist, let him do ever so many good works . . . the very gates and portcullis of God's mercy are quite shut up. . . . And in this point, if either M. Hooker or M. Some, or all the reverend bishops of the land, do stand against us, it shall little dismay us" (*ibid.* p. 505).

There is, I imagine, little need to collect passages from Romish writers to show that the Church which they represented was not wider or more liberal than the Calvinist Puritan. *Extra ecclesiam nulla salus* had passed into an axiom of theology, and the *ecclesia* was interpreted, not as being co-extensive with the company of the baptised, but as identical with the Roman "obedience." The apologists and propagandists of that Church seem indeed to have thought that they scored a point in taking advantage of Hooker's large-hearted concessions. "You admit," was the argument of the Jesuit Knott, in the book to which Chillingworth's *Religion of Protestants* was an answer, "that Romanists may be saved. We are sure that 'Protestancy unrepented destroys salvation.' It is our honest charity to proclaim that fact as with the sound of a trumpet. Is it not safer and wiser to be on the side of the Church which makes the loudest assertions that salvation is to be found in it and in it only?" Chillingworth's answer to that argument contains one noble passage which I am tempted to quote as being just one step forward in advance of Hooker, though even he stops short of the wider hope which was reserved for a later generation. "To say that God will damn men for errors as to such things, who are lovers of Him and lovers of truth, is to rob man of his comfort and God of His goodness; to make man desperate and God a tyrant. . . . If men suffer themselves neither to be betrayed into their errors, nor kept in them by any sin of their wills, if they do their best endeavours to free themselves from all errors, and yet fail of it through human frailty, so well am I persuaded of the goodness of God, that if in me alone should meet a confluence of such errors of all the Protestants in the world that were thus qualified, I should not be so much afraid of them all as I should to ask pardon of them."—*Religion of Protestants*, Answer to Preface of *Charity Maintained*, p. 36.

We shall not wonder that one who wielded this two-edged sword, striking at both Roman and Protestant dogmatists, should have been anathematized by both. It was, to say the least, a curious instance of the irony of history that the *Religion of Protestants*, which might seem to have deserved the gratitude of all Bible-Christians, should have been anathematized, not by a Romish priest or Jesuit controversialist, but by Chillingworth's Puritan antagonist, as he stood by the writer's grave, as that "cursed book"—the "corrupt and rotten book," which had "seduced so many million souls."[1]

(1) Compare the Essay on *William Chillingworth* by the present writer in *Masters of English Theology.*

VI.

THE SALVATION OF THE HEATHEN.

THE thought that the heathen as such are under a Divine education, and are not excluded, if they have been seekers after God and have followed after righteousness, from the blessedness of His kingdom, has become so much the dominant thought of the time in which we live, that we scarcely recognise, for the most part, the slowness with which that victory over the traditions of mediævalism and dark thoughts of God has been won, how those who fought for the truth which is now acknowledged by well-nigh all men have had their name cast out as evil and borne the reproach of heresy or unbelief. A survey of the history of Christian thought on this question will not be without its value, if only as teaching us to be patient with those who still linger on under the influence of the older prejudice. The wider knowledge on this or other like questions leads us into a serener region, where we find it possible to sympathise even with opinions we reject, to abstain from all hard words of condemnation, to be tolerant even of intolerance. We can think and speak as Augustine thought and spoke when he looked on the Manichæan errors by which he had been himself for many years beguiled: "Let them rage against you, who know not with what labour men arrive at truth, and with what difficulty they avoid errors. . . . . Let those rage against you who know not with what difficulty the eye of the inner man is healed so that it can gaze upon its Sun. Let those rage against you who know not through what sighings and groanings it is brought to pass that man can, in ever so small a measure, apprehend God" (*Epist. ad. Manich.* c. 2).

It is not difficult to understand how men might be led, by dwelling on one aspect of the teaching of Scripture to the exclusion of that which was its complement, to adopt either the negative or the affirmative answer to the question, Can the heathen find entrance into the eternal blessedness of God's kingdom? On the one hand we have the words which declare that "except a man be born of water and of the Spirit he cannot enter into the kingdom of God" (John iii. 5); that "he that believeth and is baptized shall be saved, and that he who believeth not shall be condemned" (Mark xvi. 16); that "there is none other name given under heaven whereby men must be saved, save only the name of the Lord Jesus Christ" (Acts iv. 12); that "no man cometh unto the Father but by Him" (John xiv. 6); that the state of the heathen is painted in the darkest colours, as that of those who are "without hope and without God" (Eph. ii. 12), "children of wrath"

(Eph. ii. 3), sunk in a fathomless abyss of evil (Eph. iv. 18, 19).

On the other hand we read that "the Gentiles which have not the Law, and do by nature the things contained in the Law, are a law unto themselves," and are therefore capable of "glory and honour and immortality" (Rom. ii. 14); that "God winked at the times of ignorance" (Acts xvii. 30); that Christ was "the Light that lighteth every man that cometh into the world" (John i. 9); and that the course of the world's history was so ordered that men might "feel after and find" Him whom they "ignorantly worshipped" (Acts xvii. 23). We have St. Peter's inference from the history of Cornelius that "God is no respecter of persons, but that in every nation he that feareth God and worketh righteousness is accepted with Him" (Acts x. 34, 35). The words of the Lord Jesus recognise the difference between the many stripes and the few, according to the measure of men's knowledge, and this implies the principle that their opportunities are the measure of their responsibilities (Luke xii. 47). The definition of the faith which from the beginning of the world has justified, as given in Heb. xi. 6, is simply that it is belief that God is and that He is a rewarder of them that diligently seek Him; and that is compatible with ignorance of any historical revelation through Moses or through Christ. If we take our Lord's teaching as to the Law by which He judges in Matt. xxv. 32 in its literal and natural sense, we have the truth that He judges the nations of the heathen world (πάντα τὰ ἔθνη as distinct from the literal or the spiritual Israel) according as they have, in their ignorance of the full significance of what they did, obeyed or resisted the law of kindness written in their hearts. In this, as in other instances, Scripture seems accordingly to present two aspects of the truth, tending to opposite conclusions, without formulating a logical reconciliation between them. It leaves them to balance each other, to be placed in their right relations as elements of the Church's faith by the teaching of history and experience, by the illumination of the intellect through the Spirit who leads men to all truth, and in that leading follows the method of the Lord Jesus, who had many things to say to His disciples which they could not as yet bear (John xvi. 12), and so fulfils Himself in many ways, wisdom being justified in each case of all her children.

It was characteristic of the Alexandrian school of Church teachers that they should embrace the wider hope as to the condition of the heathen. I do not speak now of the yet larger views of Origen, which of course embraced that hope; but it is interesting to find his master, Clement of Alexandria, adopting, as we have seen in p. 84, the interpretation of 1 Peter iii. 18 which sees in it the offer of mercy to those who, having lived according to the light they had, were capable of accepting it and coming to the conclusion that "God's punishments are saving and disciplinary, leading to conversion, and choosing rather the repentance than the death of a sinner." "Souls," he adds, "when released from the burden of the flesh, are likely to see spiritual things with a greater clearness than in the days of their life on earth" (*Strom.* vi. 6).

The mind of Augustine, however, was formed in a different mould from that of Clement. For him the maxim *Extra ecclesiam nulla salus* had the character of an axiom in all the rigour of its limitations, and there was no entrance into the Church save through the gate of baptism. Children who died unbaptized before actual sin might indeed, in their *limbus infantum*, receive a *mitissima damnatio*, but it was a damnation still, a privation of all the blessedness of the redeemed with no hope of rising out of it. As for the so-called virtues of the heathen, they were but "glittering vices" done without faith, and therefore not acceptable, deserving God's wrath and damnation. The theology of Augustine stamped itself on the mind of the mediæval Church in western Christendom. There is something almost pathetic in the way in which Dante, as the great representative of the theology of that Church, at once accepts the dogma and seeks to minimise its harshness. The children whose sighs he hears in the outer regions of the Inferno (c. iv.) have no pain but that of unsatisfied desire. The companions of Virgil seem to have elements of consolation in the region in which they dwell "full of light and clear," in the "sweet tones eloquent" of their converse with each other, in the "greeting kind" and "smile of pleasure" with which they welcome Virgil and his Florentine disciple (*Inf.* c. iv.). Still more suggestive is the form in which he states the doubt that had forced itself unbidden on his mind as to the justice of the Divine decree which thus appeared to exclude men, for no fault of theirs, from any share in the eternal blessedness. The eagle which impersonates the Divine wisdom has read that doubt, and gives the clearest possible expression to it—

> "For thou didst say, A man his first breath drew
> On Indus' banks, and there was none to tell
> Of Christ, or write or speak the doctrine true,
> And he in every wish and deed lives well,
> As far as human reason can descry,
> And sinless doth in life and speech excel.
> He without baptism, without faith doth die;
> Where is the justice, then, that damns for it?
> Where is his guilt, if he the faith deny?"

The only answer given to the doubt is that man may not dare to fathom the abyss of the Divine judgments with the plummet of his human reason—

> "Nay, who art thou, who on thy bench dost sit,
> To judge with thy short vision of a span
> The thousand miles of distance infinite?"

All that can be said in vindication of the ways of God is that baptism and the knowledge of Christ will not avail to save professing Christians from a heavier condemnation than that of the righteous heathen.

> "But look how many cry, O Christ, O Christ,
> Who at the judgment shall much further be

From Him than some who have not known the Christ:
Such Christians judged by Æthiops we shall see
Then, when the two bands take their separate way,
One rich, one poor, for all eternity."—*Parad.* xix.

The doubt which Dante thus stifled continued, in spite of the authority which repressed it, to work in the minds of men. The revival of classical studies at the Renaissance led men to recognise the virtues as well as the vices of the old Greeks and Romans. The discovery of the western continent and intercourse with men of other races who were not, like Jews and Turks, antagonistic to the faith of Christ, at least tended to enlarge the range of men's sympathies. Reason rose in rebellion against the authority which imposed a dogma that clashed with men's sense of equity. The question was clearly working in the minds of English thinkers when the theologians of the Church of England formulated her Eighteenth Article.

"They also are to be had accursed (*anathematizandi*) that presume to say, That every man shall be saved by (*in*) the law or sect which he professeth, so that he be diligent to frame his life according to that law and the light of Nature. For Holy Scripture doth set out unto us only the name of Jesus Christ whereby we must be saved."

The terms of the Article suggest three questions:—

(1.) Who were the persons aimed at in this stringent anathema?

(2.) What was the intention of the framers of the Article?

(3.) How far may the language of the Article be legitimately accepted by those who hold a belief that differs on this point from that of the framers?

(1.) Historically it seems probable that the opinion condemned had come before the English Reformers as an error of the German Anabaptists, who were the *bête noire* of the time, alarming more conservative Protestants with their extravagances. Cranmer may have thought it right to follow in the steps of the Augsburg Confession (Art. IV.), which condemns the Anabaptists who affirm that "infants may be saved without baptism and outside the Church of Christ." But the Anabaptists were not alone in repudiating the patristic axiom, *Extra ecclesiam nulla salus,* which Luther and even Calvin (each, of course, with his own narrowing, limiting definitions as to what the Church was) were ready to adopt. (Calvin, *Instit.* iv. 1, 4.)

Zwingle had proposed to himself the task of reconciling the absolute predestinarianism which he shared with Calvin, with his recognition of the good works of the righteous heathen as done by the grace of God, and therefore acceptable to Him, and attesting the salvation of the worker. And he did this by seeing in them—Socrates, Brutus, and others—those whom God had predestined to eternal life. "Nothing," he says, "hinders but that God may choose among the Heathen those who shall observe His laws and cleave to Him, for His election is free" (Zwingl. *Opp.* ii. p. 371).

There were, however, others besides the Anabaptists and Zwingle who may have been aimed at in this article. Erasmus had spoken of Cicero as inspired and as probably saved (*Ep. ad Jo. Ulatt* in Cic. Tusc. *Disput.*, quoted in Hey's *Articles*, B. IV. *Art.* 18).[1] Galeotto Martio, who died A.D. 1478, had maintained that for all nations who live justly and purely as by the law of nature, there is laid up the fruit of the life of heaven. "*Omnibus gentibus, integre et puriter veluti ex justâ naturæ lege viventibus, æternos cœlestes auræ fructus paratos*" (Hey, *ut supra*). The thought was, as it were, floating in the air.

We can, I think, enter into the feeling of jealousy and distrust with which the Lutherans and English Reformers regarded this opinion. It may have seemed to them to sanction an absolute indifference to the faith of Christ, to lead to the conclusion that we may as well leave the heathen as they are, that the Incarnation and the Atonement were not needed for man's salvation. Whether they met the error in the right way is, of course, another question. As it was they were eager, with somewhat of a morbid eagerness, in this as in other instances, to clear themselves from any complicity with Anabaptist errors, and redoubled the sharpness of their assertions. Cranmer in his *Catechism* (A.D. 1548), based upon that of the Lutheran Justus Jonas, reproduced the

(1) Comp. also the passages from the *Utopia* of Sir Thomas More, in the Study on the "History of the Wider Hope in English Theology."

language of the original. "If we should have heathen parents and die without baptism, we should be damned everlastingly." The Homily on Good Works echoes the teaching of Augustine: "If a heathen man clothe the naked, feed the hungry, and do other suchlike works, yet because he doth them not in faith for the honour and love of God, they be but dead, vain, and fruitless works to him." The *Reformatio Legum* (*de Hær.* c. 21) spoke of the opinion that salvation may be hoped for men in every religion and sect as an "*horribilis et inanis blasphemia.*" The *Institution of a Christian Man* added to the words that baptized children dying in their infancy shall undoubtedly be saved thereby, the tremendous negative, "*and else not.*"

It must be borne in mind as we record these dogmatic statements that the English Reformers, in rejecting as they did, in their general though not in their formulated teaching, the mediæval doctrine of a *limbus infantum*, and throwing into the background the thought of degrees of suffering and privation in the punishment of the condemned, left these statements in all their unmitigated harshness. Unbaptized infants, and *à fortiori* all unbaptized adults, were in hell, with all the horrors which that word connoted.

Hooker, as we have seen on p. 157, though contending with an admirable courage for his right to hope for the salvation of those who held the foundation of faith in Christ, in the midst of the errors of a corrupted Christianity, followed in the wake of the earlier Reformers as to the condition of the unbaptized heathen. It is clear, however, that by the time of the last revision of the Prayer Book in A.D. 1662, a change had passed over the mind of the leading theologians of the English Church. Then for the first time appeared the Rubric that baptized children dying before they commit actual sin are undoubtedly saved, and there is the significant omission of the words "or else not." That was no longer to be taught as a doctrine of the Church of England. Can we trace the influences by which this change had been brought about? The limits to which I must confine myself forbid an exhaustive treatment of the question, but it may be interesting to note some of the steps in the teaching of Anglican divines or others.

The doctrinal system of George Fox and his followers, as developed in the *Apology* of Robert Barclay, may be noted as a distinct step forward. It was, of course, a necessary consequence of their rejection of the sacraments as permanent ordinances of the Church that they should look on the salvation of children or adults as altogether unconnected with baptism. But they went beyond this, and in words which lie at the root of the dominant theology of our own time, from Dr. Pusey to Mr. Maurice, proclaimed that the offer of salvation was made to all men. Their three first principles are: "(1.) That God, who out of His infinite love sent His Son, our Lord Jesus

Christ, into the world, who tasted death for every man, *hath given to every man*, whether Jew or Gentile, Turk or Scythian, Indian or barbarian, of whatsoever nation, country, or place, a certain day or time of visitation, during which day or time it is possible for them to be saved and to partake of the fruits of Christ's death. (2.) That for this end God hath communicated and given unto every man a measure of the light of His own Son, a measure of grace, or a measure of the Spirit. (3.) That God, in and by this light and seed, invites, calls, exhorts, and strives with every man, in order to save him, which, as it is received and not resisted, works the salvation of all, even of those who are ignorant of the sufferings and death of Christ and of Adam's fall" (*Apol.*, Prop. v. vi.).

Extremes meet, and the doctrines of the Society of Jesus as to the *gratia sufficiens* given to every man, and which by the exercise of his will he can make "efficacious" or the reverse, against which Pascal writes from his Jansenist standpoint (*Lett. Provinc.* ii.), as adopted in words even by the "new Thomists," the Dominicans of France, was practically a testimony to the doctrine for which the followers of Fox were contending. The Jesuits also felt that they must thus vindicate the ways of God to man, and prove that those ways were equal, as judged by the reason and conscience of humanity. As limited by the additions of some of those who accepted it, that the *gratia sufficiens* was ineffectual unless it was followed by the *gratia efficax*, which was given only to the baptized, it was open to the taunt of Pascal, as to the "*grace suffisante, qui ne suffit pas effectivement;*" but it is clear that the belief was held by many Jesuit writers without that limitation, and that taken together with their other characteristic doctrine of *invincible ignorance* as an excuse for sin and unbelief, it must have tended to a very serious modification of the old patristic axiom, *Extra ecclesiam nulla salus*, of the old mediæval belief as to the damnation of unbaptized infants or of heathens to whom Christ had not been preached.

Such thoughts were at all events likely to work in that direction among followers of Laud, such as Chillingworth, or laymen of the type with which the author of *John Inglesant* has made us familiar. Everything tended to a reaction against the limitations which Calvin had inherited from Augustine, and had transmitted to his followers in a yet keener and more incisive form. Foremost among the witnesses of that reaction stands the name of Jeremy Taylor. It is a curious illustration of the extent to which the wheel had come full circle that he actually turns round, forgetting the teaching of the English Reformers, upon the Church of Rome, and charges it with a "strange uncharitableness" for teaching that "poor babes, descending from Christian parents, if they die unbaptized, shall never see the face of God," and that "of such is *not* the kingdom of heaven. . . . . The Church of England . . . . teaches no such fierce and uncharitable proposition" (*Dissuasive from Popery*, i. 8). It is clear that, so far as the Divine equity was involved in the discussion, the force of Taylor's argument could not be limited to the children of Christian parents, just as his arguments in the *Liberty of Prophesying* (*Works*, vii. p. 464, ed. Heber), as to the influences of "invincible and harmless prejudices, weakness, education, mistaken piety, anything that hath no venom or sting in it, as excusing heresy so that it is no sin;" or Chillingworth's bold statement, that if there should meet in him "a confluence of all such errors of all the Protestants of the world," whose errors were not sins of will, he "should not be so much afraid of them all as I should to ask pardon for them" (*Rel. of Prot.*, Answer to Preface of *Charity Maintained*, p. 26), stretch beyond heresies to the unbelief for which the man was not responsible. In the one case as in the other it was true that "to say that God will damn men for errors as to such things, who are lovers of Him and lovers of truth, is to rob man of his comfort and God of His goodness; to make man desperate and God a tyrant" (Chillingworth *ut supra*). Anyhow the Eastern apologue of Abraham and the fire-worshipper, whom he refused to receive into his tent, with which Taylor ends the *Liberty of Prophesying*, looks far ahead beyond the controversies that had divided Christendom to the wider question as to the condition of the heathen which was now brought before the minds of men, and was craving for an answer.

Extremes meet again, and we pass from the Anglican divines and the Jesuit schoolmen, trained in reverence for the authority of popes, fathers, councils, to the poet-theologian of the *Paradise Lost*, sitting down in the temper of an ultra-Protestantism, Bible in hand, to construct a "Christian doctrine" for himself. And we find him, consciously or unconsciously, reproducing at once the Jesuit theory of the *gratia sufficiens*, and that of the inward light, which he had learnt, it may be, from his intercourse with Thomas Elwood, and through him, with the Penns and Penningtons. "The calling of God is," he says, "either general or special. The general calling is that whereby God invites the whole of mankind in various ways, but all of them sufficient for the purpose, to the knowledge of the true Deity." The texts on which he rests his belief are John i. 9; Acts xiv. 17; Rom. i. 19, ii. 15. "It may be objected," he adds, "that all have not known Christ. I answer that this proves nothing against the doctrine that all are called in Christ alone; inasmuch as, had He not been given to the world, God would have called no one; and as the ransom He has paid is in itself sufficient for the redemption of all mankind, all are called to partake of its benefits, though all may not be aware of the source from which the benefits flow. . . . . We ought to believe that the perfect sacrifice of Christ may be abundantly sufficient even for those who have never heard of the name of Christ, and who believe only in God" (*Christ. Doctr.*, b. i. c. 17).

The next stage in the development of thought that calls for notice is that in which the hopes that were thus cherished by solitary thinkers, condemned or contemned as fanciful or heretical, or had been held by the divines of a Church antagonistic to our own, should find utterance in high places and be proclaimed as with authority. It was given to Isaac Barrow to represent that stage, preaching as Master of Trinity College, Cambridge, and it may be presumed from the University, or at least the College, pulpit. The circumstances of his life had been singularly favourable to the thoughts that widen with the years. His early Cambridge life must have brought him within reach of the influence of the group of Platonists in which we note the names, as its most conspicuous members, of Cudworth and Whichcote and Henry More; possibly also under that of the few seekers who were struggling to the wider hope even within the walls of Emmanuel (see p. 192). His line of patristic study had led him to the Greek rather than the Latin fathers—to Clement of Alexandria and Origen and Chrysostom, rather than Tertullian and Augustine and Gregory and the schoolmen. He had spent a whole year at Constantinople, and had made a special study of Mahometanism as he found it there. He had spent some time in France at the time when the Jesuit and Jansenist controversies as to the *gratia sufficiens* were at their height. And as the result of all this training, we find him in his four grand Sermons on Universal Redemption taking the position which had been maintained by Barclay and Milton and the Jesuit fathers. The doctrine of the universality of the work of Christ is asserted in all its width and fulness. He maintains that the heathen as well as Jews and Christians have been all along under a Divine education, that the grace they have received has been efficacious as well as sufficient, and adds :—

"If it be said, that having such grace is inconsistent with the want of an explicit knowledge of Christ and of faith in Him, why may we not say, that as probably (so St. Chrysostom, *vid. Mont. App.* i.) most good people before our Lord's coming received grace without any such knowledge or faith; that as to idiots and infants our Saviour's meritorious performances are applied (in a manner unknowable by us) without so much as a capacity to know or believe anything, that so we (to whom God's judgments are inscrutable and His ways uninvestigable) know not how grace may be communicated unto, and Christ's merits avail for, other ignorant persons, in respect to whom we may apply that of St. John, '*The light shineth in darkness, and the darkness comprehended it not.*' . . . . Since we are plainly taught that our Lord is the Savour of all men, and it is consequent thence that He hath procured grace sufficiently capacifying all men to obtain salvation, we need not perplex the business or obscure so apparent a truth by debating how that grace is imparted, or by labouring overmuch in reconciling the dispensation thereof with other dispensations of Providence" (*Sermon* lxxii.).

Finally he sums up in words which breathe the very spirit of F. D. Maurice.

"The undertakings and performances of our Saviour did respect all men, as the common works of nature do; as the air we breathe in, as the sun which shineth on us; the which are not given to any man particularly, but to all generally; not as a proper enclosure, but as a common; they are indeed mine, but not otherwise than as they belong to all men" (*Sermon* lxxiv.).

The teaching of theologians found an echo in the poetical literature of the time, pre-eminently in the two writers who were, one of them by birth and the other by conviction, under the guidance of the Church of Rome. Thus Dryden writes in his *Religio Laici*, written before his change. Speaking of the preaching of the Gospel, he asks—

> "But what provision could from thence accrue
> To Indian souls and worlds discovered new?
> In other parts it helps, that ages past
> The Scriptures there were known and were embraced,
> Till Sin spread once again the shades of night:
> What's that to those who never saw the light?"

He answers the question as Barrow, Milton, Barclay answered it—

> "We grant, 'tis true, that Heaven from human sense
> Has hid the secret paths of Providence,
> But boundless wisdom, boundless mercy, may
> Find, e'en for these bewildered souls, a way.
> * * * * * *
> Then those who followed Reason's dictates right
> Lived up, and lifted high their natural light,
> With Socrates may see their Maker's face
> While thousand rubric martyrs want a place."

Pope in his turn was not less explicit, and gave a yet wider popularity to Dryden's thoughts (more, one must add, from the Bolingbroke side of his mind than the Catholic) in his *Universal Prayer* :—

"Father of all, in every age,
In every clime adored,
By saint, by savage, or by sage,
Jehovah, Jove, or Lord."

And in the well-known lines of the *Essay on Man*—

"For modes of faith let senseless bigots fight,
His can't be wrong whose life is in the right."

The tale of the victory of this aspect of the wider hope over the dogmas of the older tradition is almost told. It remains only to note the utterances of two master minds separated from each other by more than a century, and representing widely different schools of thought. Butler, trained, it may be well to remember, first in the traditions of Presbyterianism, and then in those of Oxford, adopts, with a marked emphasis, Barrow's teaching as to the extent and application of the work of Redemption. He had spoken of what might otherwise have been the irremediable "destruction of human kind, whatever" (he adds significantly) "that destruction unprevented would have been." And then he adds a note expressly to protest against the limitations that men had set to that work. "It cannot, I suppose, be imagined, even by the most cursory reader, that it is in any sort affirmed or implied in anything said in this chapter, that none can have the benefit of the general redemption, but such as have the advantage of being made acquainted with it *in this present life*" (*Anal.* ii. 5). The words which I have printed in italics are, in a careful and cautious writer like Butler, who weighs the force of every syllable, singularly suggestive of what were his unexpressed thoughts as to the opportunities for more perfect knowledge that may be given men in the life that follows this.

So, in the chapter which bears the heading "Of the Want of Universality in Revelation, and of the supposed Deficiency in the Proof of it," Butler describes with some fulness the stages of knowledge in which men have in different times and countries lived, some receiving no light from Scripture, some who had only a dim and refracted light, like the ancient Persians and the modern Mahometans, some who have had the system of Christianity corrupted, and its evidence "blended with false miracles, so as to leave the mind in the utmost doubtfulness and uncertainty." And his answer to the questions raised by this state of things is plain and simple.

"Nor is there anything shocking in all this, or which would seem to bear hard upon the moral administration in nature, if we would really keep in mind that every one shall be dealt equitably with, instead of forgetting this or explaining it away after it is acknowledged in words. All shadow of injustice, and indeed all harsh appearances, in this various economy of Providence would be lost, if we would keep in mind that every merciful allowance shall be made, and no more be required of any one than what might equitably have been expected of him from the circumstances in which he was placed; and not what might have been expected had he been placed in other circumstances: *i.e.* in Scripture language that *every man shall be accepted according to what he had, not according to what he had not*" (*Anal.* ii. 6).

The last witness I shall cite is a theologian still living, conspicuous as having been for many years identified with the highest teaching of the so-called Oxford school, and for as many with that of the Church of Rome, in which, as Cardinal Manning, he has obtained so prominent a position. It may fairly be assumed that what he wrote in the former position was thought by him consistent with the Catholic faith as held by the Church of England. If he has not recalled it, directly or indirectly, since—if his language and action now are in harmony with it—it may be inferred that it is, in his judgment, in harmony with what he holds as the Catholic faith now. The passage is from vol. iv. of the sermons published by him (A.D. 1850) while he was still an Archdeacon in the English Church, not, perhaps, without leanings that were afterwards developed into act. The sermon numbered as iv. in the volume, bearing the heading "Christ preached every way a ground of rejoicing," is throughout one of great force and beauty. I quote the paragraph that bears specially on the question now under discussion:—

"Truth is given for the probation of man; the probation of man is not ordained for the sake of truth. God can prove, and from the beginning has proved, His servants in every measure of light, from the noon of night to the noon of day. We have the warrant of Holy Writ that the Gentiles who had received no revealed law did 'by nature the things contained in the law,' being 'a law unto themselves,' and that by their law they should be judged. When St. Peter said 'God is no respecter of persons; but in every nation he that feareth God and doeth righteousness is accepted of Him,' it is true that he spoke, with design, only of the admission of Gentiles to the grace given to the Jews; but he enunciated a much larger application of God's laws of grace. He denied that national distinctions were a bar to mercy, but he affirmed also that fear and righteousness are universally accepted of God. He thereby enunciated the great axioms of the kingdom of mercy, that no obedient soul can perish, no penitent be cast away, no soul that loves God be lost. If the heart be right with God, He will weigh the rest in a balance of compassion. . . . . The atonement is infinite in price; the visible Church a finite and earthly mystery. God has bound us to seek His grace through His Church; but He has not bound Himself to give grace and salvation in no other way. His mercy is boundless, His Spirit infinite, His grace always overflowing. God be praised that the fountain of living water, which makes glad the city of God, penetrates beneath the soil, and breaks up in secret springs, making pools in the wilderness. Is our eye evil because He is good? Did we not agree with Him? Shall we not take that which is ours because He may do what He wills with His own. What wantonness would this be? Whatsoever in His lovingkindness He may do out of His love, 'what is that to thee? follow thou Me.' And if He raise up saints in Midian or Samaria, or send prophets to Horeb or seers to Jezreel, where is our charity, that we would again tie the Hands that were pierced, with the bonds of our theology?"[2]

I am not aware, as I have said, that Cardinal Manning has ever formally recalled this teaching. The readiness with which he co-operates in Temperance and other philanthropic movements with men who from his point of view are in a state of formal heresy and schism, may fairly be taken as an indication that he looks on them with a hopeful charity on the grounds of their involuntary ignorance and invincible prejudice, that he still rejoices in so far as

(2) The allowance thus made for involuntary ignorance has received, it may be added, the *ex cathedrâ* sanction of the authority to which Roman Catholics look as that of an infallible guide. "We and you know," says Pius IX., in his Encyclical of August 10, 1863, "that those who lie under invincible ignorance as regards our most Holy Religion, and who, diligently observing the natural law and its precepts, which are engraven by God on the hearts of all, and prepared to obey God, lead a good and upright life, are able, by the operation of the power of divine light and grace, to obtain eternal life." And in an earlier Allocution of 1854 he repudiates the attempt to set any limits to the cases in which this plea of ignorance is admissible.—Cardinal Newman's *Letter to the Duke of Norfolk*, p. 123.

they are faithful to the light they have. But if so, can there be a stronger proof that the spirit of freedom has penetrated into the stronghold of authority, that even in the systematic theology of Rome it is impossible to maintain in the old sense the dogma that *extra ecclesiam nulla salus*, or that the heathen and unbaptized infants are for ever excluded from the blessedness of the Divine kingdom ?[3] And in like manner the dogmatic statements of the English Reformers and even of Hooker on this point have passed into "the region of things decaying and waxing old and ready to vanish away." They have been rejected alike by Dr. Pusey, who states in his sermon on the Athanasian Creed that the "gates of the kingdom of Heaven are ever open to all in every age and country who repent of their sins and seek after righteousness," and by the late Archbishop of Canterbury, who, in his *Charge to the clergy of the diocese of London in* 1866, could "scarcely credit the report that this dreadful argument was lately used by a clergyman to show the necessity for missionary effort, that at every ticking of the clock, in every four-and-twenty hours, from month to month and year to year, God sends a heathen straight to never-ending misery" (p. 39).

(3.) There remains the question how far the

(3) Mr. H. N. Oxenham seems, however, to hold to the *mitissima damnatio* of Augustine. Unbaptized infants are, from his standpoint, for ever excluded from the beatific vision—though this is no conscious loss to them, and implies no suffering of soul or body.—*Catholic Eschatology*, p. 19.

language of an Article which was *primâ facie* intended to embody the stern narrowness of the sixteenth century can be reconciled with the wider liberalism of the nineteenth. If the *animus imponentis* is to be found in what may be ascertained by collateral evidence as to the opinion of the framers of the Article, there would be no alternative for the followers of Butler and Barrow but to get rid of it, or to refuse to sign, or to sign under protest. But, on the other hand, it has never been ruled that this is the *animus imponentis* by which the consciences of men are to be bound. That would be to give a power to the "dead hand" which it has no right to claim. The *imponens* in this sense is the Church as represented by its rulers in each successive age. And in the only authoritative document which indicates the *animus imponentis* in the period that immediately followed that in which the Articles were compiled, the Declaration prefixed to the Articles under Charles I. and traceable probably to the pen of Laud, the comprehensive elasticity of the Articles, the ambiguity which admits of being construed in favour of opposite opinions, is affirmed as one of their special excellences. According to that declaration men are to receive the Articles in their "literal and grammatical sense," finding, if they choose, a protection for their own opinions, but not imposing the sense which is favourable to those opinions upon others. We are free therefore to inquire how far that literal and grammatical sense is compatible with the wider thoughts to which the Church of England has since been led, and which, so far as they have been uttered by men having the chief place of authority among her rulers, must be held as coming within the *animus imponentis* now. It may be well that, as in the case of the Articles that touch on other "curious differences," the points involved in the Calvinistic controversy, the teaching as to the Sacraments, the inspiration of Scripture, the authority of the Church, we shall find that it was designed to include other opinions than those which were held by the individual compilers, that here also the intention was one of comprehensiveness rather than exclusiveness, that, as it was said by Cardinal Newman in the 90th *Tract for the Times,* the Articles "though the offspring of an uncatholic age were themselves not uncatholic"—so it may be true of them that though the offspring of a narrow and illiberal age they were themselves not illiberal or narrow.

In the first place, then, it may fairly be said that the anathema of Article XVIII. is directed against views like those of the Deists of the eighteenth century, which asserted the sufficiency of a so-called Natural Religion in and by itself. From that point of view the Revelation in Christ and His redeeming work were superfluous and unmeaning; and, as that was a denial of the truths of which the Church is the witness, and in the acknowledgment of which her members find their blessedness, the denial (so far as it is not covered by the ignorance which God "winks at") involves the curse which consists in the privation of that blessedness and is under the anathema (*anathematizandi sunt* in the Latin Article) in which, as in the Commination Service, she proclaims her sentence upon a state which is *ipso facto* other than a blessed one. The terms of the Article do not touch those who rest their hope for the heathen on the one Name, *i.e.* on all that is signified by the Name, "whereby men must be saved," who hold that a man is saved not "in or by the law or sect which he professeth" so far as that law or sect ignores or denies the truth, but in spite of it, and by an illumination which delivers him from it, and who trace that illumination not to the "nature" in which, as being the fallen nature of man, "there is no good thing," but to the Light that lighteth every man that cometh into the world. That, it seems to me, is a natural and legitimate reconciliation of the Article with the wider and higher truth to which the Church has, in these later times, been led by the Spirit which from age to age reveals the truth as men are able to bear it.[4]

(4) It is a satisfaction to me, as before, to name Bishop Ken as a witness to the larger hope. He, in his vision of Hades, sees "infants numberless" in "the region of the happy dead," not because they have been baptized, but as being "pure from wilful sin," and "numerous souls" of Gentiles, "trophies of universal grace, who ne'er beheld the evangelic light." And Socrates is there among the martyrs, knowing at last the Name by which he had been saved (*Hymnarium* pp. 131, 132).

VII.

THE HISTORY OF THE WIDER HOPE IN ENGLISH THEOLOGY.

THE questions which meet us as to the belief of some, if not many, of the great teachers of the ancient Church, in the final restoration of all men, or at least the final extinction of evil from the universe of God, will be found discussed in the notes on "Conditional Immortality" and on the "Eschatology of the Early Church." The task on which I purpose to enter now is to trace the growth of the former thought. in its complete or incomplete stages, in the minds of English religious thinkers since the Reformation. The possibility of the extension of the redeeming work of Christ to those who have not known it, or have known it but imperfectly, will be found discussed in like manner in the Essay on the Salvation of the Heathen, and here I shall treat only of the hopes that have taken a yet wider range.

The first fact which confronts us is the well-known condemnation of the doctrine of Universal Restoration in the 42nd Article of 1553, which has for its heading, "All men shall not be saved at the length," and the text of which runs thus, in modernised spelling:—

"They also are worthy of condemnation (*damnatione digni*) who endeavour at this time to restore the dangerous (*periculosam*) opinion that all men, be they never so ungodly, shall at length be saved, when they have suffered pains for their sins a certain time appointed by God's justice."

We have but scanty *data* for forming a judgment as to the historical occasion of the Article thus framed. It forms one of a group of four Articles all of which disappeared in the Revision of 1563; the other three repudiating the errors (1) that the Resurrection was past already, "as though it only belonged to the soul;" (2) that the soul slept, "without sense, feeling, or perceiving," till the Day of Judgment; and (3) the fable of heretics called Millenarii. The experts to whom one commonly trusts assume that these were all of them Anabaptist errors (Hardwicke, *Introd. to Art.*, p. 87), and that the universalism which they are supposed to have preached rested partly on "abstract ideas of God" and partly on "new interpretations of the word 'eternal.'" This is somewhat meagre information, but the opinion has commonly been taken for granted, and was pressed by Dr. Jelf as an *argumentum ad invidiam* in his correspondence with Mr. Maurice (*Grounds for laying before the Council, &c.*, p. 60).

I confess that I do not feel satisfied that the Anabaptist thinkers were the only persons aimed at in the Article; if they had been, it would be interesting to turn to their writings and to find whether they were following in the footsteps of Origen and Gregory of Nyssa (against whom Mr. Hardwicke might have brought the charges which he brings against the Anabaptists), or fell back, as later Universalists have done, on such texts of Scripture as seemed to favour their belief.[1] As it is, it may be well to remember that there was another class of thinkers who might be suspected of these opinions. The last years of Erasmus had been given to the publication of a Latin version of Origen, for whom he professed a far deeper love and admiration than for Augustine, as "having opened to him the springs and methods of theological science" (Seebohm's *Oxford Reformers*, p. 169). It was published with a Dedicatory Epistle from Grynæus to Erastus (the Swiss physician whose name survives in Erastianism), entreating him to act as the champion and apologist of Origen against the evil tongues that attacked his fame; and by another from Beatus Rhenanus to Hermann, Archbishop of Cologne. One of Erasmus's fellow-workers was an Englishman, Laurence Humphrey (Humfridus), by whom the three Dialogues against the Marcionites had been translated into Latin. Looking to the freedom with which topics

(1) It may be noted, that in a formal recantation of Anabaptist errors under Elizabeth, no mention of this opinion is found in the catalogue. (Collier's *Church History*, vi. 553, ed. 1840). In Hooper's list of Anabaptist doctrines, one is that they "take away all hope of pardon from those who, having received the Holy Ghost, fall into sin" (Hardwicke, p. 90), and this seems inconsistent with their alleged Universalism.

outside the range of traditional orthodoxy had been discussed in Sir Thomas More's *Utopia*, it seems far from improbable that his intercourse with Erasmus may have touched on the wider hope associated with the name of Origen.[2] Anyhow it will hardly be disputed that wherever Origen was studied there was necessarily an opening made for the reception of the views with which his name was identified.

The next fact in the history we are tracing was the disappearance of the Article, with the two that had preceded it, from the text of the Articles, now reduced to thirty-nine, that were adopted by Convocation under Archbishop Parker in 1563. The Article in question appears in Parker's MS. as prepared for Convocation, but was erased as the result of discussion before the Articles were subscribed by the bishops (Hardwicke, p. 137). The grounds of that omission we are left to conjecture. It may be that the Anabaptists were now no longer looked on with the terror

(2) "He (Utopus, the founder of the ideal polity) . . . . seemed to doubt whether these different forms of religion might not all come from God, who might inspire men differently, He being possibly pleased with a variety in it" (p. 174). "Though there are many different forms of religion among them, yet all these, how various-soever, agree in the main point, which is the worshipping the Divine Essence, and therefore there is nothing to be seen or heard in their temples in which the several persuasions of them may not agree" (p. 185). He adds to this that "they believed that there was a state of rewards and punishments for the good and bad after this life" (p. 175), but defines nothing as to their nature and duration. (*Utopia*, trans. by J. H. St. John, 1838). It is obvious that this view came directly under the anathema of the Eighteenth Article. So we find More objecting to Luther that he had "revived Augustine's teaching as to the damnation of unbaptized infants" (Seebohm, *Oxf. Ref.* p. 471).

which they inspired under Edward VI., that they were dwindling into a despised sect, that it was thought better not to suggest the opinion condemned to those who might otherwise remain ignorant of it. As it is, I confess myself unable to find any traces of the wider hope in the multiplied controversies of the reigns of Elizabeth and James, and when it appears it is found where one would least have looked for it, among the Puritan students of Emmanuel College, Cambridge.

> "Via prima salutis
> Quod minime reris, Graiâ pandetur ab urbe."

Of Peter Sterry, "sometime Fellow of Emmanuel College, Cambridge, and late Preacher of the Gospel in London," there remain, so far as I know, only two volumes of sermons, published posthumously in 1683 and 1710 respectively, and a treatise on *The Freedom of the Will.* The first volume of the sermons has a long preface with the signature of J. White, who is identified with Jeremiah White, Fellow of Trinity College, Cambridge, and Chaplain to Oliver Cromwell, himself the author of an elaborate treatise on *The Restoration of all Things,* published after his death in 1712, which advocates an unrestricted universalism; the second, a shorter preface without a signature. He died in 1674. The second volume contains a list of papers that he had left behind him, and which were to have been published if there seemed sufficient prospect of a remunerative sale. And in that list we find two suggestive headings :—

"That an eternity of duration having a beginning without end is exposed to difficulties."

"Of the state of the wicked after death, and of the mystery of Divine wrath and of the devil."

As this third volume was never, so far as I know, published, we are left to infer from what is extant what Sterry's thoughts were as to these mysterious problems. For the most part the sermons are what would be described by more scholastic theologians as mystical, not without a leaning to the doctrines of Fox and Barclay. Christ as the light, the seed of eternal life in and for every man, in union with Whom the soul finds its blessedness, through Whom the Father manifests Himself and fulfils His purpose—this is the ever-recurring theme of his discourses, often presented with wonderful beauty of imagery and thought, always with a devout and rapturous tenderness which reminds one of Tauler, or of Tauler's master, or à Kempis. But it is not easy to extract formulated statements of dogma from them. He seems to shrink from views and systems and propositions. I give, however, two extracts, which seem to contradict each other, from a Catechism which he is said to have drawn up for the use of his pupils.

"*Q.* What becomes of those who believe not in Christ?

"*A.* They lie under wrath while they live. Their souls are in prison with the devils at their death. At the end of the world their bodies are raised and joined to their souls; both are brought to judgment, both are cast into the lake that burns with fire and brimstone" (ii. p. 459).

The second part of the Catechism however, written, we may presume, for those who had a greater capacity for entering into his teaching, shows that we have to read between the lines and to think of the lake of fire as that into which death and hell were to be cast. He traces the growth of evil in man: "Disorder before God, contrariety to Him, enmity against Him. So the opposition groweth higher and higher, till wrath swallow up the Sin, the Sinner, the Shadow, and all of the first Adam; when Wrath itself is swallowed up of Grace and Glory. Both these came to pass in the Death and Resurrection of the second Adam, our Lord Jesus" (ii. p. 466).

What was meant by this is set forth more fully in a letter to a friend who is addressed as "Noble Sir" (query, Sir Henry Vane the younger?):—

"Jesus Christ, as the universal Person, and Spirit in which all these subsisted, which alone truly subsisted in All, by dying, carried down the whole offending and polluted world into death; in that death all things are dissolved into their first principle, into the Divine Unity, into the Unity of the Eternal Spirit: Thus are the sins and the sinners no more for ever; thus all sins, sinners, wrath are swallowed up in the first unity of the Eternal Spirit, which is the fountain of Beauty, the fountain of Love" (ii. p. 474).

The student of Mr. Maurice's works will scarcely ail to recognise the parallelism, probably the unconscious parallelism, with Sterry's words, of the memorable passage in the *Theological Essays,* which led to his correspondence with Dr. Jelf, and ultimately to his expulsion from King's College:—

"What dream of ours can reach to the assertion of St. John that death and hell shall be cast into the lake of fire? I cannot fathom the meaning of such expressions. But they are written: I accept them, and give thanks for them. I feel there is an abyss of death into which I may sink and be lost. Christ's Gospel reveals an abyss of love below that; I am content to be lost in that" (p. 442).

I have used the term "unconscious parallelism," because I see no indication that Mr. Maurice had Sterry's words in his mind at the time he wrote this passage. On the other hand, the manner in which he mentions Sterry in his *Moral and Metaphysical Philosophy* (ii. p. 350, ed. 1874) shows that he was one of the few by whom in our time the works in question were known and studied, and there was much in all that Sterry wrote with which he must have felt profound sympathy. Of that writer's influence on his contemporaries we know but little. He was one of Cromwell's chaplains, and was with him on his death-bed (Carlyle's *Cromwell,* ii. p. 663, ed. 1845). His own deathbed was attended by Whichcote, one of the so-called Cambridge Platonists, who, as also a Fellow of Emmanuel, knew him well and had the profoundest reverence for him, wishing even to preach his funeral sermon (*Pref. to* vol. ii. of *Sterry's Sermons*). Of Whichcote himself an interesting account will be found in Canon Westcott's lecture in *Masters of English Theology*. And it will be seen that the extracts there given have much that is common with Sterry's modes of thought and phraseology. Baxter, in a passage which I have heard or read, but which I am unable to verify, couples him somewhere with Sir H. Vane the younger, and gives a summary judgment on their teaching as all "vanity and sterility." Whichcote was the contemporary at Cambridge of Milton and of Taylor, of Barrow and of Ray (Westcott, p. 150), and we may add of Tillotson. He was the friend of Cudworth and of Henry More. His writings were collected and published after his death by Shaftesbury. We may well trace the wider theology of Barrow, as seen in the extracts given in the Study on *The Salvation of the Heathen*, in part at least, to the minds with which he was thus brought into contact. It was in that school that Tillotson imbibed the tendencies which made him stand out in contrast to most of the other divines of the Revolution period. We may feel sure, with scarcely the shadow of a doubt, that there was hardly one of that company of thinkers who was not asking himself and others the question, Shall not the Judge of all the earth do right?[3]

(3) A few extracts from Whichcote's *Sermons* (1698) may be interesting as showing the general drift of his mind. "If the sinner leave off to sin, and condemn himself, then the necessity of punishment is taken away" (p. 319). "It is more according to the mind of

And there was scarcely one of the group who did not in some way or other grapple with the question and find an answer. Henry More, in a passage quoted by Dr. Farrar (*Mercy and Judgment*, p. 26), uses words that could have no other drift. "The measure of Providence is the Divine goodness which has no bounds but itself, which is infinite. . . . . As much as the light exceeds the shadows, so much do the regions of happiness exceed those of sin and misery. . . . . This is a marvel of marvels to me, that the goodness of God being infinite, the effects thereof should be so narrow and finite as men commonly conceit" (*Divine Dialogues*, pp. 479, 515). Cudworth, also quoted by Dr. Farrar (*Mercy and Judgment*, p. 27), "sees no reason why God may not as well change the course of nature and work a miracle for man's salvation as well as for his destruction." Of the leaning of Taylor's mind I have given an illustration in the note on *Conditional Immortality*. But it may be worth while to give other evidence in the following passages from his sermon on the *Miracles of Divine Mercy*:—

"I said formerly that there are many secret and undiscerned mercies by which men live, and of which

God that a sinner should repent than undergo the torments of the damned to all eternity." "The creature's suffering punishment is a very sorry amend for transgression. For what doth God gain by it?" (p. 319). "Hell arises out of a man's self. Hell's fuel is the guilt of a man's conscience" (p. 86). "Where there is wisdom and goodness in the agent all punishment is for instruction, reformation, and bettering of the offender, for example to by-standers, not for revenge upon the party" (p. 315).

men can give no account till they come to give God thanks at their publication; and of this sort is that mercy which God reserves for the souls of many millions of men and women, concerning whom we have no hopes, if we account concerning them by the usual proportions of revelation and Christian commandments; and yet we are taught to hope some strange good things for them by the analogy and general rules of the Divine Mercy. The pains of the damned are infinitely too fiery to pass lightly upon persons who cannot help themselves, and who, if they were helped with clearer revelation, would have avoided it. But as in these things we must not pry into the secrets of the Divine economy, being sure, whether it be so or not, it is most just, even as it is; so we may expect to see the glories of the Divine mercy made public in unexpected instances at the great day of manifestation."—*Works* (ed. Heber), vi. pp. 198, 199.

Or again from the sermon on *Christ's Advent to Judgment.* Here again we have a drift towards the doctrine of annihilation:—

"Origen was not the first that said the pains of the damned should cease." He then presses the words of Justin Martyr, as in the passage hereafter quoted in the Study on *Conditional Immortality,* and continues: "And whereas the general sentence is given to all wicked persons, to all on the left hand to go into everlasting fire, it is answered that the fire indeed is everlasting, but not all that enters into it is everlasting, but only the devils for whom it was prepared, and other more mighty criminals (according as St. John intimates): though also, *everlasting* signifies only to the end of its proper period."

"Concerning this doctrine of theirs, so severe and yet so moderate, there is less to be objected than against the supposed fancy of Origen; for it is a strange consideration to suppose an eternal torment to those to whom it was never threatened, to those who never heard of Christ, to those that lived probably well, to heathens of good lives, to ignorant and untaught people, to people surprised in a single crime, to men that die young in their natural follies and foolish lusts, to them that fall in a sudden gaiety and excessive joy, to all alike; to all infinite and eternal, even to unwarned people, and that this should be inflicted by God who infinitely loves His creatures, who died for them, who pardons easily and pities readily, and excuses much, and delights in our being saved, and would not have us to die, and takes little things in exchange for great: it is certain that God's mercies are infinite, and it is also certain that the matter of eternal torments cannot be understood; and when the schoolmen go about to reconcile the Divine justice to that severity, and consider why God punishes eternally a temporal sin or a state of evil, they speak variously and uncertainly, and unsatisfyingly."—*Works* (ed. Heber), v. pp. 47, 48.

It is right to add that with the characteristic

rhetorical many-sidedness, the one besetting fault of Taylor as a theologian, which hinders him from taking the place he might otherwise have claimed among the masters of those who know, he passes on, after these bold admissions, which must have startled many in his own time, as much as Dr. Farrar's sermons on *Eternal Hope* have startled many in ours, to speak of the punishments of the wicked in the old traditional tone, recalling his interpretation of the "second death," and explains it as meaning "a dying to all felicity," a being "miserable for ever."

Tillotson had but little share either in the mysticism of Sterry, or the Platonism of Whichcote and his friends, or the gorgeous rhetoric of Taylor. He was rather what one may call an "all-round" man, judicious, liberal, sympathising, comprehensive; not, perhaps, without the safe caution which characterises a man who is making his way to high places in the Church, or has already attained to them. But he, too, had not escaped the Cambridge ἦθος of his time, and may have come personally under Whichcote's teaching. And this is the answer which he has to give to the problem which weighed heavily on men's minds. I quote from his *Sermon* xxxv. (ed. 1782) on the *Eternity of Hell Torments.* He insists earnestly, as indeed any one might do, on the exclusion of impenitent sinners from heaven, but he adds, "the Judge retains the right of remitting the penalty." "If it be in any wise inconsistent either with righteousness or goodness to make sinners miserable for ever, He will not do it;" but he adds, as if half afraid of the admission, "we have every reason to believe that the punishment will be everlasting." Thomas Burnet, Master of the Charter House, had been a pupil of Tillotson's at Cambridge, and had been brought more or less under the same influences without the same motives for reticence, and he, in his *De Statu Mortuorum*, published after his death (p. 113), maintains that God neither wills nor can endure the perpetual affliction and torment of his creatures (Farrar, *Mercy and Judgment*, p. 47). Stillingfleet took Tillotson's view that God was not bound to fulfil a threatened sentence (*ibid.*). William Law, the author of the *Serious Call*, gave utterance to his hope as follows: "As for the purification of all human nature, either in this world or in some after ages, I fully believe it" (*Letters*, p. 175: 1766). Sherlock (b. 1678), Master of the Temple, and afterwards Bishop of London, carried on the Cambridge tradition of liberality of thought. I quote from his *Practical Discourses concerning Future Judgment*, which are at least as suggestive as anything of Taylor's or of Barrow's: "Some men do as peremptorily damn all the heathen world as if it were an article of their creed, and think all those enemies to the grace of Christ who do not; but for my part, I dare neither damn nor save them, for I know nothing about the matter" (p. 115). And again: "The great love I have for mankind inclines me to hope better things for them, and that strong persuasion I have of the justice and goodness of God inclines me to believe better of them" (p. 117). In the anathemas that "damned" Papists and heretics he finds that which "destroys not only Christian charity, but common humanity" (p. 119). He thinks it possible that the intermediate state of the wicked may be such that they may even flatter themselves with false hopes till the day of judgment comes (p. 161). On the whole, while rejecting Origen's view of universal restitution as not having the least countenance from Scripture (p. 218), he falls back upon the belief that the judgments of God will be seen to be righteous, and that "allowances will be made for ignorances, circumstances, and temptations" (p. 199).

A little known book, by an obscure writer, tne treatise *De Vita Functorum Statu* of James Windet, was published in 1763, with a special commendatory preface by Dr. Franck, one of the then Bishop of London's chaplains. Its character was chiefly historical, reviewing rabbinic and patristic opinions as to Sheol or Hades, as to the finite nature of the punishments of Gehenna, as to the degrees of severity in those punishments. He finally maintains his own view that the terms "aeonian," to "aeons of aeons," and the like convey the idea of indefinite, but not of infinite duration. The book is of no great value in itself, but its coming into the world under such sponsorship was sufficiently suggestive. And as the sequel shows, it fell on ground that was prepared to reproduce its germs of thought, thirty, or sixty, or a hundred fold.

In Thomas Newton (b. 1702, d. 1783), Bishop of Bristol and Dean of St. Paul's, still remembered, and perhaps to some extent read, for his *Discourses of Prophecy*, we have another link in the chain of the Cambridge succession. He was elected a Fellow at Trinity in 1723, and rose rapidly on the ladder of Court favour. His works were published in three volumes, the last of which contains a sermon on the "Final State and Condition of Men," of which it is not too much to say that it is the boldest and most startling utterance in the whole range of English theology. Having dealt with questions as to the degrees of punishment, he passes on to say that "the great difficulty of all is its duration. . . . . It is one of the most knotty points of divinity, and the hardest to be reconciled to our reason. . . . . Some assert (its endlessness) and some deny. . . . . The truth may probably lie in the mid-way between both." He rejects the theory of annihilation and the limited sense of "aeonian" (p. 717), and the view that God is not obliged to execute his threats (p. 720). "But the eternal punishment is of the wicked, and the wicked may repent and change" (p. 724). He puts the argument from analogy. "To suppose that a man's happiness and misery to all eternity should absolutely and unchangeably be fixed and determined by the uncertain behaviour of a few years in this life is a supposition even more unreasonable than that a man's mind and manners should be completely formed and fashioned in his cradle, and his whole future fortune and condition depend altogether upon his infancy. . . . . "Here it is admitted that we are free moral agents, and feel and enjoy our liberty, and shall we be deprived of this privilege hereafter, and be bound in the chains of fatal necessity? Repentance is therefore not impossible even in hell. . . . . In the end all must be subdued, so that their punishment may more properly be called indefinite than infinite" (p. 725). "It cannot consist with the mercy, or the goodness, or wisdom, or even the justice of the Supreme Being to punish any of His creatures for no end or purpose, neither for their own correction nor for a warning to others" (p. 275). He does not shrink from pushing these principles to their extremest logical conclusion. "Time and torments, much more an eternity of torments, must overcome the proudest spirit, and the devil himself must at last be subdued and submit" (p. 230), though he does not state explicitly what he believes will be the consequence of that submission.

There are, I imagine, few stranger facts in the history of English theology than that such views should have been published in the eighteenth century by a bishop of unimpeached orthodoxy, and that, so far as I have been able to trace, no notice seems to have been taken of their publication. I have not come across any sermons, or pamphlets, or treatises against them. There does not appear to have been any outcry of alarm. And in the sermon itself there is a noticeable absence of any consciousness that what was written was likely to startle or shock men's minds. He writes calmly, as one unconscious of reproach, giving his solution of what he had described, in somewhat unemotional language, as a "knotty point of divinity."

In continuing the record of Cambridge witnesses to the wider hope, I have been led to a slight deviation from chronological order, and must go back some quarter of a century to discuss the position of Butler in regard to this question. It was not to be expected that a mind like his, calm, cautious, balancing, should commit itself to speculations on the life that lies behind the veil, to us unseen and unknown. What he was most concerned with was to impress the mind of the generation in which he lived with the seriousness of life. The whole natural course of things bore its witness that God does reward good and punish evil now, and the present may legitimately be regarded as exhibiting tendencies which may hereafter attain completeness. Even in this life Nature so works with her inexorable laws that it were good for many a man that he had never been born. Who can say that that doom may not be written hereafter for these, and, it may be, for others? Efforts that men make to undo the evil past now are often unavailing. May not "too late" be their sentence hereafter? Were men wise, even with the lower wisdom of prudence, to assume that their sins were beneath the notice of a righteous God, or that his mind was one of an easy-going benevolence, not apportioning blessedness or misery according to the character of His creatures? His own temperament, and the circumstances in which he lived, led him to press these thoughts upon his readers, and so far he may be claimed as on the side of those who hold to the severer aspect of the truth as to God's judgments. On the other hand, Dr. Farrar says with truth (*Eternal Hope*, p. 185), that there is nothing that Butler says that he also does not hold, that he leaves room for the hope which yet he does not utter. Historical theology, a survey of the thoughts and opinions as to the unseen world which have found utterance in the past of Christendom, was altogether foreign to his studies, and, perhaps, to the temper of his mind. We have to gather what we can from his reticence. He is silent, then, as to the duration of punishments, silent as to their nature, except to suggest that they may be the "natural consequences" of our evil deeds, *i.e.* that they may consist in the development of evil, the memory of sins, the loss of capacity for that which is alone the satisfying blessedness of man's nature, *i.e.*, translated into theological language, the *poena damni.* He falls back upon the belief that every one will be equitably dealt with according to the standard of equity which is recognised by man's reason and conscience, and, as I have shown in the Study on *The Salvation of the Heathen*, that the atoning work of

Christ is not limited in its redeeming and restorative influences to those who have known the report of it. The arguments on which he rests the belief in a future life as the groundwork of all religion prior to revelation, show that he would have had no sympathy with the theory of Conditional Immortality. His thought that the influence of the life of the society of the redeemed might tend to work amendment in all throughout God's universe who are capable of repentance, points to an operation of the Divine love not limited to earth, of repentance as possible for the souls of men, or for other beings, elsewhere. His belief that in that society there may be scope for the activities of justice and charity suggests, as I have shown in my letter to Dr. Farrar (reprinted in this volume), the inference that that charity may find objects of its compassion as well as of its admiring or adoring love. Butler's destruction of all his MSS. leaves us to conjecture whether he had ever dealt in them with problems which must sometimes, at least, have pressed upon his mind, as on that of other profound thinkers. It may be that like others who in earlier or more recent times have been equally reticent in their public utterances, he would have acknowledged some aspects of the truth when presented to him by others to which he had not the confidence to give expression for himself.

The current of religious thought which took its start from the preaching of the great Methodist teachers, alike in the Calvinism of Whitfield and the belief in universal redemption on which the Wesleys rested, tended to give prominence to the "terrors of the Lord," to the effort on the part of individual penitents to secure salvation for themselves rather than to questionings as to the fate of others who had not secured it according to the formulæ of their systems. As in the case of Sterry, however, the preaching of the Cross of Christ in its fulness worked in some at least to a wider hope than that of the Methodist preachers. I have before me the fourth edition of a volume of *Dialogues on Universal Restoration*, by Elhanan Winchester, the work obviously of a sincere and devout believer who had found in that belief the solution of his difficulties. The book is not without a certain measure of scholarship as well as of emotional thought. It discusses the meaning of "aeonian," and arrives at the conclusion that it does not necessarily connote the idea of endless duration. It accepts the patristic view of the Descent into Hell and of the preaching to "the spirits in prison," with a fair statement of the evidence in each case. It brings together the passages of Scripture which point to the universality of the purpose of the Divine love, and suggests the hope that that purpose will not always be frustrated. The most striking passage in the volume, however, reminding us of the closing paragraph of Barrow's *Sermons on Universal Redemption*, and not without suggestive parallels in the writings of F. D. Maurice, is one in which the author narrates the manner in which he had been led to embrace the wider hope.

He had been brought to commit himself to the love and righteousness of God, and then he continues: "Immediately these words came into my mind with great power and sweetness, 'In an acceptable time have I heard thee; and in a day of salvation have I helped thee' (Isaiah xlix. 8). And I had then such a view of Christ as made me to cry out, 'Glory to God in the highest. This is salvation! I know this is salvation!' .... I saw the fulness, sufficiency, and willingness of Christ to save me and all men in such a manner, as constrained me to venture my soul into His arms; and if I had had ten thousand souls I could have trusted them all in His hands. And O, how I did long, that every soul of Adam's race might come to know the love of God in Christ Jesus!"

From this he was led on to ask, as others have been led, whether he could think of God's love as narrower than his own; whether His will to save all would be for ever frustrated; and so reached the conclusion that in the end God would be all in all, and that all the "spirits of all flesh," each according to his capacity, would be sharers in the blessedness of knowing Him as He is.

A conviction resting on a subjective emotion such as this has, of course, but a weak foundation. It may have to be balanced by facts of which the emotion takes no account, perhaps by emotion of another kind and tending to a different conclusion. But it will be allowed, I think, that the story of the way in which the conviction dawned upon the soul is not more subjective than that which we acknowledge as having a spiritual reality in a thousand narratives of conversion as wrought in every religious society, from the Church of Rome to the Salvation Army. We cannot doubt, I think, that the man believed and was saved. We cannot wonder that he should believe also that what had been possible for him was possible also for others. I have quoted the narrative as a representative instance of the way in which the doctrine of Universal Restoration commends itself to devout souls, not because they are indifferent to sin or take inadequate views of the Holiness of God, but because they have felt the misery of the one and the blessedness of the manifestation of the love of God in Christ which has translated them into the other.

That certainly must be the explanation of the adoption of the wider hope by such a man as Thomas Erskine of Linlathen. Of all the devout thinkers I have known, he was, by the evidence of all who had the happiness of knowing him, conspicuously among the most devout. No words could more adequately describe his character and life than those which speak of our having our "conversation," our "citizenship," in heaven, tasting of the good word of God and of the powers of the world to come. How far he was indebted to the teaching of any previous thinker I am unable to say. His own writings represent, almost or altogether, the workings of his own mind, without reference to or quotation from the writings of others. That he was brought up under the influences of the Calvinistic theology of the Kirk, that he found himself unable to reconcile that theology with his intuitive conceptions of the divine righteousness, or with what he learnt of that righteousness from the New Testament, that this led him to work out for himself a more satisfying and hopeful theology may, I imagine, be assumed without much risk of error. When the hope that the light of Christ might come with a power to save those who had not known or had resisted it in their life on earth first came to find distinct expression in his thoughts I do not know. Its germs seem to me to be found in two of his earliest publications, the *Natural Evidence for the Truth of Revealed Religion* (1821), and the *Unconditional Freeness of the Gospel* (4th edition, 1831). The ground of his belief is that the atonement of Christ manifested the love of the Father to all men, and secured for all a state of blessedness, not merely an exemption from punishment, which any one may therefore claim. That blessedness is not compatible with sin either in its grosser forms or in that of a spiritual selfishness. Sin left to itself is its own punishment. The condemnation of men is *ipso facto* their rejection of the blessedness thus offered them: "Sin is a disease of the mind which necessarily occasions misery" (*Nat. Evid.*, p. 197). In the book just quoted Mr. Erskine's language is consistent with the thought that death is the limit of our opportunities for embracing the salvation thus offered. "Eternity is every moment coming nearer; and our characters are hourly assuming a form more decidedly connected with the extreme of happiness or misery" (*ibid.* p. 196). "If we are placed here to be fitted for eternity, we must know God and love Him, in order that we may have pleasure in His presence" (*ibid.* p. 170). But in the other volume there is a clearer and bolder utterance. "The first hope which any man can arrive at with regard to his own personal acceptance with God, must be drawn from the great general manifestation of Divine love directed to *the destruction of evil and the restoration of the ruined race.* The individual drops are thus merged in the ocean, and self is lost in the liberty, the universality, the impartiality of redemption" (*Uncond. Freeness*, p. 84). In spite of the fact that "evil is still spread over the earth, and the serpent's crested and uncrushed head still hovers over it," he clings to this hope: "These are animating thoughts for poor wanderers in the wilderness, who have listened to the Saviour's voice. For them the fall, with all its sin and misery and darkness, will soon pass away, having served under the control of Him who bringeth good out of evil to glorify the Divine attributes, and to introduce a high and holy and happy existence—higher and holier and happier than that which Adam lost. . . . . The gate of Eden will once again be unbarred, and the banished ones brought back."

It will scarcely be questioned that this sounds almost like an echo of Gregory of Nyssa and of Sterry. It is balanced, however, by other passages which seem to set up again the limitations which the writer had swept away. There is a judgment of condemnation "at the close of this dispensation," and the final words of that condemnation is "Depart" (*ibid.* pp. 222, 223). I fail to find any passages in Mr. Erskine's *Doctrine of Election* which distinctly bears on the question of the duration of the punishment of evil. The whole book is, as one might expect, one long protest against the Calvinistic theory which the writer looked on as a perversion of the truth that every exercise of the sovereignty of God must be thought of as consistent with His righteousness and love; that He elects men to circumstances and conditions which form their probation, not to salvation or perdition; that His punishment even of the vessels of wrath is for their correction, not for their destruction; that salvation from the true curse of sin is found not in the remission of its penalty, but in the acceptance of that penalty by the sinner as that which he has deserved. Of President Edwards's famous treatise on *The Freedom of the Will* he writes: "Jesus came preaching peace by declaring his Father to be the common Father of men, prodigals and all. Edwards's book has not preached peace; it has preached perplexity and doubt. by declaring that the

Father of Jesus Christ is not the Father of all men; and that although He created all men He only loves a few of them" (*Doct. of Elect.* p. 569). Later on in life, as his published letters show, and as those know who were admitted to intimacy with him, Mr. Erskine spoke with less hesitation. The phrase "accepting punishment" seemed to him to explain almost everything. The idea of this life being a probation fell into the background as compared with that of its being an education, the first stage of a process of training which is continued after death, the punishments of which were always meant to be corrective, though men might accept or frustrate the Divine love that assigned them. I do not know that he was familiar with patristic views of the intermediate state or of the preaching to the spirits in prison. His tone in speaking of those who had passed in behind the veil was for the most part hopeful. "Poor Voltaire!" I remember his saying, on hearing that Dr. Jelf had in his controversy with Mr. Maurice challenged any one to maintain that his salvation could be thought of as possible. "Poor Voltaire! I have no doubt he thinks very differently now."

I have dwelt at some length on Mr. Erskine's teaching, though strictly speaking, of course, he can hardly take his place among *English* theologians, because to him more than to any other religious thinker Mr. Maurice had, by his own acknowledgment, stood in the relation of a disciple. He became acquainted with his writings during his undergraduate life at

Cambridge in 1830. A personal acquaintance followed in 1841, which rapidly ripened, as might have been expected with minds so congenial, into the intimacy of friendship. In 1852 he dedicated to him, with a warm acknowledgment of all that he owed to his teaching, his sermons on *The Prophets and Kings of the Old Testament.* Mr. Maurices's position was as far as possible from being that of a conscious eclecticism, but if the student of his writings were to note the three chief elements which entered into his teaching and fashioned his life, they would be found, I believe (1) in the doctrine of the Light that lighteth every man, as it was held by Fox or Barclay in the Society of Friends; (2) in the thoughts which Mr. Erskine's teaching had impressed on his mind as to the unconditional freeness of the Gospel, the nature of the Atonement, and the purpose of all Divine punishment; and (3) in that which was conspicuous by its absence in their systems, the recognition of the witness borne by the polity and the sacraments of the Catholic Church to the truths which they had maintained as from the standpoint at once of individualism and of humanity. He felt it to be his work to proclaim these truths as he held them, fused and harmonised by the experience of his own life and the width of his own sympathy, in season and out of season. The restrictions of the Divine love which he found in Calvinism, in Romanism, in Anglicanism, as ordinarily interpreted, were to be broken down, as had been of old the middle wall of partition between Jew and Gentile. The belief in a love which was educating men in this world, and did not cease to educate them when they had left it, might have been read between the lines in well-nigh every sermon that he wrote. As it was, however, it did not attract notice till he published, in 1853, the *Theological Essays* which led to his expulsion from King's College. I am not about to repeat the history of the controversy with Dr. Jelf which issued in that expulsion, but it may be well to state clearly what was then condemned, and to illustrate it by other more definite statements on the subject. The portion of the *Theological Essays* which formed the basis of Dr. Jelf's indictment occupies ten pages. The points on which special stress is laid are (1) that Mr. Maurice maintained that our Lord had excluded "the notion of duration" from the word "eternal;" (2) that the three score years and ten "of man's life" do not absolutely limit the compassion of the Father of Spirits; (3) that "we want that clear, broad assertion of the Divine charity which the Bible makes, and which carries us immeasurably beyond all that we can ask or think." This was followed by the passage quoted on p. 195. In that passage Dr. Jelf saw what seemed to him, after a protracted correspondence, a "denial of the eternity of future punishments," or at least an "atmosphere of doubt cast upon the simple meaning of the word *eternal*, and a general notion of ultimate salvation for all."

Part of that correspondence included a letter from Mr. Maurice to a friend, whom the publication of his *Life* (ii. p. 15) enables us to identify as Professor J. F. A. Hort, of Cambridge, which I think it right to add as a fuller and more specific statement of Mr. Maurice's teaching. It was written, it may be added, in 1849, four years before the publication of the *Theological Essays*:—

"My duty then I feel is this:—

"(1) To assert that which I know, that which God has revealed, His absolute universal love in all possible ways, and without any limitation.

"(2) To tell myself and all men that to know this love and to be moulded by it is *the* blessing we are to seek.

"(3) To say that this is eternal life.

"(4) To say that the want of it is death.

"(5) To say that if they believe in the Son of God they have eternal life.

"(6) To say that if they have not the Son of God they have not life.

"(7) *Not* to say who has the Son of God, because I do not know.

"(8) *Not* to say how long any one may remain in eternal death, because I do not know.

"(9) *Not* to say that all will be necessarily raised out of eternal death, because I do not know.

"(10) *Not* to judge any before the time, or to judge other men at all, because Christ has said, 'Judge not, that ye be not judged.'

"(11) *Not* to play with Scripture by quoting passages which have not the slightest connexion with the subject, such as 'Where the tree falleth it shall lie.'

"(12) *Not* to invent a scheme of purgatory, and so take upon myself the office of the Divine Judge.

"(13) *Not* to deny God a right of using punishments at any time or anywhere for the reformation of His creatures.

"(14) *Not* to contradict Christ's words, 'These shall be beaten with few, these with many stripes,' for the sake of maintaining a theory of the equality of sins.

"(15) Not to think any punishment of God's so great as the saying, 'Let them alone.'"

It will be seen from these propositions (1) that Mr. Maurice was justified in saying that he did not hold a theory of Universalism; (2) that he excludes, to the extent of ignoring, the doctrine of a so-called Conditional Immortality; (3) that he held that God's punishments of evil, though they may include a retributive element, are also designed to be reformatory; (4) that he held that the state after death is one in which, with some exceptions, it is possible for the souls that are under punishment to turn from darkness to light, and from death to life.

As it was, for good or evil—we may believe for good rather than evil in the long run, however wanting in courage or justice the course may have seemed at the time—the Council of King's College shrank from formulating any statement of the doctrines they condemned. They contented themselves with the vaguest language of alarm. There were in the Essay in question certain "opinions and doubts" as to "certain points of belief" on the "punishment of the wicked and the final issues of the Day of Judgment" which were "of dangerous tendency and calculated to unsettle the minds of the theological students." The "continuance of Mr. Maurice's connexion with the college" would therefore "be detrimental to its usefulness." The Council rejected a proposal made by Mr. Gladstone for an inquiry by competent theologians "how far the writings of Professor Maurice, or any propositions contained in them which have been brought under [the notice of] the Council, are conformable to or at variance with the three Creeds and the formularies of the Church of England." We are left to conjecture the grounds of the refusal. It may be that they felt it would be difficult to prove a distinct charge of teaching at variance with the Creeds. It may be that they felt that their functions were limited to the protection of the college committed to their care, and that they had no authority to assume anything approaching to a judicial interpretation of the formularies of the Church of England. Anyhow, the natural inference from the fact that Bishop Blomfield took no further action, and left Mr. Maurice undisturbed in the chaplaincy of Lincoln's Inn, is that his teaching did not seem to him, however unsettling it might be to the minds of students, or however detrimental it might prove to be to the interests of the college, to be outside the limits of the comprehensiveness of the Church of England.

A more important fact has recently been brought to light in the recent lives of Bishop Wilberforce and Mr. Maurice. Mr. Gladstone stated in a letter written at the time to Lord Lyttelton (*Life of Maurice*, ii. p. 195) that he cherished the hope that the inquiry which he proposed would issue in the arrangement of some "*formula concordiæ* which might avert the scandal and mischief" of the dismissal on which the Council of King's College determined. Such a formula was actually prepared by *the* Bishop whose aim it was to represent all that was most catholic, most Anglican, most evangelical, in the English Church. The formula thus tendered by Bishop Wilberforce was accepted by Mr. Maurice without hesitation, and its importance in the history of the controversy justifies its insertion here.

"I cannot but think that in contending for a truth you have been led into an exaggeration of its proportions. Will you, then, suffer me to try whether I can aid you to make that truth more plain?

"(1) What, then, I understand to be charged against you is this: That you teach 'that the revelation of God's love given to us in the Gospel is incompatible with His permitting any of the creatures He has loved to be consigned to never-ending torment; and that you therefore do, with more or less clearness, revive the old doctrine of the Universalists, that after some unknown period of torments all such must be restored.' Now *I* do not understand you to intend to advocate any such view. What I do understand you to say is this: That to represent God as revenging upon His creatures, by torments through never-ending extensions of time, their sinful acts committed here is (1) unwarrantably to transfer to the eternal world the conditions of this world. For that time is of this world; and that eternity is not time prolonged, but rather time abolished, and that it is therefore logically incorrect to substitute in the Scriptural proposition for 'eternal death' 'punishment extended through a never-ending duration of time;' and (2) as this is unwarranted, so it is dangerous: (*a*) because by transferring our earthly notions of such prolonged vengeance to God it misrepresents His character; (*b*) because as men recoil from applying to themselves or others such a sentence, it leads to the introduction of unwarranted palliatives which practically explain away the true evil and fatal consequences of sin. What I understand you to mean affirmatively to teach is this: (*a*) That the happiness of the creature consists in his will being brought into harmony with the Will of God. (*b*) That we are here under a Divine system in which God, through the Mediator and by the Spirit, acts on the will of the creature to bring it into harmony with His own Will. (*c*) That we see in this world the creature, in defiance of the love of his Creator, able to resist His merciful Will.

and to harden himself in opposition to it, and that misery in body and soul is the result of that oppotion. (*d*) That it is revealed to us that our state in this world is, so to speak, the seminal principle of what it is to be in its full development in that world which is to come, and that therefore a will hardened against His must be the extremest misery to the creature both in body and soul; that this hardened separation from God, with its consequent torments, is the 'death eternal' spoken of in Scripture — the lake of fire 'where their worm dieth not, and the fire is not quenched,' &c., of which we know no limits, and from which we know of no escape; concerning which, therefore, it is unsafe to dogmatise as if it was subject to earthly conditions; and that in any contemplation of its horrors we must always contemplate God's exceeding love, and remember that He is striving through the Gospel to deliver every sinner from it who against his own sin will appeal to Him through Christ. (*e*) Finally, that to conclude that after a certain period of such sufferings God's vengeance would be satisfied and the lost forgiven future suffering would be one phase of the error against which you write, and therefore as remote as possible from your teaching."

This statement of his teaching was accepted by Mr. Maurice "entirely and unreservedly." He "could not improve it by any alterations or additions." The letter was sent to Bishop Blomfield, but there is no record of its having met with any answer or attention. The result was that the Council of King's College was led to condemn as "unsettling" and of "dangerous tendency" teaching which Bishop Wilberforce had "all along" believed, and still more, of course, after the acceptance of his statement of it, to be "entirely orthodox."

It lay in the nature of the case that the moral and spiritual influence of Mr. Maurice was widened and not narrowed by the position which he thus occupied as the protomartyr of the wider hope. Disciples gathered round him who proclaimed from the house-tops what till the publication of the *Theological Essays* he had spoken in the closet. Foremost among these one has to place the honoured name of Charles Kingsley. There are, I take it, few instances in the history of theology of more loving and loyal discipleship. One feels as one reads the letters that passed between them that the master and the scholar were worthy of each other, that each presented elements of character which were complementary to those of the other. To him Maurice turned from older friends and teachers as to a man like-minded with himself, destined to carry on his wishes as a destroying Thalaba of the false *eidôla* of popular theology. A comparison of the two biographies suggests the thought that it was the more impetuous character of the scholar that led the master to speak out the thoughts that were seething in the minds of others. Mr. Kegan Paul records that it was through Kingsley in 1854 that he first learnt to entertain the wider hope of a repentance and a restoration as possible after death (Kingsley's *Life*, i. p. 228). And it was to this point that Kingsley gave a special prominence in all his teaching, notably in the correspondence with Thomas Cooper, the Chartist, which appears in his *Life* (i. 392—396). It was on this ground, and with the desire to obtain from the leaders of the Oxford School (Pusey, Liddon, and their followers) an explanation of the Damnatory Clauses of the Athanasian Creed which should include this, that in 1872 he joined, after having signed a petition for the removal or for an authoritative exposition of those clauses, in a protest against a proposal for its disuse (*Life*, ii. 395). That precise explanation he did not obtain. For the explanations which were actually given I refer the reader to the Study in this volume on *The Damnatory Clauses of the Athanasian Creed.*

The next stage in the history we are tracing is found in Mr. H. B. Wilson's contribution to *Essays and Reviews* in 1861. His Essay on *The National Church* ended with a paragraph on the question, "What shall become of 'the many' who at the close of their life on earth are but rudimentary spirits—germinal souls?" And his answer to the question is this: "The Roman Church has imagined a *limbus infantum*; we must rather entertain a hope that there shall be found, after the great adjudication, receptacles suitable for those who shall be infants, not as to years of terrestrial life, but as to spiritual development—nurseries, as it were, and seed-grounds, where the undeveloped may grow up under new conditions, and the perverted be restored. And when the Christian Church in all its branches shall have fulfilled its sublunary office and its Founder shall have surrendered His kingdom to the Great Father, all, both small and great, shall find a refuge in the bosom of the Universal Parent, to repose, or be quickened into higher life, in the ages to come, according to His will."

It is noticeable, whatever be the explanation of the fact, that in the elaborate indictment presented to the Lower House of Convocation by Dr. Jelf, and afterwards published under the title of *Specific Evidence of the Unsoundness of Essays and Reviews*, no notice was taken of this passage. As far as he was concerned, Mr. Wilson's words on this matter did not seem to him to call for special notice. It was not so, however, with others, and in the well-known case of Fendall *v.* Wilson it was the leading point on which stress was laid by the prosecution. Judgment was given against the defendant by Dr. Lushington, as judge of the Arches Court, but was reversed by the Judicial Committee of Privy Council, which consisted on that occasion of the Lord Chancellor (Westbury), the Archbishop of Canterbury (Dr. Longley), the Archbishop of York (Dr. Thomson), the Bishop of London (Dr. Tait), Lord Cranworth, Lord Chelmsford, and Lord Kingsdown. The decision of the Court on this point, after stating that it might be said that the effect of sustaining the judgment of the Court below would be to restore the 42nd Article of 1552 that had been withdrawn in 1562, was con tained in the following words: "We are not required, or at liberty, to express any opinion upon the mysterious question of the eternity of final punishment, further than to say that we do not find in the formularies to which this Article" (of the prosecution) "refers any such distinct declaration of our Church upon the subject as to require us to condemn as penal the expression of a hope by a clergyman that even the ultimate pardon of the wicked, who are condemned in the Day of Judgment, may be consistent with the will of Almighty God."

It was natural that this decision should be welcomed by Maurice and Kingsley and Stanley and others who, in greater or less measure, shared their views. Others who did not share them, who like Bishop Tait held that "the Gospel revelation does distinctly tell of a never-ending privation of God's favour for the lost" (we note the carefully chosen phraseology), maintained that the decision of the Privy Council said "not one word antagonistic to the sober, scriptural view," to which he thought the clergy would be wise to adhere in their preaching (*Charge*, 1866). In his often expressed admiration of Mr. Maurice, in his institution of him, in spite of the protest of many influential clergy, to the incumbency of Vere Street Chapel, we may find proofs that he at least must have rejoiced in the protection which the judgment gave to him and others like him. Dr. Pusey, on the other hand, put himself at the head of a movement which was to unite High Churchmen and Low in a league against the Privy Council decision. He preached an university sermon at Oxford on the Eternity of Punishment in a tone of fierce denunciation. It was noticeable, however, that his picture of the horrors of that punishment dwelt almost wholly on the unchecked development of moral evil, consequent on the *pœna damni*, as distinct from the *pœna sensus*, with only a passing reference to the "terrific physical miseries" of the fire and the worm. The natural consequences of sin were supposed to be its sufficient punishment. Hatred of God was, as indeed it must ever be, its own exceeding torment. The same emotion showed itself in the preface to the *Case as to the Legal Force of the Judgment of the Privy Council* (1864), which was submitted to Sir Roundell Palmer and Sir Hugh Cairns, and in which they were asked to advise whether a certain number of propositions supposed to be deduced from the judgment, six of which referred to the section on everlasting punishment, were or were not covered by it. The answer given by those distinguished lawyers was that they could not say. The judgment of the Privy Council furnished no "means of determining in the abstract any of the legal questions" which Dr. Pusey had raised. The white heat of that preface, which seems to have sent a shudder through the soul of good Bishop Patteson,[4] and which showed itself in Dr. Pusey's declaration that he and Mr. Maurice worshipped different Gods, and that the latter "blasphemed" his God, led him to urge that men should bring the Inspiration of Scripture and the Punishment of the Wicked into the "cries" of a general election, refusing to support any candidate for Parliament who would not pledge himself to reform the Court of Final Appeal, and supporting persons of whatever politics (query, Home Rulers and Liberationists?) who would so pledge themselves (p. 22).

But there is one passage of the preface which has not, I think, received the notice it deserves. Dr. Pusey, it appears, could have accepted Mr. Wilson's own statements as admitting of a tenable explanation. His "hope" or "opinion" might be only "a modification of the doctrine of Purgatory," and "the question whether that modification was consistent with Art. XXII. was not before the Court."—"Mr. Wilson did not deny hell."—Nay, he himself, in his defence, took the word "everlasting in its natural sense." The whole fierceness of Dr. Pusey's indignation was poured out on Lord Westbury for having gone beyond a simple acquittal, or verdict (such as the Primate had given) of "not proven," with "no temptation, except the pure love of the heresy, and the desire

(4) See *Life of Bishop Patteson*, ii. p. 127. It may be remembered that the Bishop's father, Judge Patteson, had supported Mr. Gladstone's amendment in the King's College Council of 1853.

of throwing open an Article of Faith against which Rationalism rebels" (pp. 10, 11). I content myself with referring to the passage now. Its bearing will be seen more clearly when we come to consider the discussion which followed after an interval of fourteen years between Dr. Pusey and Dr. Farrar.

The next memorable contribution to the literature of the question came from a prominent leader of the Evangelical school, the Rev. T. R. Birks, who, after the publication of his views, succeeded Mr. Maurice in the chair of Moral Philosophy at Cambridge. His mind also had worked its way, through much anxiety and perplexity, to what seemed to him a true solution of the great problem of the Mystery of Evil, and in 1867 he published his conclusions in a volume that bore the title of the *Victory of Divine Goodness.* In not a few passages it presents so close a verbal identity with the language of Mr. Maurice's *Theological Essays*, that in a writer of inferior calibre it would suggest the thought of a literary plagiarism. To him also the announcement "that death and hell should be cast into the lake of fire, is a work of redemption, a triumph of Divine love" (p. 171). He asks as to those who suffer the punishment of their sins, "Will they not be saved in a strange mysterious sense, when the depth of their unchangeable shame and sorrow finds beneath it a still lower depth of Divine compassion?" (p. 191). He rejects the notion that "lost souls are their own mutual tormentors, and given up to Satan to be tormented by him for ever," as "making hell the scene of Satan's triumphant malice, just as heaven is that of the Creator's triumphant love" (p. 47). He thinks it credible that the lost, "with the utmost personal humiliation and shame and anguish," may have "a contemplation of a ransomed universe, and of all the innumerable varieties of blessedness, such as would be fitted in its own nature to raise the soul into a trance of holy adoration" (p. 45). "Must not such a vision," he asks, "be unutterably blessed, in spite of all personal loss and ruin, shame and sorrow, and so death may be swallowed up in victory?" (p. 48). "Alike in the case of the saved and the unsaved, the heirs of glory and of shame, the Son of God will not have borne the curse and endured shame and agony in vain" (p. 171). This victory over evil extends even to Satan and his angels. "Ever-during, self-tormenting wickedness, unrestrained by the hand of God, belongs rather to the death which is God's last enemy, and which Christ has come to destroy and abolish for ever. . . . . It is the common boon which the Atonement secures to all mankind, the saved and the unsaved alike, that this awful, mighty enemy of God, the sum of all possible evil and misery in a God-forsaken universe, is destroyed, abolished, and done away with for ever" (p. 169). "The forbearance towards evil, while it lasts and seems to triumph, is a perfect forbearance. The victory over evil, when that forbearance is full, must be a perfect victory. The issues of judgment, however solemn, are such, and must be such, that . . . . the All-good, whose mercies are over all His works, can acquiesce in them with a deep complacency and delight." In this view "the doom of the lost is the object of acquiescence and holy contemplation to all the unfallen and the redeemed" (pp. 178, 179). He lays stress in interpreting the words, "Good were it for that man if he had never been born," that the word used for good is *καλόν*, not *ἀγαθόν*. "The honour is lost for ever, but the being remains a good, better than not being" (p. 195). He admits that Scripture is silent on the matter, but thinks that this "is no real presumption against the presence of a further truth, secretly implied in its statements, though not expressly and openly revealed" (p. 93), and he holds that "such a state of the Church and the world seems now to have come, that a further unfolding of God's purpose of love towards all men may now be, in the fullest sense of the word, 'meat in due season.'"

It will be admitted, I think, that these speculations, though they retain the idea of endless punishment, are as novel and startling in their contrast to popular theology as any that have met us in the long course of this history of thought. It does not appear, however, that any action was taken in the matter beyond that of reviews in the *Record* and other papers, and his maintenance of these views was no bar to his election to his professorship at Cambridge.

Nor was Mr. Birks alone in these thoughts. Mr.

E. H. Bickersteth, whose *Hymnal Companion* is adopted in a large number of our churches, published in 1866 a poem under the title of *Yesterday, To-day, and for Ever*, which occupies in the literature of our own time much the same position as Young's *Night Thoughts* or Pollok's *Course of Time* did in that of our fathers, and in which he sets forth his views of the last Judgment and the life that follows it. It is hardly too much to say that the eleventh and twelfth books of that poem are little more than metrical paraphrases of the passages which I have quoted from Mr. Birks' treatise. Satan, after the judgment has plunged him and his angels and the souls of the lost

> "Beneath Gehenna's burning sulphurous waves
> In the abyss of ever-during woe,"

utters his last soliloquy. In it he acknowledges the goodness and mercy which restrains him from further "suicidal wickedness." Now that he and his hosts are fettered they can

> "safely gaze
> On that, the final victory of love,
> Evolving out of darkness light in heaven.
> Thus only to the prisoners of despair
> Can mercy, which is infinite, vouchsafe
> Far glimpses of the beauty of holiness."

And therefore he and they can join in

> "That multitudinous tide of awful praise,
> 'Glory to God who sitteth on the throne,
> And to the Lamb for ever and for ever.'"
>
> Book xi. *ad fin.*

So in book xii. (563—568) the spirits of the

blest are represented as gazing into the "awful deep"—

> "Couching beneath; and there they saw the lost
> For ever bound under His dreadful eye
> Who is eternal and consuming fire,
> There in the outer darkness. And the view
> So wrought in them, that perfect self-distrust,
> With pity not unmixed and tender tears,
> Lean'd ever on their God for perfect strength."

In the notes on the former passage he states his conviction that the teaching of Scripture "stands inflexibly opposed to that mediæval tradition which represents devils tormenting men and men blaspheming God for ever, and assures us of the eternal repression of every act of evil and of the eternal silencing of every word of rebellion." Most readers will, I think, acknowledge that there is an element of truth and beauty in this conception of the ultimate victory of goodness; but the question rises, and is not, I think, adequately answered, whether the state of mind thus described does not fulfil all the conditions of a true repentance accepting its punishment, and whether it is consistent with our thoughts of the unchangeableness of the Divine character that that repentance should never meet with pardon, never pass out of hopeless and irremediable torments both of body and soul. Might it not even be said that there is a *higher* spiritual excellence in the character which rejoices that others are in a blessedness which it cannot share than in that of the blessed who contemplate the torments of the lost with an undisturbed complacency?

I am reluctant to speak of myself or to quote from my own writings; but in tracing the history of the controversy I am compelled to notice what I have myself contributed to it. Like Mr. Bickersteth, I threw some of the thoughts which were working in my mind into the form of verse, and in 1864 published a volume, *Lazarus and other Poems,* in which the disciple of Bethany was made to tell the lessons he had learnt in his four days' sojourn in the world behind the veil. From that poem I will quote as little as I can:—

"The worm, the fire, the darkness, and the scourge,
These are but signs and figures of the truth.
The enduring pain
Is memory of evil seen at last
As evil, hateful, loathsome. . . . . .
. . . . . . To the souls that sinned
In ignorance of God His grace may come
In mercy, wide and free, revealing light
To those in darkness, blotting out the guilt
Of sins of wild confusion. . . . . . .
* * * * * *
I cannot tell how evil first began,
Or why, through all the mystery of the world
It runs its course, and all creation groans
In bondage, panting, struggling to be free.
I cannot tell if it shall cease to be,
Or when, or how, the final victory won,
The conquering Christ shall yield his throne to God
Or if the conquest shall destroy the works
Of sin and death, or leave them as they are,
His curse upon them. All I know is this
That God is holy, and His righteous wrath
Must fall for ever on the soul that sins;
That God is Love, and willeth not the death
Or here, or there, of any soul of man."

The "conclusion of the whole matter," the only solution of the problem by the conflicting hopes and fears that rise out of the teaching alike of Scripture and experience, was to be found in the words—

"Impossible with man, but not with God."

My chief motive for calling attention to words that do not claim the merit of any special originality is to note how the influences of the time were working where they might least have been expected to find entrance. The poem from which I have quoted was published while Dr. Jelf was still Principal of King's College. It was placed in his hands, and remained unchallenged by him or by the Council.

From the sermon with which this volume opens, and which was preached in St. Paul's Cathedral in 1871, I need not quote. The reader can judge for himself. I name it here (1) because it led to a correspondence with a Roman Catholic priest of some eminence as a theologian, which was published in the *Contemporary Review*, and is reprinted in this volume, and which indicates how far its teaching could be accepted from that standpoint; and (2) because it drew forth what, as far as I know, is the one solitary judgment given by him on the questions discussed in it, from one of the great thinkers of our time. Bishop Thirlwall had shared, as might have been expected, Julius Hare's indignation at the action of the council of King's College in 1853 (*Life of Kingsley*, i. p 376), but he had not touched upon the matter in any public utterance. In the *Charge* of 1866, which dealt elaborately with many of the questions raised by *Essays and Reviews*, he had passed over the paragraph in Mr. Wilson's Essay which had been the ground of the prosecution to which he had been subjected. When I sent him the sermon on the *Spirits in Prison* he thanked me for it in terms for him of unusual warmth. It was "admirable and memorable." He looked on it as "one of the most valuable gifts the Church has received in this generation" (Letter of June 6th, 1871). Those who accept its teaching are entitled, I think, to know that they have the support of a far higher authority than that of the writer. I pass over other works which all witnessed of the wider thoughts which were stirring in men's minds—the *Restitution of All Things*, by the Rev. Andrew Jukes, the *Ultimate Triumph of Christ's Kingdom*, by the Rev. A. R. Symonds, and the like, including a whole *Universalist's Library*, edited by the Rev. David Thom, D.D., which were written from the standpoint of Universalism pure and simple—and come to the latest phase of the question presented by the controversy between Dr. Farrar in his *Eternal Hope* and Dr. Pusey in *What is of Faith as to Everlasting Punishment.* Like Mr. Maurice, Dr. Farrar distinctly disavows the position of the Universalists. He lays stress, as I have done, on the truths involved, directly and indirectly, in the preaching to the "spirits in prison." He denounces with all his glowing eloquence and overflowing richness of quotation the popular conceptions of endless torments that serve only to harden, and of a state stereotyped, for all the future ages, at the hour of death, and the spirit that hurls its anathemas at heresies or denials which may be the result of inevitable ignorance or invincible prejudice. But I need not dwell on the characteristics of a book which has been read far more widely than this volume is ever likely to be. The fact that Dr. Farrar, with the warm affection of an old pupil, dedicated his *Eternal Hope* to me, and inserted in his Appendix a letter (reprinted here) in which I endeavoured to point out the bearing of Butler's teaching on one portion of his subject, makes me reluctant either to praise or criticise. What it is worth while to note is the altogether unlooked-for result of the discussion with Dr. Pusey to which *Eternal Hope* gave occasion. At first, it would seem, he was stirred to something of the same heat of spirit as had been roused in previous years by Mr. Maurice's teaching and the Privy Council judgment in Fendall *v.* Wilson. He writes to Mr. James Skinner that he is answering "Farrar's mischievous book." He accepts, as it were, the challenge which had been given by the Westminster Abbey sermons, and comes forth as the champion of the older orthodoxy, in a volume that bore the title *What is of Faith as to Everlasting Punishment* And behold! the prophet who came to curse was constrained to bless, and here also there was a *formula concordiæ.* Dr. Farrar found himself "entirely in accordance with Dr. Pusey on every essential point," and "read his essay with unspeakable thankfulness" (*Mercy and Judgment,* p. 18). Dr. Pusey in his turn admits that the substitution of the idea of a future purification (instead of a state of probation) would put Dr. Farrar "in harmony with the whole of Christendom." Had he known how ready Dr. Farrar was to make this substitution he would have "re-written his book," and "would have said, You seem to me to deny nothing which I believe." Both thinkers, *i.e.*, admit that a man may so indurate himself in evil in this life as to extinguish all capacity for goodness, *i.e.*, in our Lord's language, that he may commit the sin against the Holy Spirit which hath never forgiveness. Both admit that, short of that sin, there may be countless cases of seeming failure, heresies, unbelief, denial, that arise from ignorance or prejudice, enfeebled and stunted capacities, which yet do not exclude men from salvation, and therefore leave them as possible subjects for the process of purifying education which leads up to it. In words which Dr. Pusey had used in a sermon on *The Responsibility of Intellect in Matters of Faith,* but which read almost as if they were an echo of Mr. Maurice's teaching, he replies to those who objected to the Damnatory Clauses of the Athanasian creed as wanting in charity.

"No! ask any tolerably instructed Christian person, and his instinct will respond what every teacher of the Church everywhere knows to be truth. Ask him, Will any soul be lost, heathen, idolater, heretic, or in any form of hereditary unbelief or misbelief, if in good faith he was what he was, living up to the light which he had, whencesoever it came, and repenting where he did amiss? All Christendom would answer you, God forbid! He would not be 'saved by that law which he professeth,' but he would be saved in it, by the one Love of God the Father who made him, and of God the Son who redeemed him, and God the Holy Ghost who drew and in his measure sanctified him" (p. 45).

With this approach to a reconciliation of views that seemed to tend to an irreconcilable divergency this historical sketch may well close. I do not wish to undervalue the learning or the thought of which we find evidence in Mr. H. N. Oxenham's *Catholic Eschatology,* mainly against Universalism and the theory of Conditional Immortality, upholding the Romish doctrine of purgatory, or Mr. F. N. Oxenham's *What is the Truth as to Everlasting Punishment,* mainly an answer to Dr. Pusey, but it can scarcely be said that they make a fresh stage in the controversy. The outcome of what I have endeavoured to present is, I take it, that there has been a constant drift during the last three centuries to a wider hope, to a larger charity, to a more cautious reticence. Routine or sensational preachers may use the old language, but the great masters of theology, though at first they may anathematise each other's creed, at last come to understand how much they hold in common. They can hardly realise the force of the current by which they have been borne along. They seem, as in the last quoted extract, to forget how different the language of the majority of Christian teachers in the past has been from what they now represent as the teaching of all Christendom. Lastly, the thought comes across one's mind, as one tracks the wanderings of men's minds in the mazes of labyrinthine questions, how far the keenest intellect has been from more than an approximate solution of the great problem—

> "Our little systems have their day,
> They have their day, and cease to be."

In that illumination which we believe to be given to all who have sought for light, in the calm wisdom of the world behind the veil, remote from the strife of tongues, the disputants have, we may hope and believe, found something more than a *formula concordiæ.*

VIII.

MODERN GERMAN THOUGHT IN ITS RELATION TO ESCHATOLOGY.

IT may be of some service to bring together, if not exhaustively yet with a certain measure of fulness, the views which have been held as to the punishment of the wicked by the deeper and more reverential thinkers of foreign Protestant theology in our own times. I confine myself to those who acknowledged fully the authority of Scripture as a rule of faith, who opposed in various forms the Rationalism of their time, and whose names are held in honour as among the leaders of the Lutheran and Reformed Churches.

I. I take as among the earliest of these the *Christian Doctrine* of Carl Nitzsch, and give two extracts from it.

(1.) "The thought of an eternal condemnation (Mark ix. 44 ; Matt. xxv. 41, 46) is so far a necessary one that there can be in eternity no constrained holiness, no happy unholiness. But there is no ground for saying that the truth of God's word or God's kingdom necessitates the existence of beings eternally condemned, or that God perpetuates any personal existence only to deprive it of the possibility of becoming holy and therefore happy." (*Christliche Lehre*, p. 376.)

(2.) "The apostolic teaching is that for those who on this side the grave have been unable to know Christ in His truth and grace, there is, on the other side, a knowledge of God never purposeless or fruitless, but working either for judgment or as giving life. To confine this work to the three days of the descent into Hell is monstrous." (*Ibid.* p. 377.)

"The possibility of evil still exists (in the unseen state) but it is for the sake of good, and if it is not altogether annihilated through the grace of redemption, yet it will be relatively annihilated and subserve only for the glory of God. If there is eternal punishment, even that must cease with the full working out of salvation. The redeemed cannot desire the damnation of any man, but they may well yearn after the judgment, as a revelation, a dividing point, a limit of all dominion of evil, a close of all mixed and therefore imperfectly pure conditions." (*Ibid.* p. 378.)

It will be seen that Nitzsch adopts the interpretation of the Spirits in Prison which I have given in my sermon, that his teaching on the intermediate state and the final close of all things is in substantial agreement with that of Mr. Maurice and Archdeacon Farrar, or even goes beyond it.

II. The *Christian Dogmatics* of Dr. H. Martensen, Bishop of Seeland, takes its place side by side with the book just cited, or perhaps as standing on even a higher level as to clearness of vision and profoundly reverential thought. I take from it some eminently suggestive passages.

(1.) "Their kingdom (that of departed souls) is not one of works and deeds, for they no longer possess the conditions upon which works and deeds are possible. Nevertheless they live a deep spiritual life; for the kingdom of the dead is a kingdom of subjectivity, a kingdom of calm thought and self-fathoming, a kingdom of *remembrance* in the full sense of the word, in such a sense, I mean, that the soul now enters into its own inmost recesses, resorts to that which is the very foundation of life, the true substratum and source of all existence. Hence arises the purgatorial nature of this state. As long as man is in this present world he is in a kingdom of externals, wherein he can escape from self-contemplation and self-knowledge, by the distractions of time, the noise and tumult of the world; but at death he enters upon a kingdom the opposite of all this. The veil which the world of sense, with its varied and incessantly moving manifoldness, spreads with soothing and softening influence over the stern reality of life, and which man finds ready to his hand to hide what he does not wish to see—this veil is torn asunder from before him in death, and his soul finds itself in a kingdom of pure realities. The manifold voices of this world, which during this earthly life sounded together with the voices of eternity, grow dumb and the holy voice now sounds alone, no longer deadened by the tumult of the world; and hence the realm of the dead becomes a realm of judgment. 'It is appointed unto men once to die, and after that the judgment' (Heb. ix. 27). So far is the human soul in this state from drinking Lethe that it may evermore be said 'their works do follow them' (Rev. xiv. 13); those moments (*qu.* 'elements'?) of life, which were hurried away and scattered in the stream of time, rise again, collected together and absolutely present to the recollection—a recollection which must be viewed as bearing the same relation to our temporal consciousness as the true visions of poetry bear to the prose of finite life; a vision which must be the source either of joy or terror, because it presents to view the real and deepest truth of consciousness, which will not only be a comforting and life-giving, but a judging and condemning, truth also. As, therefore, their works thus follow departed spirits, they not only live and move in the elements of bliss or woe which they have formed and prepared for themselves in time, but they continue to receive and work out a new state of consciousness; because they continue spiritually to mould and govern themselves in relation to the *new* manifestation of the Divine will now first presented to their view." (*Christian Dogmatics*, p. 460, Clark's *Foreign Theological Library*.)

I have transcribed this somewhat long extract because it states, as it seems to me, with great clearness and beauty, the law of continuity to which natural reasoning points, as seen in the light of revealed truth, and so clears the way for the fuller development of the thought of a work of discipline, purification, and even, in a measure, of probation, in the unseen world. To that development the teacher passes on:—

"The state of the soul in Hades thus depends upon its relation to Christ, the centre of all souls. Before the appearance of Christ in glory this state must be different from what it will be after that event. It must be a different state for those who have hoped in Him and believed in Him, from what it is for those who have not believed on Him, whether these last be persons who have never known the Lord, or persons who had not decided for Him, or persons again who had been His avowed enemies. . . But none of these states can be considered to be fully and finally closed, for even the blessed have still an inner history; they still need a purifying, an increase and growth in holiness and in bliss. While conversion must still be possible for the unconverted in Hades, it is also the region in which evil may imprint its whole essence, because there it must assume the impress of pure spirit." (*Ibid.* p. 463.)

In regard to the further question whether we may look beyond this possibility of change to the actual restoration of all moral beings, Martensen's language is singularly calm and temperate.

"The Church has never ventured upon this inquiry. The Christian consciousness of salvation in all its fulness would lose its deepest reality were the doctrine of eternal condemnation surrendered. It must, however, be allowed that the opposite doctrine of universal restoration has been espoused at various periods in the history of the Church, and, moreover, that it too finds some foundation and sanction in the language of Holy Scripture; that it has not always sprung merely from levity, as has often been the case, but from a deep conviction of humanity, a conviction growing out of the very essence of Christianity. We have full warrant therefore for saying that the more deeply Christian thought searches into this question, the more does it discover an ANTINOMY, *i.e.* an apparent contradiction between two laws equally divine, which, it seems, cannot find a perfectly conclusive and satisfactory solution in the present stage, the earthly limits, of human knowledge." (*Ibid.* p. 475.)

He finds this Antinomy at once in the language of Scripture, pointing now (as in Matt. xxv. 46; Mark ix. 43; Matt. xii. 34; 1 John v. 16) to an endless condemnation, and now (as in 1 Cor. xv. 26, 28; Eph. i. 10) to universal restoration, and in the conclusions of human thought, which "starting from the idea of God's Fatherly character, lead on to the doctrine of universal restoration," while "the anthropological, psychological, and ethical method, *i.e.* life and facts, conduct us, on the other hand, to the dark goal of eternal damnation." But that damnation presents itself to him under other aspects than those of the symbols which popular theology has accepted with a crude literalism. It "must depend upon the fact that the lost creature, as made in God's likeness, possesses the inextinguishable capability of good, but that this capability is absolutely cut off from all conditions of activity necessary to its development, or to adopt the language of the Gospel, 'The door is shut' (Matt. xxv. 10). For the lost there is no future; he can have no more history, he is shut up in the retrospect of a lost past, of a squandered existence. And as the mind's capacity of goodness incessantly demands its satisfaction, while all the means of this satisfaction are wanting both within the man and without him, this unceasing yet unsatisfied demand of the conscience may be described as 'the worm which dieth not, and the fire that is never quenched.'" (*Ibid.* p. 479.)

I do not say that I altogether accept this teaching. It seems to me more in harmony at once with the teaching of experience and the analogies presented by the laws of nature recognised by modern science, to think of the condition of the lost as that in which a capacity for goodness has been extinguished, rather than as one in which the capacity remains but can find no environment in which to develop its promise and potency of life into energy and act. The consciousness of such a lost capacity, with a clearer vision than before that the loss involves an irremediable privation, seems to have been present to the mind of the Roman moralist when he wrote, as his sentence upon evil-doers-

"Magne Pater Divum, sævos punire tyrannos
Haud alia ratione velis, quum dira libido
Moverit ingenium, ferventi tincta veneno,
Virtutem videant, intabescantque relicta."
PERSIUS, *Sat.* ii. 38.

"Father of all; be this Thy gracious will
Thus to avenge the tyrant's deeds of ill,
When evil lust envenomed stirs his blood
And leads him on to war against the good,
That he should look in darkness and in gloom
Upon the good he left, and mourn his doom."
E. H. P.

It is at all events suggestive as to the altered attitude and temper of men's minds on this matter that Martensens's view of the final condition of the impenitent evil-doers coincides with that which Dante represents as the lot of the righteous heathen, who are placed in the outer *limbus* of the *Inferno*, that they are as those

"Who without hope live ever in desire."—*Infern.* iv.

III. I pass from the great Danish theologian to Dorner, who is chiefly known to English students by his profound and exhaustive treatise on the Doctrine of the Person of Christ. Compared with that treatise the most elaborate works of our own English theologians on the same subject, Bull's *Defensio Fidei Nicenæ*, and Pearson *On the Creed*, are hardly more than epitomes and manuals. Recently, however, Dorner has applied the same boundless learning, the same depth and subtlety of thought, to the wider problems of the work of Christ in its nature and extent, and his *System of Christian Doctrine*, which fills four volumes of the second series of Clark's

Foreign Theological Library, may well be commended to the student as more complete and thorough than that of any dogmatic system from the pen of English thinkers. From this work I take two passages closely connected in their subject matter.

(1.) The Descent into Hell. On this point Dorner begins by saying that "it may be accepted as a result of modern exegetical research that, in harmony with the faith of the ancient Church, Peter really contemplates Christ, after His death, probably before His resurrection, as active in the region of the dead, and therefore not in the place of torment, but in the intermediate region." He rejects "the application, found among Reformed theologians of the school of Calvin, of the descent into Hades to the torments of Hell, which had to be endured by Christ," and Luther's view that "Christ presented Himself as a victorious Lord to the devil and the damned in hell, thus making a mere epideictic triumphal procession there." "It is rather," he says, "to be regarded as the application of the benefit of His atonement, as seems to be intimated by the κηρύττειν ('preaching') among the departed. But this relegates us to the prophetic office. The Descent into Hades is, therefore, not to be regarded as primarily an act of the high-priestly or kingly office. The preaching of the Grace of God in Christ, His presentation of Himself 'as the efficient cause of Salvation, able to atone and actually atoning,' pertains primarily to the prophetic office. . . . . His life in Hades is not a shadowy life; but, according to Peter,

He intervenes mightily by His words and carries on His work. . . . . But no more detailed construction of the necessity and mode of this activity on behalf of the departed is to be attempted; the New Testament passages must be left in their simple form. Nevertheless, the following elements contained in the Descent into Hades are important. While the notions of the Hebrews respecting Sheol contain truth, the world of the intermediate state—not merely the notion of it—has a progressive history. Even the pious, in the Old Testament, tremble at the kingdom of the dead, just as in the Middle Ages also humanity fell back into pre-Christian dread of death. For Purgatory, again, is a Hades which even Christians did not transcend, more terrible than Sheol, its gloomy issues overspreading the whole life of those days like a black cloud. Now, through Christ, the intermediate state of the departed has experienced a movement, nay, a transformation, through the manifestation of His person and His work. The ceasing of this preaching, begun by Christ with *His* preaching at that time, is neither recorded nor reasonably to be supposed. The ancient Church supposed the preaching on behalf of the departed to be continued through the Apostles. The Apostles knew that with the completion of the atonement deliverance is given from the terrors of Hades and the fear of death; and the same consciousness found expression again in the strongest way at the Reformation. No power, not even death and Hades, can separate us from fellowship with Christ. But this further implies that Christ's appearance among the dwellers in the region of the dead was the work of His free spirit-power—no passive subjection to a mere physical necessity. And a further consequence is, that the Descent into Hades expresses the universality of Christ's significance, even in respect to former generations and the entire kingdom of the dead. The distinction between earlier and later generations, between the time of ignorance and the time when He is known, is done away by Christ. No physical power is a limit to Him. The future world, like the present, is the scene of His activity. Combining these farthest extremes in His person, He constitutes Himself the centre transcending all physical limits; in presence of which all distinctions of time and space vanish, one distinction alone having significance, that between faith and unbelief." (Dorner, *System of Christian Doctrine*, vol. iv. pp. 130, 131.)

(2.) In a later section Dorner treats of the Intermediate State as seen in the light of this teaching :—

"There is an INTERMEDIATE STATE before the decision of the Judgment. The Reformation, occupied chiefly with opposition to the Romish Purgatory, leaped over, as it were, the middle state, *i.e.* left at rest the questions presenting themselves here, gazing with unblenched eye only at the antithesis between the saved and the damned, on the supposition, retained without inquiry (in opposition to more ancient tradition), that every one's eternal lot is definitely decided with his departure from this present life. This is in keeping with the high estimation put on the moral worth of the earthly life. Nevertheless, this view is untenable, and that even on moral grounds. Not merely would nothing of essential importance remain for the judgment if every one entered the place of his eternal destiny directly after death, but in that case also no space would be left for progressive growth of believers, who yet are not sinless at the moment of death. If they are conceived as holy directly after death, sanctification would be effected by separation from the body; the seat, therefore, of evil must be found in the body, and sanctification would be realised through a mere suffering of death as a physical process instead of through the will. Add to this that the absoluteness of Christianity demands that no one be judged before Christianity has been made accessible and brought home to him. But this is not the case in this life with millions of human beings. Nay, even within the Church there are periods and circles where the Gospel does not really approach men as that which it is. Moreover, those dying in childhood have not been able to decide personally for Christianity. Nor is the former supposition tenable exegetically. As to the Old Testament, it does not teach that all men enter directly after death into blessedness or damnation. They rather pass into Sheol, which is described as an abode of the departed, who are without power and without true life. The pious and godless are not thought of as separated therein. This agrees with the statement (John xiv. 3) that Christ was the first to prepare the place of blessedness to which His person and work belong. Further, what was said above respecting the Descent into Hades applies here, implying that a salvation through knowledge of the Gospel is possible also for the departed. Christian grace is designed for human beings [as such], not only for the inhabitants of earth. It is not said he that hears not shall be damned, but 'he that believes not' (Mark xvi. 16). Jesus seeks the lost; the lost are to be sought also in the kingdom of the dead. The opposite view leads to an absolute decree of rejection for all who have lived and died as heathen, whereas Christian grace is universal. . . . . And if Tyre and Sidon, had they seen what the Jews saw, would have repented in sackcloth and ashes, they would have been saved; which therefore implies that if the time of grace expired for them with death, they would have been damned for not seeing and knowing Christ, which was not their fault. When, further, Christ says of a sin that it is forgiven neither in this nor in the next life (Matt. xii. 32), whereas other sins are forgiven in this world without limitation, this contains a testimony that other sins, save the sin against the Holy Ghost, may be forgiven in the next world. How, moreover, can the *place* alone decide as to moral worth in the capacity of redemption? When the Epistle to the Hebrews says: It is appointed to man once to die, and after this the judgment (Heb. ix. 27), we must not with the old dogmatists take this to mean that the eternal salvation or woe of every one is decided immediately after death. As to the time of the final judgment after death, the passage says nothing. Add to this that not merely is the last judgment *a* crisis,[1] but death also brings one in its own way. . . . . The passages which make the pious enter at once a better place exclude a Purgatory as a state of punishment or penance, but by no means exclude a growth in perfection and blessedness. Even the departed righteous are not quite perfect before the resurrection. Their souls must still long for the dominion of Christ and the consummation of God's kingdom. There is, therefore, a *status intermedius* even for believers, not an instantaneous passage into perfect blessedness." (*Ibid.* pp. 409, 410.)

In regard to the wider question of the *Apokatastasis*, or Universal Restoration, Dorner speaks in much the same temperate tone as Martensen. He states the arguments for it, both scriptural and *à priori*, with fairness and force, but confesses that he "has been unable to find the dogmatic grounds for it decisive," and the "objective reason for this inability is found in the fact of human freedom." It does not admit the assertion of a universal process leading *necessarily* to salvation, because such process

(1) It is not called *the* judgment. Commonly the definite article is used in the New Testament when the last judgment is intended.

is and remains conditioned by non-rejection and free acceptance (p. 424). The doctrine of the annihilation of the ungodly he treats as a "mere hypothesis," and "we must be content with saying that the ultimate fate of individuals remains veiled in mystery, as well as whether all will attain the blessed goal or not" (p. 427). Lastly, he sums up his conclusions on the whole matter in the following dogmatic propositions:—

"(1.) There is a judgment, which maintains the divine justice, and also, by excluding everything hostile, subserves the consummation of the kingdom of God.

"(2.) There is no predestination to damnation, only continued impenitence can be the cause of that; hence no one who has, or can have, the will to be converted is damned for ever.

"(3.) The process of grace can never fall into the physical sphere; therefore rejection of grace remains possible, and every hope of *apokatastasis* (restitution) that passes into the physical sphere is to be rejected, as well as the hope of personal salvation apart from Christ.

"(4.) There may be those eternally damned so far as the abuse of freedom continues eternally; but without the possibility of the restoration of freedom man has passed into another class of beings, and, regarded from the standpoint of the idea of man, is a mere ruin.

"(5.) Blessedness can only exist where holiness

exists. As there is no condemned penitence, so there is no unholy blessedness." (*Ibid.* p. 428.)

The treatise *On the Christian Doctrine of Sin*, by Dr. Julius Müller, may well claim a place side by side with Dorner's profound volumes. The nature of sin in its antagonism to God is traced from its genesis, through all its manifold developments, to its close. And this is what he has to say as to that ultimate issue. He dwells upon the nature of the culminating point of evil as seen in the blasphemy against the Holy Spirit (Matt. xii. 31). That sin excludes, he says, forgiveness, because it destroys the capacity of repentance. "For the way of return to God is closed against no one who does not close it against himself; therefore those who have not yet closed it against themselves, in that the means of salvation, the redemption in Christ, has not yet been offered to them, will indisputably hereafter, when beyond the bounds of this earthly life, be placed in a condition to enter upon this way of return to God if they choose. And this of course also refers to those to whom, although belonging to the outer sphere of the Christian Church, the real nature of the Gospel has nevertheless not been presented; indeed we may venture to hope that between death and the judgment of the world many deep misunderstandings, by which numbers were withheld from the appropriation of the truth, will be cleared away." (Clark's *For. Theol. Library*. vol. ii. p. 483.)

He holds it to be possible, however, that there may

be an endless persistence in evil on the part of those who have by their own act extinguished the capacity for repentance, that the Divine love cannot work except through human freedom, that "the doctrine of an universal restoration is decisively excluded by the declaration of Christ under our consideration respecting the blasphemy of the Holy Ghost" (p. 481); but then he finds also in that declaration the ground of a wider hope than that dominant in Roman Catholic or Protestant theology. Maintaining the full significance of the future "shall be forgiven," "there is," he adds, "according to these words, a time to be expected when all the sins of mankind, with the single exception of the blasphemy of the Holy Spirit, will find forgiveness. If they are only few who find the narrow way to life, many, on the contrary, who travel the broad road to destruction (Matt. vii. 13, 14)—this destruction, however, is not absolutely identical with the eternal damnation. Many are lost in this earthly life, and therewith lost with respect to the condition immediately following their death, for whom there yet impends a deliverance. The *αἰὼν μέλλων* ('world to come') is by no means the time and state which immediately follow the death of the individual, but the period of the manifested, consequently of the perfectly realised, Messianic kingdom, which first of all takes place after the Resurrection and the judgment of the world." (*Ibid.* p. 487.)

He (Müller) is not, however, a Universalist. There is a power to resist the drawings of the Divine love throughout the æons, as well as the power of yielding to them. "The development of evil completes itself in a condition in which the not-willing the good has become at the same time a perfect non-ability, in which personality persistently averted from God has become, as it were, a petrifaction in sin. This is the worm which dies not, the fire which is not quenched; self-love, which will not bow itself in order to become truly exalted, which will not die in order to live, nothing but hatred and yet completely powerless, incessantly raging against God, whom it is, nevertheless, compelled to recognise as the Almighty Creator of all being." (*Ibid.* p. 488.)

F. Delitzsch, in his *Biblical Psychology*, occupies a position in part identical with that taken by Mr. E. White and other advocates of the doctrine of conditional immortality. For him "immortality exists only as a future spiritual gift to those who are re-united with God the Immortal (1 Tim. vi. 16). . . . . It is this which the oldest teachers of the Church opposed to philosophical heathenism. 'The soul,' cries Tatian, 'is not in itself immortal, O ye Greeks; and Justin Martyr says, 'It participates in life so far as God wills it to live.' 'For God alone,' says Athanasius, 'has immortality, and is Himself immortality.'" (Clark's *For. Theol. Lib.* p. 474.)

He does not, however, accept the conclusion to which Mr. White and his followers have been led from this starting-point. "Annihilation, in view of the personality which distinguishes the human soul from the brute soul," is for him "an idea of extreme improbability." With even more emphasis he rejects the doctrine of the *apokatastasis* (restitution) as contradicting Scripture (p. 352). On the other hand, he recognises (p. 483) the full significance of the descent into Hades and the preaching to the "spirits in prison." And what was then seen in act remains potentially at all times. "We dare not place the limit" (beyond which atonement and conversion are no longer possible) "arbitrarily at any point within the range of time. . . . So long as there is time, conversion must be possible, for it is actually the Christian idea of the significance of time that it is a period of trial and of grace; and as long as the sinner finds himself within the range of time he exists under the long-suffering of God." It is only when what we call time ceases with the final advent of the Lord, that the state of the blessed and the condemned becomes, from his point of view, fixed for ever (p. 553).

The five writers from whom I have quoted may fairly be considered as representing the philosophical theology of those who take their place in popular estimation among the orthodox teachers of the Lutheran Churches. They are profoundly reverent in their treatment of Scripture; they have mastered, in a measure to which few English theologians can lay claim, the theology of the Fathers and the schoolmen; they have grappled with the difficulties presented by modern thought; they are as far as possible from thinking of the character of God as one in which benevolence dominates over holiness or as tolerant of evil; they are penetrated with the thought of evil in all its hatefulness as a direct antagonism to His nature. Were I to pass beyond these into the wider list of those who are conspicuous chiefly as interpreters, I might fill many pages with quotations. I content myself now with quoting a suggestive note from Stier on Matt. xii. 31, 32.

"Of the utmost importance, when the words are taken exactly as they ought to be, is the demonstrable inference *ex vi oppositi* that other sins are forgiven also in the world to come. Nay, Christ has already maintained much more than the mere possibility of forgiveness for some sins even in the world to come, when he declared that all sin except this one *shall really be forgiven*, at all events in the world to come. And there is good ground for this; indeed it cannot be otherwise, for as there can be no standing still either in good or evil, but there must be a development outwards to the full degree of ripeness for the eternal fire or for eternal life, so also, in the other world, it goes on to the last judgment in the same way as here upon earth: all sin which belongs to a man at death develops itself either into the blasphemy against the Spirit, to the Satanic sin, which alone casts down to eternal fellowship with Satan, or it is through means of not yet ceasing grace taken away and forgiven. But, let it be observed, it is *forgiven* also in the world to come, by no means expiated, discharged, purged away by fire, or forced away. All 'salting with fire' (Mark ix. 49) and all purifying pain can only awaken in the freely acting creature the penitent faith which lays hold on grace, in that world not otherwise than in this." (*Words of the Lord Jesus,* in Clark's *For. Theol. Lib.* ii. p. 169.)

IX.

PRAYERS FOR THE DEAD.

THERE is, so far as I know, no direct evidence as to the time when the thought first entered into a human heart that the prayers which he had offered for friend or brother during his life need not cease, and ought not to cease, at his death. We can enter, without much effort of imagination, into the workings of such a heart as the man gazed on the cold, calm face of the dead, who was soon to be buried out of his sight. Assuming that he believed in the soul's immortality and in the love of the God of the spirits of all flesh for the souls that He had made, assuming that he looked forward to a final resurrection to everlasting life, the impulse to pray as he had prayed before, in the absence of a direct Divine command to the contrary, would be practically irresistible. Had not the soul needed his prayers, and found help from them, up to the time when the separation came? Was there any ground for thinking, apart from the denial of the Sadducee, that death had made that profitless and wrong which was before profitable and right? Had death so transformed the character as by a lightning flash, that it was from that moment in an absolutely fixed state, from which hope and fear were alike excluded by having passed into certainty? To fix the origin of the prayers for the dead which the Christian Church received as a full-grown traditional practice from the Jewish is, as I have said, a task for which we have no adequate data.[1] We can, however, point with approximate accuracy to the time when it first took deep root in the religious life of Israel, and became a recognised and honoured usage. The Second Book of Maccabees contains, as is well known, the *locus classicus* on the subject. The history with which that book deals lies within the limits of B.C. 187—161. The book itself is ascribed by experts to an Alexandrian writer of about B.C. 50; but it purports to be an epitome of a larger work by Jason of Cyrene, which is assigned to about B.C. 100. The evidence which the book gives as to the usage in question has accordingly every note of universality. It testifies to its existence among the Jews of Palestine, and of Egypt, and of Western Africa, for at least a century and a half before the time of Christ. The circumstances of the period of which the book narrates the history were emi-

(1) The writer of a scholarly and thoughtful article on *The Church of England and Prayers for the Departed* in the *Church of England Quarterly Review* for April, 1880, finds an instance of such prayers in the opening words of Psalm cxxxii. 1: "Lord, remember to David all his anxious care." The inference rests, of course, on the assumption of the post-Davidic date of the Psalm.

nently calculated to foster, if not to originate, such a practice. The resistance of the Maccabæan leaders to the idolatrous tyranny of Antiochus had developed the martyr-spirit, and that spirit rested on and intensified the belief in immortality. The speeches of the sufferers form a prominent element in the induction by which Dr. Pusey endeavours to prove that there is a concurrent witness from the *Acta Martyrum* to the endlessness of the pains of hell (*What is of Faith* . . . ., p. 62). Then, almost for the first time, we hear of "a resurrection unto everlasting life" (2 Macc. vii. 14), of a covenant under which that life is promised to those that keep the law (2 Macc. vii. 36). And with this there is the belief that that life is not shut out from fellowship with this. There had been a battle with the enemies of Israel, and they had been defeated. Some of the followers of Judas Maccabæus had been slain, and their leader gave orders for their burial. And lo! it was found that "under the coats of every one that was slain were things consecrated to the idols of the Jamnites." The temptation to plunder had been too strong for them. In the very act of resistance to idolatry they had robbed an idol's temple. They had been guilty of the sin of Achan, which of old had brought defeat and disgrace upon the armies of Israel (Josh. vii. 12—26). Can we not enter into the thoughts of the Jewish hero as the hidden guilt came to light? Have not like thoughts passed through the minds of many a Christian soldier as he has seen his comrades fall around him in the heat and stir of battle? Have they not their counterpart in the feelings which stir within us, as we contemplate the deaths of all but the exceptionally righteous or the exceptionally wicked? What are we to think, how are we to act, in relation to those in whom the elements of good and evil—in this instance the temper of the martyr and the temper of the freebooter—are so strangely mingled? Judas and his warriors, at all events, knew what to do and to think. "All men, therefore, praising the Lord the righteous Judge, who had opened the things that were hid, besought the Lord that the sin committed might wholly be put out of remembrance." They accepted the death of their comrades as a righteous punishment, and acknowledged that God was just in all His ways. But that was not all. Falling in with a practice which was clearly already of long standing, he "made a gathering throughout the company, to the sum of two thousand drachms of silver," and "sent it to Jerusalem to offer a sin-offering, doing therein very well and honestly, in that he was mindful of the resurrection." The writer of the book sees in the practice a witness against the Sadduceeism which was already in his time beginning to undermine the faith of the wealthier and more cultivated classes in Judæa, and which at a later date found its way even among the priesthood (Acts. v. 17). "If he had not hoped that they that were slain should have risen again, it had been superfluous and vain to pray for the dead" (2 Macc. xii. 40—45).[2]

What has been said of the teaching of Hillel and Shammai is in full accordance with the belief thus implied, and with the practice of prayers for the dead which is thus recognised. There can scarcely be a shadow of doubt that such prayers were offered in every synagogue, or repeated by mourning kinsmen to whom the duty of right belonged, during the whole period covered by the Gospels and the Acts. The inscriptions in the Jewish cemeteries at Rome, with their brief supplications for peace, tell the same tale (Garrucci, *Cimitero degli Ant. Ebrei*, pp. 33, 34), as also do those from a Jewish cemetery in the Crimea, the inscriptions in both cases being of the first or second centuries after Christ.[3] In the judgment of many Protestant commentators (Ellicott, Bengel, Alford, De Wette), the prayer of St. Paul for Onesiphorus as distinct from his household that "he may find mercy of the Lord in that day," is probably a sample of such prayers (2 Tim. i. 16—18).

(2) A less certain evidence of a like practice and feeling has been found by some interpreters in Tobit. iv. 17. "Pour out thy bread on the burial of the just, but give nothing to the wicked." (Comp. Spencer, *De Leg. Hebr.* bk. iv. ch. 9, §. 3.)

(3) I copy from Dr. F. G. Lee's *Christian Doctrine of Prayer for the Departed*, p. 33, some of the inscriptions which he gives from Chwolson's *Memoires de l'Academie Imperiale de St. Petersbourg*, ix. 7:—"May he enter into peace and rest on his couch. . . . May his soul be bound fast in the bundle of life with the Everlasting. . . . May his rest be Paradise. . . . May his soul abide in happiness." Of these the formula of "the bundle of life" is of most frequent recurrence. The inscriptions given by Garrucci are like in character, "May his sleep be in peace" being the ever-recurring formula.

According to the rules of the Rabbis it was the duty of the son or next of kin to say the *Kaddisch*, or prayer for the soul of the deceased, for eleven months after his death, the limit of time being clearly connected with the thought of the twelve months of corrective punishment in Gehenna, as taught by Hillel, and Shammai, and Akiba. We turn to the prayer thus enjoined, and we find it singularly undogmatic. There is no specific mention of the deceased for whom the prayer is offered. It is mainly indeed of the nature of a doxology, said, as it were, with what in the language of Roman ritual is called an "intention." "Blessed and honoured and praised be the name of the Holy and Blessed One. May His name be exalted for ever and ever," and so on, with manifold variations. What there is of prayer is wide and general. "May His kingdom come quickly, in the days of your life and of the life of the whole house of Israel! May the prayer of the whole house of Israel be accepted by their Father who is in heaven!" (Eisenmenger, *Entdeckt. Judenth*, ii. p. 360.) It was natural that a prayer so general should in course of time be modified in its form, or supplemented by other prayers. In the usage of modern Judaism I find the following: "May God in His mercy remember M. or N., for the welfare of whose soul I this day offer . . . [sum of money to be invested for works of mercy]. May his soul be united in eternal life with the souls of Abraham, Isaac, and Jacob, Sarah, Rebecca, Rachel, Leah, and other holy men and women in the Garden of Eden" (McCaul, *Old Paths*, p. 408, *Gebete für die Israel. Jugend.* Vienna, 1861, p. 390). Other forms substantially identical are given by Dr. F. G. Lee in the work already referred to. The popular belief of the Christians of the first two centuries showed itself in the ever-recurring formulæ of the inscriptions in the Catacombs of Rome, in cemeteries in Gaul and elsewhere. *Vivas in pace. Vivas in pacem. Vivas in Christo. In æternum vivatis. Spiritus tuus bene requiescat. Deus Christus Omnipotens spiritum tuum refrigeret* (Martigny, *Dictionnaire Archæologique, s.v. Acclamations, Purgatoire, Rafraichissement,* and the works on the Catacombs by De Rossi, Northcote, Maitland, *passim*, Luckock's *After Death*, chap. vii.). These simple prayers for peace, life, refreshment were the utterances of a child-like faith and hope, and do not in themselves determine the belief of those who used them in either the endlessness of the ultimate punishment of the wicked, or any definite theory of purgatorial chastisements. They belong generally to the second or third century after Christ. It is obviously improbable that at that period, or at any time after A.D. 50, the Christian Church should have borrowed any new practice introduced by the Jews, or adopted any new belief from the traditions of the Rabbis. It is as improbable that Judaism and its teachers should have adopted any practice introduced by Christians, whether growing up spontaneously within the Church or under the pressure of a heathen environment. The inference is accordingly natural and legitimate that the prayers for the dead, which we find in both, were derived from an earlier source, prior to the time of the separation, *i.e.* from the earlier traditions of the Jewish Church, which passed, without question and without blame, into those of the Christian. How far those traditions went back we cannot determine. The Maccabæan history gives us one fixed date with certainty, but the practice may have existed much earlier, probably soon after or during the Captivity.

The liturgies of the ancient Church expand the hope into greater fulness. That which bears the name of St. James contains a prayer as "for the return of the erring, the health of the sick, the deliverance of the captives;" so also "for the rest of the fathers and brethren that have fallen asleep aforetime" (*Early Liturgies.* Clark's *For. Theol. Library*, p. 23). The eucharistic sacrifice is offered as a propitiation "for our transgressions and the sins of the people, and for the rest of the souls that have fallen asleep aforetime" (p. 26), or more fully thus, "Remember, O Lord God, the spirits of all flesh, of whom we have made mention and of whom we have not made mention, from righteous Abel unto this day; unto them do thou give rest there in the land of the living, in the joy of paradise, in the bosom of Abraham, and of Isaac, and of Jacob, our holy fathers; whence pain, grief and lamentations have fled; there the light of thy countenance looks upon them and enlightens them for ever" (*ibid.* p. 34). In the Liturgy of St. Mark we have the following as part of the *Anaphora*, or prayer of oblation. "O Lord our God, give peace to the souls of our fathers and brethren who have fallen asleep in Jesus, remembering our forefathers of old, our fathers, patriarchs, prophets, apostles, martyrs, confessors, bishops, and the souls of all the holy and just men who have died in the Lord" (*ibid.* p. 60). Like passages are found in the Liturgies that bear the names of St. Basil and St. Chrysostom (Neale, *Anc. Lit.* pp. 18, 19, 65, 122, 136). In the Liturgy which forms the last book of the *Apostolic Constitutions* (viii. 41), but which seems to have the character of an ideal pattern rather than to represent the actual use of any historic Church, the prayer assumes a more individual form, and its exceeding beauty will justify, I think, a quotation *in extenso.*

"O Thou who art by nature immortal, and hast no end of Thy being, from whom every creature, whether mortal or immortal, is derived; who didst make man a natural creature, the citizen of this world, in his constitution mortal, and didst add the promise of a resurrection; who didst not suffer Enoch and Elias to taste of death, the God of Abraham, and the God of Isaac, and the God of Jacob, who art their God, not as of dead but of living persons; for the souls of all men live with Thee, and the spirits of the righteous are in Thy hand, and no torment can touch them, for they are all sanctified under Thy hand, do Thou now also look upon this

Thy servant, whom Thou hast chosen and received into another state, and forgive him, if voluntarily or involuntarily he has sinned, and afford him merciful angels, and place him in the bosom of the patriarchs, and prophets, and apostles, and of all those that have pleased Thee from the beginning of the world, where there is no grief, sorrow, or lamentation, but the peaceable region of the godly, and the undisturbed land of the upright, and of those that see the glory of Thy Christ."

Here also the argument from the universality of the practice to its primitive antiquity is absolutely irresistible. If the Liturgies of Jerusalem, Antioch, Alexandria, Rome, Carthage, Gaul, agreed in this respect; if there was no difference between the Ritual of the orthodox and the heretics as regards these prayers, we cannot avoid the conclusion that they must have been found in the original type of Liturgy of which all these were, each with special variations, natural developments, and which can hardly be assigned to a later period than the age of the apostles, or that which immediately succeeded it.

The teaching of the mediæval Western Church is sufficiently represented by the language of the missals that were in use in England before the Reformation, in which we find the priest offering the bread, even prior to the act of consecration, "pro salute vivorum et requie fidelium defunctorum" (Maskell, *Anc. Lit.* p. 56), while after consecration and communion we have with slight variations the formula, "Remember, O Lord, the souls of Thy servants and thine handmaidens, who have gone before us with the sign of faith, and who sleep in the sleep of peace; Grant unto them, O Lord, we beseech Thee, and to all that rest in Christ, a place of refreshment, of light, and of peace, through the same Jesus Christ, our Lord" (*ibid.* p. 101—103). Numerous other examples are given by Dr. F. G. Lee (*ut supra,* chap. v.), and by Canon Luckock in his *After Death,* chap. ix.

But the character of the prayers for the dead which were offered by the pre-Reformation Church is best seen, as might be expected, in its Burial Service. The whole tone presents a marked contrast, in its trembling humility, its blended tone of hope and fear, to the almost unmingled confidence and assurance of that which has been in use in the English Church since A.D. 1552. I quote some passages which in many cases, if I mistake not, would be as an echo of thoughts that pass through the minds of mourners as they stand by the open grave and think of the possibilities of good and the actualities of incompleteness or of evil which they have known in those whom they have lost. I translate from the Latin original.

". . . . O God, we humbly beseech Thee that whatever this Thy servant may have contracted of evil contrary to Thy will, by the deceit of the devil or his own iniquity and frailness, Thou, in Thy pity and compassion, wouldest wash away by Thy clemency, and command that his soul be borne by the hands of Thy holy angels into the bosom of Thy patriarchs, of Abraham Thy friend, and Isaac Thy chosen, and Jacob Thy beloved, where grief and sorrow and sighing flee away and the souls of the faithful are in joy and felicity. . . ." Anthems are interspersed. "Give unto them eternal rest, O Lord, and let thy perpetual light shine on them.'" "May the angels lead thee into paradise, and the martyrs receive thee into their company and bring thee to the city, the heavenly Jerusalem." And then there follow more prayers of the same character. "Grant, O Almighty Father, to the spirit of this our brother whom Thou hast called from the troubled waves of this world, a calm bright place of refreshment and of calm. Let him pass by the gates of hell and the pains of darkness, and remain in the abodes (*mansionibus*) of the saints and in the holy light which Thou didst promise of old to Abraham and to his seed. Do Thou blot out all his sins to the uttermost farthing, that so he may attain with Thee to the life of Thy immortality and to Thy eternal kingdom. . . ." And so on through manifold variations of thought and phrase, but all in the same tone. (Maskell, *Monum. Ritual*, i. pp. 114—129.)

Most readers will, I think, admit that if prayers for the dead are admissible at all, these, in their exceeding beauty and tenderness, meet the wants and feelings of those who offer them, and may claim a high place among the devotional utterances of the piety of past ages. They must have come from one of wide sympathies and wide hopes. They must have been the expression of the thoughts of a mourner who felt the incompleteness of all human holiness, the anxious uncertainty which men must for the most part feel as to the spiritual state of the dead at the moment of their departure. Few prayers that I know equal them in their tenderness and pathos, in the beauty and richness with which all scriptural imagery bearing on the state of the dead is brought together and melted, as in the fire of a divine charity, into an admirable unity. It will be seen, moreover, that in their terms they are confined for the most part to those who have died in the true faith, and that they do not in themselves imply the *Romish* doctrine of purgatory.

Another prayer of great beauty, found in the *Fifteen O's*, a devotional manual published by William Caxton (reprinted by Griffith and Farran in 1869), is also, I think, well worth translating as showing the dominant tone of English religious feeling in the age immediately preceding the Reformation. "Be merciful, O Lord, through Thy glorious resurrection to the souls of all the faithful departed; be merciful to those souls who have none to intercede for them, for whom there is no consolation or hope in their torment, save that they were made in Thine image. Spare them, O Lord spare them, and defend Thy work in them, and give not the honour of Thy name, we pray Thee, to another. Despise not the work of Thy hands in them, but put forth Thy right hand, and free them from the intolerable pains and anguish of hell, and lead them to the fellowship of the citizens on high, for Thy holy Name's sake." The prayer is given as one to be said on entering a church or churchyard.

The first Prayer Book of 1549 did not break off abruptly from the continuous usage of fifteen hundred years. What is now the prayer for the Church militant on earth had then a wider range. It had no limiting title, and it contained, in reference to the dead, both a commemoration of thanksgiving and a prayer, the latter running thus—

"We commend unto Thy mercy, O Lord, all other Thy servants, which are departed hence from us with the sign of faith, and do now rest in the sleep of peace: Grant unto them, we beseech Thee, Thy mercy and everlasting peace, and that at the day of the general resurrection, we and all they which be of the mystical body of Thy Son, may altogether be set on His right hand and hear that His most joyful voice: Come unto me, O ye that be blessed of my Father, and possess the kingdom which is prepared for you from the beginning of the world."

The office for the Burial of the Dead, in like manner, keeps up the continuity of the traditions of the past in nearly as manifold a variety of forms as those of the service from the Bangor use already quoted.

"We commend into Thy hands of mercy, most merciful Father, the soul of this our brother. . . .

Grant, we beseech Thee, that at the Day of Judgment his soul and all the souls of Thy elect, departed out of this life, may with us, and we with them, fully receive Thy promises, and be made perfect altogether through the glorious resurrection of Thy Son Jesus Christ our Lord." Psalm xlvi. was put into the mouth of the mourners, with all the new significance which the occasion gave it. "Return unto thy rest, O my soul; for the Lord hath dealt bountifully with thee: for Thou hast delivered mine eyes from tears and my feet from falling. I will walk before the Lord in the land of the living. . . . Precious in the sight of the Lord is the death of His saints." The Lord's Prayer is followed by versicles which contain the petition, "From the gates of hell, Deliver their souls, O Lord." The office ends with a fuller prayer, which is an almost verbal echo from the pre-Reformation service.

"O Lord with whom do live the spirits of them that be dead: and in whom the souls of them that be elected, after they be delivered from the burden of the flesh, be in joy and felicity: Grant unto this Thy servant, that the sins which he committed in this world be not imputed unto him, but that he, escaping the gates of hell and pains of eternal darkness, may ever dwell in the region of light, with Abraham, Isaac, and Jacob in the place where there is no weeping, sorrow, nor heaviness, and when that dreadful day of the general resurrection shall come, make him to rise also with the just and righteous, and receive this body again to glory, then made pure and incorruptible. . . ."

A special office for "the celebration of the Holy Communion when there is a Burial for the Dead," though containing no special prayers, is yet suggestive as adapting the mingled sorrows and hopes and aspirations of Psalm xlii., with which it opens, to the feelings of the mourners.

In the Prayer Book of 1552 all these elements of prayer are, as is well known, omitted; but the omission seems to have been effected with the tendency to oscillation and compromise which marks so much of the action of the reformers of the English Church. On the one hand they swept away, presumably under the influence of the foreign divines with whom they were in correspondence, all that directly implied that the souls of the dead in their intermediate state could in any degree be helped by the prayers of the living.[4] The evidence of intention supplied by these acts of omission was emphasised by the teaching of the *Second Book of Homilies*, which, in the *Third*

(4) It has been suggested that the words "we with them," *i.e.* with those who have died in the true faith and fear of Christ, in the existing Prayer for the Church militant, were intended to leave a loop-hole for what had been formally struck out. I confess that I see no evidence of such intention, and that the title "militant here in earth" seems deliberately intended to exclude it. The same explanation applies, if I mistake not, to the analogous phrase, "that we, with all those that are departed in the true faith," in the present Burial Office. It is not a prayer for them, but that the living may share a blessedness which is assured for them. It is possible, however, that this may be another instance of a deliberately "ambiguous formulary." (See Luckock's *After Death*, pp. 241—243.)

Part of the Sermon concerning Prayer, commonly ascribed to Bishop Jewell, not only associated purgatory and prayers for the dead as inseparably connected ("Where is then the third place"—as distinct from heaven and hell—"which they call purgatory? or where shall our prayers help and profit the dead?") but practically denies the whole teaching of the ancient Church as to any intermediate state.

"Let these and other places" (texts of Scripture and quotations from the Fathers) "be sufficient to take away the gross error of purgatory out of our minds: neither let us dream any more that the souls of the dead are anything at all holpen by our prayers: but, as the Scripture teacheth us, let us think that the soul of man, passing out of the body, goeth straightways either to heaven or else to hell, whereof the one needeth no prayer and the latter is without redemption." And of this Second Book of Homilies it was said, and still is said, in the Thirty-nine Articles, that it "doth contain a godly and wholesome doctrine and necessary for these times," and therefore it, as well as the First Book, was ordered to be read in churches (Art. XXXV.). So far the foreign reformers would seem to have triumphed all along the line. On the other hand, the words of the Act of Uniformity which ratified the Prayer Book of 1552 were framed, designedly or otherwise, in a form which supplied the admirers of that of 1549 with a sufficient weapon of defence. It pleaded for the work of revision that "divers doubts had arisen for the fashion and ministration of the services," but said that they originated "rather by the curiosity of the ministers and mistakers than of any worthy cause," and it declared the First Prayer Book to be "a very godly order, agreeable to the Word of God and the primitive Church, very comfortable to all good people desiring to live in Christian conversation, and most profitable of this realm." It might reasonably be contended, I apprehend, on the strength of this language, of any service contained in the book thus described, as the Thirty-sixth Article affirms of the Consecration and Ordination Services set forth in the time of Edward VI., that it "hath not anything that of itself is superstitious and ungodly," even though it might be admitted that some things in it tended, through long association, to perpetuate superstition.

Something like a check to the more vehemently Protestant party may be found also in the fact that in the draft of the Latin Articles of 1552 prayers for the dead had been included, with purgatory, &c., in the condemnation of Art. XXII., but were omitted on revision. The more deliberate judgment of the majority of the framers of the Articles was that it was not expedient to identify them with purgatory, or to declare that they were repugnant to the Word of God.

As it is, the silent acquiescence of the Church of England since 1552 in the omissions that characterised the Prayer Book of that year must, I take it, be regarded as a sufficient proof that she has not thought it desirable to revive the practice of prayer for the dead, even though many of her most conspicuous theologians have defended those prayers as in conformity with primitive usage and not contrary to Scripture. The assertion of the Article as to the Second Book of Homilies, however, cannot be looked upon as more than a vague and indeterminate commendation, and does not bind those who sign the Articles to an unreserved acceptance of every historical or dogmatic statement in them.

And in this instance, as is urged by the writer of an able article in the *Church Quarterly Review*, No. xix. p. 11, the publication of a *Primer*, or Manual of private Devotion, in 1559, and later on in the reign of Elizabeth, which contains three prayers for the dead of the same type as those in the Prayer Book of 1549, and of a Latin Prayer Book in 1560 with like devotions at the end, may be taken as a sufficient proof that such prayers were not looked on as in themselves wrong or unscriptural. Dr. F. G. Lee (in Appendix xi. to the work already cited) gives a long list of a hundred and seventy-five monumental inscriptions which witness, in every decade of years since the Reformation, to the continuance of the practice. Sir H. J. Fust, in his memorable judgment in *Breeks* v. *Woolfrey*, cites one which is specially interesting from the tomb of Bishop Barrow, in the cathedral of St. Asaph, in 1680: "*O vos transeuntes in domum Domini, in domum orationis, vestro orate pro conservo ut inveniat misericordiam in die Domini.*" The judgment in question, affirming that prayers for the dead are not a violation of the articles, canons, and constitution of our Church, was not appealed against, and stands therefore, for the present, as the recognised exposition of the law of the Church on this question.

I have so far traced the course of the worship of the Church as the expression of its thoughts. It will have been seen that that worship implies the belief in a state between death and the resurrection in which progress is possible, in which the soul grows in holiness and is capable of greater blessedness, and shares in varying degrees in the light and peace of God; that the prayers thus offered have been limited to the baptised who had kept their faith and had not hardened themselves in evil. As a matter of fact, indeed, they were offered for the highest saints, for prophets, apostles, martyrs, even for the mother of the Lord (Ambr., *Serm.* 20 *in Psalm.* cxviii., Hilar., *in Psalm.* cxviii.). It remains to trace the history of thought as apart from worship, reflecting on it, seeking to explain it. We are compelled to confess, as we examine those thoughts, that they lead us into a region of thought belonging in great measure to the unknown and the unknowable. At first prayers for the dead appear to have been connected, as *e.g.* by Tertullian, with the thought of a millennial reign of Christ on earth, and of a "first resurrection," in which all baptised persons who had not fallen into deadly sin were to be sharers, but a "*modicum delictum*" will be punished by a proportionate delay and mitigated by a "*refrigerium*" (Tertull., *De Anim.* c. 58), which may, in its turn, be shortened by the prayers of the faithful (Tertull., *De Monog.* c. 10). The belief continued till at least the fifth century. Ambrose, praying for departed emperors, asks for them a "*matura resurrectio*" (*De Obit. Valentin. ad fin.*), speaks of them as "*beati si quid meæ orationes valebunt,*" and goes indeed one step farther, and says of those who are not sharers in the first resurrection at the beginning of the millennial kingdom, that they will continue "burning" till the second, or at least remain longer in their punishment (*in Psalm.* i.).

Millennial expectations, however, though not formally abandoned, fell into the background, and the great theologians of the fourth and fifth centuries had to find a theory about prayers for the dead which did not depend on them. Chrysostom was content, for the most part, with an emotional rhetoric. The prayers "were not in vain;" the dead, even if sinners, might be helped by them, and not by them only, but by alms and oblations (*Hom.* 41 *in* 1 *Cor.*). They were to be used only for the baptised; for all others, the uninitiated (ἀμύητοι), there was only Gehenna. Even catechumens, dying with the intention of baptism, were to be helped (one does not see the logical ground of the distinction) by alms rather than by prayers (*Hom.* 3 *in Philipp.*, *Hom.* 24 *in Johann.*). Gregory of Nyssa, adopting the hypothesis of a penal discipline after death for souls imperfectly righteous, which had meantime gained ground in the East, not without the marked tendency which we have seen (see p. 139) to a belief in universal restitution, says that those who are not purified by prayer and wisdom in this life must pass through the "cleansing fire" after their departure (*De Anim.* iii. p. 255, ed. 1637). Aerius (circ. A.D. 356—376) cut the knot of the difficulty by anticipating the Protestant conclusion that prayers for the dead are not useless only, but pernicious, leading men to relax their efforts after holiness during life, and to trust in the purchased prayers and offerings of their surviving friends, and for this and other opinions was classed among heretics by Epiphanius (*Hær.* 75) and Augustine (*Hær.* 53). Augustine himself, at once more logical and more emotional, had to reconcile his impulses and his theory, and was led to speculations more or less novel on the unseen state. He has no doubt about his mother's salvation, yet he prays after her death that her sins may be forgiven her; that God will not enter into judgment with her; that his father, who was less advanced in holiness, may be forgiven also (*Confess.* ix. 13). The growing tendency to the *cultus* of saints led him indeed to think it wrong (in this respect not in accordance with the liturgical language of the Church) to pray for martyrs, who ought rather "*quia impleverunt caritatem,*" to be entreated to pray for us (*Serm.* 17, *de Verb. Apost. Tract* 84 *in Joann*). He recognises, so far at least as to say that he does not reject it, "because it is perhaps true," "purgatorial chastisement" for the sins of some men (*De Civ. Dei,* xx. 25), a fire which the souls of men will feel in proportion as they bring with them into the unseen world the wood, hay, stubble, sins, and errors which, though venial as not involving condemnation, require to be burnt up by a temporary tribulation there, if they have not been put away on earth (*De Civ. Dei.* xxi. 26.) In the small treatise known as the *Enchiridion* (c. 107 — 110) he enters into fuller detail. The souls of the dead may be relieved by the eucharistic sacrifice, or by alms in the Church, or by the prayers of survivors, if their state at death made such relief possible. They were at least a consolation to the living, who were thus able to intercede for them, either, in words singularly suggestive, "that they might have full remission, or that their condemnation (*damnatio*) might become more tolerable."

The seeds of speculation thus sown developed, as might be expected, in the Western Church in proportion as, in the Pelagian and other controversies, it placed itself under the guidance of the great Bishop of Hippo. It is noticeable that the whole discussion of the question of Prayers for the Dead by Thomas Aquinas (*Summa. Theol.* 8, iii., *Suppl. qu.* xxxi.) turns mainly upon the passages just cited. It is decided, after weighing the arguments on each side, that such prayers, including those implied in the eucharistic sacrifice, do not avail for those in hell, nor for the saints in paradise, nor for the unbaptised infants in their *limbus*, but only for those in purgatory. Practically, in consequence of this teaching, the usage involved, not the undefined conceptions with which it had been associated in the Church of the first four centuries, but the formulated dogma of "purgatory," that also being a development or corruption of an earlier less definite belief in the early Church, and in the fact of this association may be found the best *apologia* for those who thought they could only get rid of the corruption by a rigid eradication of every germ of speculation or of feeling by which it had been fostered.[5] To those who had witnessed the abuses which we connect specially with the name of Tetzel, but which were found, and more or less are found still, in every church in Western Christendom, it might not unnaturally seem that the abuse in this instance was a sufficient reason for the disuse. It remains to be seen how far, if not by a formal act on the part of the English Church, yet by the teaching of individual thinkers, we can restore what was primitive or scriptural in the practice or the theory on which it rested. With this in view we can pass on to what will require a

(5) Canon Luckock's judgment (*Studies in the History of the Prayer Book*, p. 90) of the personal character of the reformers who left their mark on the Prayer Book of 1552—"their boast was that they cared little for antiquity, and had no reverence for the past; the guidance to which they trusted was that of private judgment, which many of them came at last to believe in as infallidla"—seems to me, though I agree with much that he says on the question of the prayers for the dead which he defends, somewhat over harsh.

separate study, the history of the belief in purgatory.

NOTE.—I may add an interesting testimony from a letter of Bishop Heber, published in the *Diary of a Lady of Quality*, p. 255. He maintains, as I have done in this paper, the primitive and apostolic character of the practice, speaks of prayer for departed friends as "neither unpleasing nor unavailing." "The earlier Christians, most of them, believed that the condition of such persons" (*both* classes of souls in Hades) "might be made better, and a milder sentence be obtained for their errors and infirmities from the Almighty Judge by whom the doom of all creatures shall be finally settled (p. 1, ch. 1—4). Heber had forerunners in the *Preces Privatæ* of Bishop Andrewes (Day I.). "Have mercy, O Lord, on the living and the dead," and the saintly Ken, who prays for those who "were in the flesh or sleeping in Christ," and that the soul of a dear friend "might rest in peace" (Bowles, *Life of Ken*, ii. 303). I take the references from Dr. Luckock (*After Death*, p. 247—249). Ken's epitaph, written by himself, though not placed on his tombstone, is also worth quoting. "May the here interred Thomas, late Bishop of Bath and Wells, uncanonically deprived for not transferring his allegiance, have a perfect consummation in Blisse, both of body and soul, at the Great Day, of which God keep me alwaies mindful." (*Life*, by a Layman, p. 505.)

X.

THE DOCTRINE OF PURGATORY.

THE germs of a belief in a temporary, and therefore disciplinary, punishment after death may be found in the traditions of the schools of Hillel and Shammai that there are some who "go down to Gehenna and moan and rise up again," and in the practices of prayer and sacrifices founded on it (see p. 54). The words which spoke of the "many stripes and the few" (Luke xii. 48), of the "payment of the uttermost farthing" (Matt. v. 26), of the "more tolerable judgment" on the sins of relative ignorance (Matt. xi. 22, 24), fell in, as we have seen, with such a belief, though it cannot be said that they prove it. The same holds good of St. Paul's language as to the "fire" which "shall try every man's work of what sort it is," and burn up the wood and hay and stubble while it purifies the silver and the gold (1 Cor. iii. 13). When that fire shall do its work, when the penal discipline shall begin, whether in the intermediate state or at the final day of judgment—whether the fire is material or symbolic of mental and spiritual discipline—are ques tions left, as it were, deliberately among the things unrevealed.

Whatever floating thoughts of this kind were working in men's minds were likely to take a more definite shape when the teachers of the Christian Church came to be men of a wider culture, conversant with the philosophers and poets of the Greek and Roman worlds. In the teaching of Plato, to which they were wont to turn, in Tertullian's phrase, as to a *testimonium animæ naturaliter Christianæ*, in the *Gorgias* (pp. 523—526), the *Phædon* (p. 113), and the *Republic* (the Vision of Er the Armenian, in B. x. pp. 614—621) and the *Timæus* (pp. 42, 43), they found a thought not unlike that which they had received from Judaism, that, while some were incurably evil and had sinned against light and knowledge, others were punished for a time according to their deserts, and were then brought back to another period of earthly life. The doctrine of a metempsychosis, which this belief implied, though it would seem to have found a home in the teaching of the Pharisees and Essenes (Joseph., *Wars*, ii. 8; *Wisdom* viii. 20; Philo., *de Gigant*, p. 222; and John ix. 2), was never adopted by any Christian teacher, but that of a reformatory punishment appealed alike to men's sense of natural equity and their belief in the righteousness and love of the God of the spirits of all flesh. The poetic representation of that belief in Virgil (*Æn.* vi.) may or may not have been known to the fathers of the Alexandrian Church, but it could scarcely have been without its influence on the mind of Augustine; and both for that reason and for the fact that at a later period, as notably in the case of Dante, it fashioned the belief of men, it may be worth while to quote it.

> "When life is o'er, and man's last hour has come,
> Not even then does evil cease to harm,
> Nor are the taints of flesh cleansed all at once;
> It needs must be that much will linger still,
> Through o'erlong use, in fashion wonderful.
> Hence comes it that by sufferings they are taught,
> And pay in torments debts of sins of old:
> Some on the tempest-winds float vaguely on;
> Of some the guilt is cleansed in waters deep,
> Or by keen fire burnt out; so, each of us,
> We bear our soul's due portion; thence at length
> Some few to the Elysian plains pass on,
> And dwell in fields of blessing, till at last,
> When the full time is come, the long, long day
> Has cleansed each deep-dyed stain, and leaves the sense
> Ethereal, pure, the immaterial fire."
>
> Virg., *Æn.* vi. 735—747.

With these facts in mind, it is interesting to trace the evolution of the thought in the great Fathers of the Eastern and Western Churches, and at the risk of reproducing, in part, what has been already brought before the reader in the Study on *Eschatology*, I will cite some of the more striking passages. Thus Clement of Alexandria teaches that "the punishments of God in Hades are remedial and reformatory, and lead to repentance" (*Strom.* vi. c. 36), and recognises in the conflagration to which the Stoics looked as the end of the world an anticipation of the Christian doctrine of purification by fire (*Strom.* v. c. 9), and speaks of the souls that are at once punished (κολαζομεναι) and purified in the fire. The teaching of Origen, though he went beyond the thought of a cleansing suffering for those who were capable of receiving it, to the conclusion that all were capable, takes up the same language: "We do not deny the cleansing fire and the destruction of the world and the annihilation of evil and the renovation of the universe" (*Cont. Cels.* iv. p. 174). The fire which will burn, but not burn up, will serve at once as a punishment and a means of healing (ἰατρεία) (*Cont. Cels.* v. p. 241). Gregory of Nyssa, as shown in the Study on *Eschatology,* follows in the same strain. The idea of human life as an education rather than a probation, as being the latter only so far as it subserves the former, is dominant throughout his writings. "Those who are not sharers in the purification of baptism will be purified by fire" (*Orat. Catech.* xxvi.). It is more significant that the same line of thought was followed by many great teachers who were as far as possible from holding the universalism of Origen. Gregory of Nazianzus (*Orat.* xl. 6) could speak of the "benignant, the philanthropic fire worthy of Him who chastises (κολάζοντος)," by which men were to be purified from evil. Tertullian speaks of the payment of the last farthing of the sinner's debt as possible after death (*De Anima,* c. 58). Cyprian held that the souls of some who are sent into the prison-house may in like manner be liberated from it, that they are thus cleansed and purified by fire, *i.e.* by long-continued suffering, waiting for the judgment of the great day (*Ep.* lv.).[1] Jerome speaks of Christians who are to be saved after punishment (*Dial. c. Pelag.* c. 28), and adopts the general opinion that the fire and the worm are the symbols of memory and conscience (*in Esai.* cxvi. 24). Augustine, as we have seen (*Enchirid. ad Laur.*), speaks boldly of a purgatorial fire, of cleansing punishments, of a fire that is not eternal, that purifies but does not destroy. Prudentius, the great hymn-writer of the fifth century, is content in his humility to pray that he may have a portion in that discipline of healing, however sharp. In words which almost anticipate the spirit of Cardinal Newman's *Dream of Gerontius*, he utters his prayer thus :—

"Within thy Father's home
In different order come,
O Christ, the mansions meet,
Each soul's assigned retreat.
I ask not with the blest
To gain eternal rest;
* * * *
For me, for me, 'tis well
If no dread form of Hell,
No face that fills with fear,
Shall meet my spirit there;
If only Thou restrain
Gehenna's fire and pain,
Nor leave my soul to flit
All hopeless to the pit.
Enough,—if fleshly stain
Require the cleansing pain—
That in the lake of fire
I purge each foul desire
* * * * *
The boundless realms of light,
The crown of glory bright,

(1) See the note in Dr. Pusey's *Translation*, p. 128.

This meed let others gain;
Enough if I obtain
Beneath Thy pitying eye
A lighter penalty."[2]

Hamartig, ad fin.

The sentences which I have quoted from Augustine stamped themselves upon the memories of men, and were the starting-point of a new development.

Gregory the Great (*Dial.* iv. 34) reproduced the phrase of the "purgatorial fire," limiting its use, however, to very venial faults, such as immoderate laughter. It is noticeable that when we come to the elaborate speculations of the schoolmen, the *Sentences* of Peter the Lombard, the *Summa* of Thomas of Aquinum, these are the passages which are perpetually reappearing. The former indeed seems to feel that there was already a risk like that which Aerius had anticipated, that men might come to trust in the posthumous atonement of the alms and prayers of those on earth, and warns them earnestly that these will not avail them unless they have had in their life the faith that worketh by love. The limits of the efficacy of such prayers are that they bring a mitigation of punishment to the moderately wicked, a fuller absolution to the moderately good. Apostles and martyrs do not need them. Others, such as the unbaptised, heretics, evildoers, cannot profit by them (Lombard., *Sent.* iv., *Dist.* 45). In the *Summa* itself, as it came from the hands of Aquinas, it

(2) A fuller translation of the whole passage may be found in the volume *Master and Scholar*, and other poems, by the present writer.

might almost be said that the doctrine of purgatory is conspicuous by its absence. What meets us in modern editions of the *Summa* as giving his judgment on the questions that had been mooted as to the intermediate state of discipline is a compilation from his *Commentary* on the fourth book of the *Sentences* of Peter Lombard. That teacher had contented himself with adopting the words of Augustine in the *Enchiridion* (c. 19) already quoted (*L.* iv., *Dist.* 45) as to the efficacy of prayers for the departed, the legitimacy of the hope that the divine compassion may find some alleviation of the penalty incurred even by the impenitent, whose loss of the beatific vision of the sweetness of the love of God is, in its nature, everlasting (Pet. Lomb., *L.* iv., *Dist.* 46). Aquinas, with a more speculative and exhaustive subtlety, discusses the manifold questions to which this thought gave rise. He holds that for those who depart this life without grace and without love there is no conversion afterwards, though he too admits the possibility of a diminished punishment (*Summ.* p. iii. *qu.* 99). He teaches that for unbaptised children there is no pain of sense, but only the loss of the blessedness which is the special inheritance of the baptised (*App. qu.* 1.), resting his conclusion on the authority of Gregory Nazianzen (*Orat.* 40, *de Bapt.*). Of the pains of purgatory, he affirms with Augustine (*Serm.* 4, *de Defunct.*) that they are greater than any that can be felt or imagined in this present world; that the souls that are in it accept their punishment, so that it becomes voluntary, as welcomed by the will; that it is possible that angels may take part in the work of purification, that they may be led by them to the place of torment, that even the demons may be allowed to exercise a power to inflict pains which shall turn to good (*App. qu.* 2, *s.* 3.); that the sins which are thus cleansed are venial and not mortal (*Art.* 4); that while the purgatorial fire cleanses primarily from the power and the foulness of sin it also avails as a satisfaction for its guilt (*Art.* 5); that the duration of the punishment varies with the measure of the guilt (*Art.* 6); that neither Scripture nor reason enables us to determine the locality of the purgatorial region, or whether the fire, which for the souls that are purified is temporal, is the same as that which is eternal for the lost (*App. Art.* 10, *qu.* 2). A comparison of these propositions with the *Purgatorio* of Dante will show how closely the great poet of the Middle Ages has followed in the steps of the great schoolman.

I have brought together these questions, subtle and, to use Bacon's phrase, "vermiculate" as they are, as showing the width of the range of thought in the great scholastic thinkers of the Middle Ages; how easy it was for them, as it has been for others in later times in dealing with other controversies, to "find no end in wandering mazes lost;" how needful it was that men should be taught, through the failure of the intellect to solve the problems which it had the courage to face, or through the experience of the practical results of such speculations, to keep within the limits of the knowable.

The history of those practical results will soon meet us, and will account for, if it does not altogether justify, the attitude which Protestantism has for the most part taken in reference to these questions. But before entering on that history, it remains to look at what is beyond all question the most wonderful and beautiful of all embodiments of the belief in a purgatorial discipline after death. Popular belief or pulpit rhetoric might represent to itself a purgatory which hardly differed, except in its duration and its hope, from hell, with the same material flames, the same outer darkness. Visions like those of St. Patrick's purgatory had filled men's minds with the "lurid dreams" of the sufferings of the imperfectly righteous. The mind of Dante could not rest in such conceptions, and took a path of its own, where the teaching of Aquinas, the great master whom he followed, had left the question indeterminate. For him purgatory was not in the same region as hell, was altogether different in its character. I have thought it well, as a student at once of Dante and of mediæval theology, to work out, so far as I could, what the great Florentine had been taught by his personal experience in this life of what he found available for the cleansing of the soul, to think of as possible constituents of the purifying process of the life to come. And I may refer the reader to the article on the *Purgatorio,* in the *Contemporary*

Review for September, 1884, for the result of my labours. What will strike every one is, if I mistake not, the supreme originality of his conception. The mountain which rises from the sea, open to the sky and light, not without its pleasant resting-places and the solace of sweet song, is as unlike the dark visions of others who had pictured the unseen world to their own coarser imaginations as Cardinal Newman's *Dream of Gerontius* is to those which still haunt the minds of the peasants of Italy or Spain, or are presented *in terrorem* by the perfervid rhetoric of Jesuit mission preachers.

The history of the Council of Florence presents, as is well known, a marked stage in the development of purgatorial doctrine. Till then it had been an individual opinion, a tradition of the Fathers, a doctrine of the schoolmen, recognised in the common speech of men and in the practices of the Western Church. Now, for the first time, it assumed the character of a dogma of the faith, stamped with the authority of a Council representing both East and West, claiming to be œcumenical, and held under the immediate sanction of the Pope. For the most part writers on the Thirty-nine Articles and Church historians[3] are content to note the fact that the Council of Florence (A.D. 1434) sanctioned the doctrine of purgatory; that as an attempt to bring about an union of the East and

(3) So Bishop Harold Browne in his *Exposition of the Thirty-nine Articles*, art. xxii.; Taylor, *Dissuasive from Popery*, part ii. book ii. 21; vol. xi. p. 82, ed. Heber.

West it was a complete *fiasco*; that its teaching as to purgatory was rejected by the Eastern Church, and that that Church, so far, on this question casts in its lot with the Anglican and Protestant and Reformed Churches in their controversy with Rome. That representation of the results of the Council of Florence is, however, it will be seen, incomplete, and so misleading.

The history of the Council of Florence was written in full by one of the Greeks, Sylvester Sguropulus (or Syropulus), who accompanied the Patriarch of Constantinople as one of his cross-bearers and counsellors, and was published in A.D. 1660 by Robert Creyghton, one of my predecessors in the deanery of Wells. It appears to have been freely used by Gibbon (ch. cxvi.) and Milman (*Lat. Christ.* B. xiii. ch. 13, 14) in their narratives of the Council, but is little noticed by other writers. Neither of the two has taken note of the significance of the passages to which I now call attention.

The four points which had been formulated for discussion were: (1) The use of unleavened bread at the communion. (2) The nature of purgatory. (3) The supremacy of the Pope. (4) The "double procession" of the Spirit involved in the addition of the *Filioque* to the Creed of Constantinople (Syrop. p. 123). Of these we are concerned only with (2). Of the ecclesiastics who took part in the discussion the most conspicuous were Cardinal Julian Cesarini and John the Spaniard, the Master of the Papal Curia, on the side of the Italians; Bessarion (afterwards Cardinal), Archbishop of Nicæa, and Mark, Archbishop of Ephesus, on that of the Greeks. Of the two latter the first, as his subsequent history showed, represented the party of concession and conciliation. Mark, for his part, was the uncompromising champion of his Church, ever eager to score a point in favour of the East. It was agreed that purgatory should be discussed, and Mark began by asking, in the loud voice of opposition, whence the Latin Church had derived its traditions, and how many centuries they had lasted, and what really was the Latin doctrine of purgatory (*ibid.* p. 125). The discussion came on, and was opened by Cardinal Julian. He calmly traced the dogma to St. Peter and St. Paul, with a continuous chain of teaching, through all the doctors of the Church, from their time to the present. He states it in the terms which had been familiar in the West since the days of Augustine. The souls of the saints ascend straight to heaven and enjoy eternal rest. Others who have sinned and have not completed on earth the full measure of their penance, nor brought forth good works as its fruits, are cleansed by the purgatorial fire, and are freed from it, some more quickly, others more slowly, according to the measure of their guilt, and then join the company of the blessed. For those who died unbaptised or in deadly sin there was simply the punishment of hell. He was answered by the Archbishop of Ephesus, and the answer was every way remarkable. "This shows," says Mark, "how the mountains of controversy dwindle into molehills when men meet for mutual explanations. We had heard that the teaching of your Church was different from what we now hear from you. As you have set it forth I find but a small difference between us on this point, and that, I hope, if God wills, will soon be set straight" (*ibid.* p. 131). It is true that afterwards, in the by-play of personal irritation, Mark drew back from this assent, and maintained, both at Florence and afterwards at the Council of Basle, that there was a greater difference than it implied between the two Churches ; but his defection was supplied by Gregory, the Grand Penitentiary of Constantinople, who maintained that the Latin doctrine was laudable and good. Andreas of Rhodes, on the side of the Latins, appealed to the authority of Gregory of Nyssa, and, by implication, of his brother, Basil of Cæsarea. Their arguments were met by silence, and Mark had to content himself with promising to give a definite answer on another day, which, however, never came (*ibid.* pp. 134—140).

This episode will, I think, be admitted to show that, apart from the over-subtle questions that had been raised by the schoolmen and the practical abuses connected with indulgences, there was in the current belief of the Eastern Church in the fifteenth century a substantial agreement with the Western. The relation between the two Churches on this point was indeed parallel to that between Jews and Christians, orthodox and heretical liturgies, on the point of prayers for the dead. Their agreement bore witness to the belief which they held in common as having been taught by the universal Church, that included East and West prior to their separation. The Council in due course formulated its decision, but, as the narrator complains, it was done by the Latins in the absence of the Greeks and without their knowledge. The definition is, as might be expected, on the same lines as those followed by Cardinal Julian in his speech: "If men have died truly penitent and in the love of God, but before they have made satisfaction for sins of omission and commission by worthy fruits of repentance, their souls are purified after death by the pains of purgatory, and to the relief of those pains avail the prayers of the faithful, the sacrifices of masses, supplications, alms, and other offices of piety; the souls of those who die after baptism and without actual sin, and those which after contracting the stain of sin have been cleansed either in their bodies or after they have left them, are then received into heaven and have the vision of the Triune God, one more perfectly than another according to the diversity of their merits; while the souls of others who die in mortal sin, or even in original sin only (*i.e.* the unbaptised), descend into hell, to be punished with unequal punishments" (Richard, *Anal. Concil.* iv. p. 671).

The teaching of the later Greek Church, though it rejected the decrees of Florence as such, is very far from repudiating the theory of the intermediate state of which its early Fathers had been the great defenders. I quote from the writings of one of its most distinguished teachers, Macarius, Bishop of Vinnitza and Rector of the Ecclesiastical Academy of St. Petersburg. He recognises, on the contrary, a resemblance in the fundamental idea: "In fact, the orthodox Church teaches, like that of Rome, (*a*) that the souls of some, *i.e.* of those who die in faith and repentance, but without having had time in their life to bring forth fruits worthy of repentance, and consequently to merit from God a complete pardon from their sins, and to be actually purified from them, undergo torments till they are judged worthy of such a pardon, and are duly purified; (*b*) that in such a case the souls of the dead profit by the prayers of their brethren who are still alive, by their works of charity, and especially by the oblation of the unbloody sacrifice" (*Theologie Dogmatique*, ii. p. 726). It will be admitted that this hardly warrants the statement that the Greek Church altogether rejects the teaching of the Council of Florence.

Another doctrine, however, was coming to the front, had been gaining ground, indeed, for two centuries or more before the Council of Florence, which gave a new character to the belief in a purgatorial state, and tended to vulgarise and corrupt it. The idea of a quantitative satisfaction in act or suffering for all things wrongly done or left undone had always been an over-prominent element in the theology of the Western Church. It had fashioned its theory of the Atonement and brought it down to the conception of the payment of a debt, by the transfer of merits to the debtor side of the sinner's account with the Divine righteousness, till the debt was cleared. But the merits of Christ were actually infinite, and, it was argued, that the Church could dispense them as it pleased for the good of souls. With this there was united the thought that the saints and martyrs of the Church, having done more than was necessary for their own salvation, had acquired a store of merits which, in union with those of Christ, and in subordination to them, might in their turn be added to the treasury of merits and transferred at the Church's pleasure, as its chief ruler, the vicar of Christ, the successor of St. Peter, might determine. Might not that indulgence, that remission of the satisfaction due for sin according to the strict rule of penance, be made an incentive to prayer and good works? Was not any great occasion of rejoicing or solemnity in the history of the Church—a jubilee, a pilgrimage, a festival, the exhibition of relics—an opportunity for granting such indulgences? And was the power of the Church limited to the satisfaction made by the penances of earth? Could it not transfer its merits to those who were behind the veil? Might there not be a partial, why not even a plenary, indulgence of what remained of temporal punishment not only in this life, but in that to come? And so indulgences of this kind were issued, varying in their measure of time, remitting days or years or centuries of purgatorial punishment as of the discipline of penance on earth. Historically the practice is not traceable to an earlier date than that of Pope Alexander III., at the end of the twelfth century. The general indulgence issued in A.D. 1300 by Boniface VIII. gave a fresh impulse to the practice. Clement VI. formulated more fully than before the theory of an accumulated treasure of merits, transferable for a consideration which might be almost nominal, and as by cheques payable to bearer. Good works or penalties, the discipline of suffering, might be commuted for a money payment, just as in the Salic and other barbaric codes, from which this idea of commutation was probably derived, all crimes, of whatever nature, were punished by fines (Smyth, *Mod. Hist.*, Lect. ii.). To that point of degradation had the theology of the Western Church fallen in its commercial theory of satisfaction. The sale of pardons became the crying scandal of the fourteenth and fifteenth centuries, bringing in a treasure of a more palpable kind to the papal coffers, rousing the indignation of all who had any clear vision left of true repentance or of true righteousness. The satires of Langland and of Chaucer, the protests of Wiclif and Huss, all pointed to this as the crying evil of the time. It is not more than a conjecture, but it is, I think, a probable surmise, that it was the absence of this theory, or of any defence of the practices resting on it, in the plausible statement of Cardinal Julian as to purgatory, that at first astonished the Greek theologians at the Council of Florence, and reconciled them to what they heard from him. Remonstrances, warnings, satires were, however, in vain, and the abuse culminated in the sale of indulgences under the bull of Leo X. for raising money for the building of St. Peter's. "When the tale of bricks is doubled, then Moses is born," ran the old Jewish proverb; and it was when Tetzel presented to men the corruptions that had been growing for centuries, in their most monstrous and corrupted form that Luther arose in his might, and pointed, as St. Paul and Augustine had done before him, to a truer source of righteousness, to faith in a righteous Person, who imputes or imparts (I use both words as presenting the two aspects of Protestant theology) His righteousness to us. It would seem as if it were the penalty of the ambition and the avarice of the Church of Rome that it has, in part at least, materialised and vulgarised almost every truth of which it was the keeper or the witness. *Nihil tetigit,* we might almost say *quod non fœdavit.* It has degraded the reverence for saints and the mother of the Lord into a homage that verges on idolatry. It has rationalised and localised the true thought of our communion with Christ in the eucharistic sacrifice into the dogma of transubstantiation and the worship of the outward sign. It has painted to eye and ear in coarsest colours the horrors of the intermediate state of purification, and then, when it had alarmed men for their own souls or the souls of their kindred and their friends, it has said to them, almost as in the very words of Tetzel, "Down with your cash, and as the money clinks in the box the soul that you care for is delivered from its torments."

When the Council of Trent met in 1545 it was in the spirit of conservative reformers, eager on the one hand to correct all proved abuses, and to take from the hands of their opponents the weapon which the popular abuse of indulgences in connexion with the doctrine of purgatory had placed in them, and on the other unwilling to concede that much had been proved, or to surrender the main points at issue in deference to their opponents. They dealt with the two questions now before us in this temper. In regard to purgatory, they recognise that there is an intermediate state for those who are neither at once admitted to the fellowship of the saints nor delivered over to eternal torments, in which severity and clemency are blended by the Divine righteousness. Those who have suffered little in this life and who are free from deadly sins are thus able to make satisfaction (*compensatio*) by temporal and not eternal punishment. The "sound doctrine" of purgatory, and of the help given to the souls detained in it by the prayers of the faithful and the sacrifice of the altar, is to be diligently taught. On the other hand, difficult and subtle questions which do not make for edification are to be avoided. Practices that tend to over-curious speculation, or superstition, or greed of gain, are to be avoided as scandals.

Bishops are to see that all endowments for masses and prayers for the dead are to be solemnly and faithfully applied according to the intentions of the founders (*Conc. Trid. Sess.* xxv. *Decr. de Purgatorio*). In regard to indulgences they take the same line. The practice was to be retained as ancient and resting on a Divine authority. An anathema was pronounced on those who denied their utility. But they too needed to be guarded against abuses which had given occasion to the blasphemies of heretics. They were not to be sold for money, nor so given as to interfere with the discipline of the Church. The whole system was to be placed under the control of the bishops of each diocese, and then of provincial synods, and lastly of the Pope (*Conc. Trid. Sess.* xxv. *Decr. de Indulg.*).

How far these decrees have been effectual in checking the abuses which they were meant to correct I will not now inquire. The open sale of indulgences for the living or the dead is, it may be, no longer prevalent. But one would like to know what is practically the working of the system on the faith and life of those who live under it, what conceptions they form, according to their culture and their knowledge, of the indulgences which are still scattered broadcast over Western Europe, for those who take part in this or that festival, in pilgrimages to this or that shrine. Anyhow, the root-error of the treasure-store of merits dispensed at the pleasure of the Pope is still there, and the idea of a quantitative satisfaction to be made primarily by sufferings in this life or the next, but capable of being commuted for the ceremonial utterance of a prayer or the visit to a shrine, each good for a given number of days, or years, or centuries, remains as an apparently ineradicable element of the Romish system. The office of the Consolidated Merits Stock is still open, and transfers are effected on payment of the registration fee.

It remains to ask how far the Church of England has definitely pronounced her judgment on the subject. Her twenty-second Article condemns the "Romish doctrine (*doctrina Romanensium*) concerning purgatory, pardons, &c., as a fond thing vainly invented and grounded upon no certain warranty of Scripture, but rather repugnant to the Word of God." But the Article does not formulate the doctrine which it thus condemns. As a matter of fact the Article of 1553, as Cardinal Newman urged in Tract XC., cannot have been directed against the Tridentine definition of 1663. The change of the opening words of the article, at a time when no such change was made without a purpose, from the *doctrina Scholasticorum* (the "doctrine of the school authors") as it stood in 1553 to the *doctrina Romanensium* of 1562, indicates that it was directed not so much against the formulated statements of Lombard or Aquinas, still less against the earlier teaching of the Greek and Latin Fathers, as against the popular current teaching of the Romish theologians of the time, and so far as the Tridentine decrees, with whatever reserves and limitations, embodied that teaching, they come under that condemnation. On the other hand, the association of purgatory with pardons, and the fact that prayers for the dead were (as shown in p. 279), deliberately exempted from the censure in which some of the more vehement reformers had sought to include them, may legitimately be urged in favour of a certain latitude of interpretation. Separate the doctrine of an intermediate state of progressive purification and growth in holiness from the false theories and the corrupt practices of the *doctrina Romanensium,* fall back upon the earlier and purer conception of a Divine education, a work of healing, and then the belief in the communion of saints comes into a natural activity. There is no *à priori* reason why we should not pray for the growth in holiness, and therefore in blessedness, of those who are behind the veil as well as for those who are still militant on earth. Popular Protestantism cuts the knot which it has not the skill to unloose. Grant, as fully as you please, that a man is justified by faith, and that one who dies in faith (I do not now discuss the nature of that saving faith) is therefore saved, it yet remains a fact of experience that the great majority of men die with characters imperfectly developed, with many weaknesses and sins. Are we to assume, and if so on what ground of Scripture or of reason, that death, as in a moment, transfigures the whole man into the likeness of the Lord, and effects a complete sanctification? It can scarcely be supposed that the character, with all its weaknesses, or worse than weaknesses, continues stereotyped, as it were, at the hour of death, even though men may conter[illegible] that its condition at that hour determines its destiny [illegible] ever. Is it not far more according to the laws of [illegible]tinuity, on which Butler rests the main argument of his *Analogy*, to believe in a gradual growth in wisdom and holiness under the new conditions of existence, in the development of what existed before in germ, the coming into light of what before was latent? In any case it seems clear that so far as we cherish the belief in an intermediate state of consciousness at all, it will assume, under the law of progress in theology to which all the teaching of history bears its witness, a very different shape from the *doctrina Romanensium* of the sixteenth century. The teachers of our time—Roman Catholics like Cardinal Newman, Cardinal Manning, and Mr. H. N. Oxenham; English theologians like Dr. Pusey, Mr. Maurice, Dr. Farrar, and many others; Nonconformists like Mr. S. Cox and Mr. Baldwin Brown—all drift in one direction, and that direction is one of a larger charity and a wider hope. Our purgatory, if we may venture to seek to rehabilitate that abused and dishonoured word, will not be confined to the baptised or to those who have known historically and through human teachers the revelation of God in Christ, but will include all who have lived according to the light they had, and have, in however feeble a manner, repented of their sins and followed after righteousness. It will not exclude, as the *doctrina Romanensium* then excluded, those who through involuntary ignorance or invincible prejudice have fallen into heresy or lost their way in controversies about the essentials or non-essentials of the faith. It will not consist in the torture of material flames or be measured according to the theory of a quantitative satisfaction. We shall refrain from asking questions which we have no *data* for answering, as to the nature and duration of the sufferings that may be needed for the discipline of the soul, and shall be content to leave the whole work of discipline to the great Teacher, the whole remedial process to the great Healer. We shall not think that the souls of the dead are cut off from the sympathy and fellowship of which prayer is the expression, but we shall dismiss the dream that the gift of God can be purchased with money. We shall associate their memory with that of the sacrifice and death of Christ in our Eucharistic communion, but we shall remember that the sacrifice was made once for all, for the living and the dead (Heb. ix. 28), and that the Victim rose again that He might be Lord over the dead and the living (Rom. xiv. 9), that He has the keys of Hades and of death (Rev. i. 18), and that He visits the prisoners of hope with the glimpses of his compassion (Zech. ix. 12).[4]

(4) A volume, by the Rev. H. J. Coleridge, S.J., under the title of *The Prisoners of the King* (1882), may, I suppose, be fairly regarded as representing more or less completely the popular *doctrina Romanensium* of our own time as o purgatory, and of that doctrine I am compelled,

in spite of my respect for the manifest devoutness and tenderness of the writer, to say that it seems to me a "fond thing vainly invented." It teaches that the more lavish grant of indulgences is *the* great blessing of our time, and that their efficacy does not depend on the merits of those who may gain them (p. 363); that it stands on the same, if not a higher, level as that of prayers, communions, alms-deeds (p. 372); that it is "the opinion of many doctors that when our Blessed Lady was dying she obtained from her Son the liberation of all who were then in purgatory; that she exercises her loving power in favour of the souls in purgatory on every feast of the Assumption, and even on all her feasts;" that "privileges of the same kind are attributed by holy writers to some of the saints—as St. Laurence, who delivers a soul every Friday, and St. Francis of Assisi, who is allowed to deliver his own religious children on his annual feast-day" (p. 126). And this teaching, and much other, of the nature of a sick man's dreams, or an old wife's fables, is made to rest mainly, not on the authority of the great Fathers of the early Church, but on the visions and revelations of St. Bridget, St. Catharine of Bologna, St. Catharine of Genoa, and Anne of St. Bartholomew, the companion of St. Teresa (pp. 291, 336, 337, 353). These are the teachers to whom, in the modern developments of Jesuitism, the intellect and conscience of Christendom are invited to submit themselves.

XI.

CONDITIONAL IMMORTALITY.

1. THE belief that the punishment of impenitent evil-doers, after a period of punishment commensurate with their guilt, would consist in utter privation of all conscious being, which has in later times been maintained, notably in our own time by Mr. Edward White in his *Life in Christ* (1876), by Mr. Samuel Minton in his *Harmony of Scripture on Future Punishment*, and in a long list of other publications, and by Dr. William Huntington of the American Episcopal Church in his *Conditional Immortality*, either as the result of an elaborate induction from the teaching of Scripture, or of an *à priori* conviction that evil, as being only a blot, a taint, a discord, in God's creation, not made by Him, having no permanent ground of being, could not have the perpetuity of existence which belongs to God and His goodness and those who share in it, was not without its witnesses in the early ages of the Church. Hints are dropped which admit of no other interpretation than that the writer cherished the belief more or less fondly, and looked on it as con-

sistent with the language of Scripture, though in his popular teaching he was content to use the imagery of undefined terms with which that language supplied him. Thus we find Justin at one time speaking of an "eternal (*æonian*) chastisement," as contrasted with the millennial period which Plato (*Phædr.* p. 249) had assigned for the punishment of the wicked,[1] and of Satan with his hosts and human followers as destined to the fire to be punished for "a limitless period"[2] yet at another stating the fact with a strange limitation. "The soul," he argues, "is created, brought into being, and therefore is not naturally immortal." He will not affirm that the souls of men cease to exist at death, for that would be, in Plato's phrase, which he quotes (*Phæd.* p. 107), a "stroke of luck" (ἕρμαιον) for evil-doers, but "the souls of the righteous remain in a better place, the unjust in a worse, waiting for the time of the judgment. Thus the one, deemed worthy of God, die no more; the others are punished, *so long as God wills both their being and their punishment.*"[3]

Irenæus repeats the same thought with somewhat more of metaphysical subtlety. All life, from his point of view, is the gift of God. There is no natural immortality. "He who shall preserve the life bestowed upon Him, and give thanks to Him who imparted it, shall receive also length of days for ever and ever. But he who shall reject it, and prove himself ungrateful to his Maker, . . . deprives him-

(1) Apol. i. 8. (2) Ibid. c. 28. (3) Dial. c. Tryph. c. 5.

self of continuance for ever and ever, . . . shall justly not receive from Him length of days for ever and ever."[4] Elsewhere, it is true, he speaks in the current language of Christianity as to the "eternal" (*æonian*) duration of punishment, and it may be contended that he refers here only to the loss of the blessedness which alone constitutes the length of days of which the Psalmist speaks. *Primâ facie,* however, it will hardly be denied that his language tends towards the thought of a possible annihilation, and it has certainly been so understood by both Roman Catholic and Protestant writers.[5]

2. Whatever doubt may attach to the two testimonies just quoted, that of Arnobius is free from all ambiguity, and following, as it does, the same line of thought as that taken by Irenæus, throws light on what was obscure in him. Arnobius, too, contends against the Platonic notion of man's natural immortality, and charges him with philosophical inconsistency in holding that belief, and yet making the soul, thus immortal and everlasting, susceptible of punishment and pain. "What man does not see that that which is immortal, which is simple, cannot be subject to any pain; that that, on the contrary, cannot be immortal which does suffer pain? And yet his opinion is not very far from the truth. For although the gentle and kindly disposed man thought it inhuman cruelty to condemn souls to death, he yet

(4) Iren., *adv. Hær.* ii. 34.
(5) Huet., *Origeniana.* Taylor, *Christ's Advent to Judgment, Works,* v. 47 (ed. Heber).

not unreasonably supposed that they are cast into rivers blazing with masses of flame, and loathsome from their foul abysses. For they are cast in, and, being annihilated, pass away vainly in everlasting destruction. . . . . And to make manifest what is unknown, this is man's real death, this which leaves nothing behind. For that which is seen by the eyes is (only) a separation of soul from body, not the last end, annihilation—this, I say, is man's real death, when souls which know not God shall be consumed in long-protracted torment with raging fire."[6]

These utterances of an earlier date found an echo of sympathy in our English Chrysostom. With one of those strangely bold outbursts in which we trace a yearning for something more satisfying than the narrowness of the schools of Laud on the one side and Ussher on the other, Taylor utters his wider hope. He has spoken incidentally of Origen and his teaching. "However," he adds, "Origen was not the first that said the pains of the damned should cease. Justin Martyr, in his dialogue with Triphon expresses it thus: . . . [Then follows the quotation *ut supra*]. But I observe that the primitive doctors were very willing to believe that the mercy of God would find out a period to the torment of accursed souls; but such a period, which should be nothing but eternal destruction, called by the Scripture 'the second death.' . . . And Irenæus disputes it largely 'that they that are unthankful to God in this short life,

(6) Arnobius, *Adv. Gent.* ii. 14.

and obey him not, shall never have an eternal duration of life in the ages to come,' '*sed ipse se privat in sæculum sæculi perseverantia,*—he deprives his soul of living to eternal ages;' for he supposes an immortal duration not to be natural to the soul, but a gift of God, which He can take away, and did take away from Adam, and restored it again in Christ to them that believe in Him and obey Him: for the other, they shall be raised again to suffer shame and fearful torments, and according to the degree of their sins, so shall be continued in their sorrows, and some shall die, and some shall not die; the devil and the beast, and they that worshipped the beast, and they that were marked with his character, these, St. John saith, 'shall be tormented for ever and ever.' He does not say so of all, but of certain great criminals, ὅπως ἂν θεὸς θέλῃ, 'all so long as God please'—some for ever and ever, and some not so severely; and whereas the general sentence is given to all wicked persons, to all on the left hand, to go into everlasting fire; it is answered, that the fire indeed is everlasting, but not all that enters into it is everlasting, but only the devils for whom it was prepared, and others, more mighty criminals (according as St. John intimates); though also *everlasting* signifies only 'to the end of its proper period.'

"Concerning this doctrine of theirs, so severe and and yet so moderate, there is less to be objected than against the supposed fancy of Origen; for it is a strange consideration to suppose an eternal torment to those to whom it was never threatened, to those who never heard of Christ, to those that lived probably well, to heathens of good lives, to ignorant and untaught people, to people surprised in a single crime, to men that die young in their natural follies and foolish lusts, to those that fall in a sudden gaiety and excessive joy, to all alike; to all infinite and eternal, even to unwarned people; and that this should be inflicted by God, who infinitely loves His creatures, who died for them, who pardons easily, and pities readily, and excuses much, and delights in our being saved, and would not have us to die, and takes little things in exchange for great; it is certain that God's mercies are infinite, and it is also certain that this matter of eternal torments cannot truly be understood; and when the schoolmen go about to reconcile the Divine justice to that severity, and consider why God punishes eternally a temporal sin, or a state of evil, they speak variously, and uncertainly, and unsatisfyingly."[7]

He goes on to re-state the arguments for this conclusion, pressing the terrors of the torments even if they end, and of that ultimate privation of all being and blessedness, and then adds: "This is the gentlest sentence of some of the old doctors. But the generality of Christians have been taught to believe worse things far concerning them and the accursed souls." And then he dwells with all his wonted force of

(7) Taylor, *Christ's Advent to Judgment* (*ut supra*). The passage has been already quoted in p. 199, but it seems worth while to reproduce it, as in its proper place, in this connexion.

rhetoric on the "second death, which is no dying, but a being tormented, burning in a lake of fire," and yet afterwards returns as if with a lingering fondness to the theory of annihilation as at least possible.

In this, as on other questions, it is obviously easy enough to quote Taylor on both sides. His largeness of sympathy, his power of seeing what was the strength of either side in a discussion, perhaps also a half-unconscious satisfaction in the exercise of that power, and in thus being a better advocate than the most zealous unwavering partizan, led him to change his tone from time to time, according as the mood swayed him. But it will hardly be denied, I think, that the feeling of the above extracts is that of a man who in his secret soul cherishes the belief for which he pleads so warmly, but who treats it, more or less, as an esoteric truth,[8] to be reserved for those to whom the popular belief has become a source of perplexity, not to enter into the public teaching of those whose main work it is to persuade men with the terrors of the Lord.

Tillotson stands, to some extent, in the same position as Taylor. For the most part his language is

(8) So S. T. Coleridge (*Notes on English Divines*, i. p. 265). "I often suspect that Taylor, *in abditis fidei* ἐσωτερικῆς, inclined to the belief that there is no other immortality but heaven, and that hell is a *pœna damni negativa, haud privativa.* I own myself strongly inclined to it; but so many texts against it! I am confident that the doctrine would be a far stronger motive than the present; for no man will believe eternal misery of himself, but millions would admit, that if they did not amend their lives, they would be undeserving of living for ever."

strong and deciding as to the perpetuity of punishment. But in the Sermon[9] in which he deals with the subject he throws out, parenthetically, the suggestion (as if it had been a relief to his own mind, and might be a relief to others) that though the exclusion of impenitent sinners from heaven was proclaimed as the Law of Judgment, yet "the Judge retains the right of remitting the penalty;" and that, "if it be in anywise inconsistent with righteousness or goodness to make sinners miserable for ever, He will not do it." It should be added, that after this he proceeds to show that "we have every reason to believe that the punishment will be everlasting."

The old arguments have been reproduced in our own time. It has been urged that Scripture nowhere represents the soul as naturally immortal; that the Church has wrongly adopted that belief from the teaching of Plato and his followers; that it asserts that "God alone hath immortality," and that He bestows it only on those who seek for it by "patient continuance in well-doing;" that the word *αἰώνιος*, which is commonly urged as affirming perpetuity, implies an indefinite rather than an infinite duration, a completion of an appointed period rather than an endless succession of ages, which can never be completed; that the word *'απώλεια* (*destruction*, or perdition) and its cognates, which are used more than any other in the New Testament to describe the doom of the lost, convey as their natural meaning

(9) Serm. XXXV., *On the Eternity of Hell Torments.*

the thought of "perishing," in the strictest sense, the passing out of being, the annihilation of what gave the soul a living, personal existence. This thought, it is urged, satisfies all our conceptions at once of the righteousness and the mercy of the Divine government, excludes from blessedness those who have no capacity for sharing it, and yet avoids the conclusion that evil is perpetuated by a Divine decree only in order that the doer of the evil may suffer a penalty which is not, and cannot be, restorative, and which, the great drama of the world's history being brought to its close, can no longer serve as an example to other created beings of the retribution which evil brings down upon its own head.

I have thought it right, in justice to the momentous nature of the question at issue, in justice also to the many thoughtful and devout men who have thus reasoned, to state their case with all the clearness and calmness in my power. It is, as Taylor says, one that calls for all thoughtful consideration. But the case, I am compelled to add, fails to bring conviction. Prior to our entrance upon the region of revealed truth, all arguments for the immortality of the soul, drawn from the simple, uncompounded oneness of consciousness, from the law of continuity, from the exercise, up to the hour of death, of all or nearly all the faculties of the soul's life, from the instinctive yearnings or fears which take possession of the soul and assert their power, tell as much for the continued being of those who have done evil as of those who have wrought righteousness. To concede that there is no natural immortality in the soul of man given by God as the Creator, and that it comes as a superadded gift through Christ, is, it may be urged, to admit the main principle of materialism. The theory of Conditional Immortality assumes, it is true, the continued existence of the soul after death, prolonged, it may be, for ages of penal suffering till the Day of Judgment and after it, till at last, when the "uttermost farthing" is paid, it ceases to exist. But against this theory it may be urged (1) that the perpetuated existence of evil which continues persistent in its rejection of good, is not more incompatible with our conceptions of the Divine goodness than its existence for a few short years or for long ages, though it would be so if the evil itself were perpetuated, then or now, by a Divine decree. (2) Annihilation, the dreamless sleep of death, which many souls would welcome after life's fitful fever, or after the allotted period of punishment, would, it may be urged, have little or no deterring power to restrain men from evil, and would not serve adequately to vindicate the Divine law of retribution. And when we pass into the region of revealed truth, the answer is, that as "life," in its application to the future recognised as "eternal," is more than mere existence, is nothing less than that knowledge of God which we have come to speak of as the beatific vision, so "death," "destruction," "perdition," involve the privation, not of "existence" as such, but of that which makes it a true and blessed life. A fair induction from all the passages in which such words occur will, it may be affirmed, prove that this is the dominant, if not the exclusive, meaning of them all; that the thought of annihilation is seldom, if ever, present to the mind of the writer.

Three elements of inquiry enter into any complete investigation as to the meaning of any word which has played an important part in the history of thought. There is (1) the meaning of the root out of which it has been formed, so far as our knowledge enables us to trace that meaning. (2) There is the history of the word, as it passes from the lips of men in their current speech, generation after generation, modified in its meaning by new associations, now widened and now narrowed, now elevated and now depressed, becoming more definite by the action of the desynonymising process of which the history of language presents so many instances, or gathering round it so many *nuances* of meanings that it is scarcely possible to find in one language any one and the self-same word which will serve as an invariable equivalent for it as used in another. (3) There is the meaning, new wholly or in part, which may be stamped upon a word in common use by the mind of a poet or a thinker, through which it gains a special consideration and significance which it had not before. In proportion to the controversies, theological, philosophical, political, which have gathered round any words, such, *e.g.*, as life, death, soul, spirit, election, procession, eternal, justification, atonement, is it important to explore, as far as may be, each region of the inquiry.

In dealing with the words ἀπόλλυμι, 'απώλεια, and their cognate forms, for which we find English equivalents in "lose," "destroy," "perish," "ruined," "undone," "lost," "waste," "perdition," "destruction," and the like, I am not aware that we can gain anything by going farther back than the simple form ὄλλυμι, as it appears in Homer. Even there, however, the meaning of that form and that of the compound and intensive verb are hardly distinguishable from each other. The former appears in the familiar phrase of battle, which speaks of the din

ὀλλύντων τε καὶ 'ολλυμένων.—*Il.* iv. 451; viii. 65; xi. 83.

where it is used of "the slayers and the slain" in battle. So Andromache speaks of its having been the fate of her Hector.

'απ' αἰῶνος νέος ὤλεο.—*Il.* xxiv. 725.

But this "perishing from the world," though it involved the destruction of the mortal body, the cessation of its natural life, was, as far as possible, from connoting non-existence. "The dead" were *οἱ 'ολώλοτες*, but then the souls of those dead, or lost ones, appear in Hades, with a distinct, personal existence, capable of sorrow and of joy, of perception and of thought. (*Od.* b. xi.) But even in its earliest known stage, the word has a sense stretching beyond physical death.

αὐτῶν γὰρ ἀπωλόμεθ' ἀφραδίῃσιν.

"We were undone by their unwisdom" (*Od.* x. 27.), says Odysseus in his narrative to Alcinoös. And it was this meaning which almost more than any other fixed itself in the colloquial usage of classic Greek, of which it will be sufficient to refer to Aristoph., *Clouds*, 1442; *Peace*, 555, Of any approach of its use in regard to men, of the destruction of conscious existence, there is, so far as I know, not a single instance.

The Greek of the New Testament was, however, connected with that of what we may speak of as the classic period, through the medium of the Septuagint version of the Old Testament. What light does that version throw upon the meaning of the words in question?

(1.) It is noticeable how often the verb, even in its past and perfect tenses, is used of that which, though lost, may yet be recovered. In Ps. cxix. 175, we have the "*lost* sheep" ('απολωλὸς), who can yet pray that Jehovah will seek him out. In Ezek. xxxiv. 4, the crime of the shepherds of Israel is that they have not "sought out that which was *lost;*" while the work of the true shepherds (Ezek. xxxiv. 16) is, of course, the opposite of theirs. So in Isai. xi. 12, it is the work of the true King to "assemble the outcasts, the 'perished ones' (ἀπολομένους) of Israel." And it is the glory of Jehovah in Job v. 11, that he raises up the lost (ἀπολωλότας). Even the noun ('απώλεια) is used in Lev. vi. 3, Deut. xxii. 3, for the lost thing that has been found.

Both noun (as in Num. xx. 3) and verb (as in Ezek. ix. 11) are used of "death." In 1 Macc. ii. 37, the latter is used of the rout of armies; in Prov. xi. 6, the noun stands as the equivalent of the "naughtiness" of the A.V. In Job xi. 20, it is said that "the hope of the wicked is destruction," where ’*απώλεια* stands for the "puff of breath" of the margin, or the "giving up of the ghost" of the text. In Job vi. 18 (A.V.), which runs in the first person in the Septuagint version, we have ’*απωλόμην καὶ* ”*εξοικος ἐγενόμην* ("I was undone and became an exile"), where it stands as the equivalent for the Hebrew, "I came to *tohu*," *i.e.* "to confusion." In three somewhat striking passages—Job xxvi. 6; xxviii. 23; Prov. xv. 11—the noun, standing for the Hebrew *Abaddon* is found with *Hades* (standing for *Sheol*), "Hell and destruction," in the A.V., as with a kind of personification for the powers of the world of darkness.

It was with this range of significance that the New Testament writers found the word when they accepted it into their vocabulary. How did they use it, either as the rendering of words probably spoken in Aramaic, or as the expression of their own thoughts? Prominent is their use of the verb, as before, in the Septuagint, in its perfect tense, for that which though lost is yet recoverable. The Son of Man comes to "seek and save *that which was lost*" (Matt. xv. 4; xviii. 11). The same participle is used of the "*lost* sheep of the house of Israel," whom the twelve were sent to find (Matt. x. 6), of the *lost* sheep, the *lost* shekel, the *lost* son of the three parables of Luke xv. 6, 9, 24. It is used, in the present tense, in 2 Cor. ii. 15, iv. 3, 2 Thess. ii. 10, for those who are on the way to such a state, and here therefore the "perish" and "are lost" of the English version are obviously misleading. It is used of physical death in Matt. xxvii. 26; Luke xi. 51; John xviii. 4; 2 Peter iii. 6; Jude v. 11; of failure and frustration in Acts v. 37; in Rom. xiv. 15; 1 Cor. viii. 11. In John iii. 15, xvii. 12, it is contrasted with "eternal life," and its meaning may therefore depend in part on St. John's use of that term,[10] but in the latter of the two passages it was understood by the apostle to refer to physical death (John xviii. 9). In 2 Peter iii. 6 it is used of the "destruction" (*i.e.* the "breaking up") of the old world that it might appear in a renewed form. In such phrases as the question of the demons, "Art thou come to *destroy* us?" (Luke iv. 34), it obviously means increase of misery and not annihilation. Passing from the verb to the noun, we find 'απώλεια ("destruction") used of the *waste* of the ointment, in Matt. xxvi. 8, Mark xiv. 4, *i.e.* of another than was thought to be its right use. In the "Son of *perdition*" of John xvii. 12, 2 Thess. ii. 3, its use is determined by the parallel phrase of "children of *perdition*" ("children of transgression" in A.V.) of Isai. lvii. 4; *i.e.* men who fail of the proper aim of their being, who ruin themselves and others; and that

(10) See Study XIV., *On the Meaning of the Word "Eternal"*

meaning is prominent in the "fitted for *destruction*" of Rom. ix. 22, and "draw back unto *perdition*" of Heb. x. 39; and the "heresies of *perdition*" ("*damnable* heresies" in A.V., "*destructive* heresies" in Rev. Vers.).

I submit as the result of this induction (1) that there is absolutely no ground for identifying the words, "destroy," "perish," and their cognate forms, as used by the New Testament writers with the cessation of conscious existence; (2) that as used by them they speak (1, of a state of failure, ruin, frustration, not necessarily irremediable, and (2) of physical death.

There is, it should be added, one marked exception, which I have reserved to the end of this induction, as to the use of the words now under discussion in classical Greek, and that exception is found in the *Phædo* of Plato. It is an admirable example of the third element of inquiry of which I have spoken, that of tracing the new meaning which has been stamped upon a word by the mind of an individual thinker. In the passages cited by Mr. White in his *Life in Christ*, and upon which he rests the main stress of his argument, pp. 390—393 (from *Phæd.* xiv., xxiii., xxix., xxxvi., xxxvii., xli., xliv., lv.) they are used repeatedly of that which is to the soul what death is to the body. The terms "imperishable" and "immortal" and "incorruptible" are treated as almost if not altogether synonymous, the one predicate at least connoting the existence of the other

The force of the induction as regards the meaning which the words have in the *Phædo* is, I admit, complete. But then there comes the question (1) whether that meaning was likely to be the one attached to the words by those who, like the writers of the New Testament, or the Greek translators of the Old, were as remote as possible from the influence of Plato and his disciples; and (2) whether the induction which I have endeavoured to present from the latter of its actual significance as used by them is not sufficient to determine its meaning as employed by the former. The language of the New Testament is obviously in a much closer connexion with that of the Septuagint than either of them is with that of Plato; and if the meaning of annihilation is altogether absent from the one, if the other presents passage after passage in which the words are used, either of misery and ruin, or of loss, failure, frustration from which recovery is still possible, it is surely at variance with the true methods of interpretation to force that meaning upon them in such passages as that which speaks of God or the enemy of God,[1] as having "power to destroy both soul and body in Gehenna" (Matt. x. 28), or of the One Lawgiver who is able to save or destroy" (James iv. 12).

(1) I put the alternative because the latter interpretation has been adopted by theologians of repute, as, *e.g.*, Stier, *Words of the Lord Jesus* (in vol. i p. 43, Clark's *Foreign Theological Library*), and F. D. Maurice (*Theological Essays*, 2nd edition, pp. 469, 470). My own judgment agrees with that of the majority of commentators in adopting the former view.

And if this meaning does not necessarily lie in ἀπόλλυμι and its cognates, still less can it be found in "death" as applied to the soul (John v. 24; viii. 51, 52; Rom. vi. 4, 21; vii. 10, 13; 2 Cor. ii. 16; James i. 15, 24); for "death" is the opposite of "life," and if "life" be, in this connexion, something more than mere existence, as it is in John xvii. 3, 1 John iii. 14, involving the idea of the blessedness which consists in knowing God, then "death" must stand for the loss of that blessedness rather than for absolute non-existence. Whether that loss is irretrievable after the "death" of the body is a question to be determined on its own evidence, but it is at least noteworthy, that the word does not in itself convey that significance. As with the word "lost," so with "death," as in John v. 24, 1 John iii. 14, James v. 20, "death,"—the "death" of the soul—is a state from which a transition to life is possible. Whether the "second death" which is one with "the lake of fire (Rev. ii. 11; xx. 14; xxi. 4, 8), implies annihilation or punishment, and whether that punishment is, in its nature, endless for all who are condemned to it, is a distinct question, but it will scarcely, I think, be questioned that, in the passage where the term occurs, it suggests the thought of existence continued under conditions of suffering rather than of the loss of the consciousness of existence.

It should be borne in mind, however, that Mr. White, the chief representative teacher of the doctrine of Conditional Immortality, adopts the interpretation of the preaching to the Spirits in Prison (1 Peter iii. 18) which I have maintained in my sermon (*Life in Christ*, p. 344). The soul, *i.e.*, has its existence prolonged during the interval between death and the final judgment, in order that it may have other opportunities of accepting life in Christ than it has had during its sojourn upon earth. If it makes a right use of those opportunities it may even there receive the new gift of immortality; if it persists, in spite of them, in its own evil, it is then, at the final judgment, re-united to the body, and both soul and body are then cast into the Gehenna of fire, *i.e.* in "the long agony of the remembrance of their sins," in which, after a period of suffering proportionate to its guilt, it is, in the full sense of the term, as Mr. White accepts it, destroyed, *i.e.* is annihilated, and ceases to exist (*Life in Christ*, p. 433). This, it is contended, sufficiently vindicates at once the righteous government of God and the infinite compassion which will not perpetuate evil only that it may endure an endless misery. In maintaining this view, Mr. White, of course, accepts, though he says that he "builds no argument" upon it, the limited sense of the word *αἰώνιος* as applied to the punishment of the wicked, and so comes round to the position suggested or maintained, as we have seen, by Justin, Irenæus, and Arnobius, and half accepted by Taylor. Archbishop Whately, it may be added, seems inclined to adopt this view. He teaches that "no promise of eternal life is held out to any but Christians," that "of others revelation does not speak;" that the final destruction of the impenitent is, at least, possible (*Future State*, ch. viii.). He inclines to the belief that the soul sleeps in unconsciousness between death and the resurrection, and excludes growth and change of any kind from the intermediate state (ibid. chap. x.).

NOTE.—The reader who desires to go further into the question may be referred to two works, each of them marked by considerable power and by wide and reverential thought: (1) *The Doctrine of Annihilation in the Light of the Gospel of Love*, by the Rev. J. Baldwin Brown (1875); and (2) *Catholic Eschatology and Universalism* (pp. 65—69), by H. N. Oxenham. The former writes from the standpoint of Universal Restoration, the latter from that of the Purgatorial teaching of the Tridentine decrees. I agree with him in his conclusions, but it seems somewhat exaggerated language to speak of the doctrine of Conditional Immortality as "ghastly misbelief," a "dark and atheistic creed."

NOTE.—Mr. White has called my attention to the fact that the statement in page 330, as to the "other opportunities of accepting life in Christ" which may be offered to the soul after death, is limited, in the passage to which I have referred, to those who have not heard the gospel of that life during their earthly probation. In that class, however, he includes the "departed heathen millions;" and "perhaps," also, "not only the untaught victims of European priestcraft, but the numerous persons who in all ages since Christianity was radically corrupted by its professional teachers, have been driven into scepticism by the darker perversions of its doctrine and morality;" in other words, all those whose life on earth has not given them an adequate probation. I leave the reader to judge how far this agrees with my own teaching as to the possibilities of the intermediate state throughout this volume.

XII.

THE TEACHING OF BISHOP BUTLER AS TO THE LIFE AFTER DEATH.[1]

A LETTER TO DR. FARRAR.

MY DEAR FARRAR,—The passage in Butler's *Analogy* to which I referred as bearing on the great question with which this volume deals is in part i. c. 3:—

"Virtue, to borrow the Christian allusion, is militant here, and various untoward accidents contribute to its being often overborne: but it may combat with greater advantage hereafter, and prevail completely, and enjoy its consequent rewards in some future states. Neglected as it is, perhaps unknown, perhaps despised and oppressed here, there may be scenes in eternity lasting enough, and in every way adapted to afford it a sufficient sphere of action; and a sufficient sphere for the natural consequences of it to follow in fact. . . . . And, one might add, that suppose all this advantageous tendency of virtue to become effect amongst one or more orders of vicious creatures in

(1) Reprinted from Archdeacon Farrar's *Eternal Hope*.

any distant scene or period throughout the universal kingdom of God; this happy effect of virtue would have a tendency, by way of example, and possibly in other ways, to amend those of them who are capable of amendment and being recovered to a just sense of virtue. If our notions of the plan of Providence were enlarged in any sense proportionable to what late discoveries have enlarged our views with respect to the material world, representations of this kind would not appear absurd or extravagant."

It seems to me that these remarkable words throw light on the teaching of the previous chapter, in which Butler dwells very solemnly on the warning thought, suggested by the natural course of things, that the punishment of evil-doers may, if the evil has reached a certain measure, be final and irreversible. He holds very strongly the truth that this life is a state of probation, and that after it each man will receive according to his deeds, and "in *exact proportion* to the good or evil which he has done." He does not deal directly with the problems presented by cases in which, as with infants, idiots, and, we must add, the vast multitudes who have lived and died in the times of ignorance, there has been, as far as we can judge, no real probation. He enters his protest against those who "forget or explain away, after acknowledging it in words," the truth that "every one shall be *equitably* dealt with." He maintains that "all shadow of injustice, and indeed all harsh appearances, in this various economy of Providence would be lost if we would keep in mind that every merciful allowance shall be made, and no more be required of any one than what might have been equitably expected of him, from the circumstances in which he was placed" (part ii. chap. 6). He expressly protests (part ii. chap v. note D) against the dogma that "none can have the benefit of the general redemption but such as have the advantage of being made acquainted with it in the present life." He describes that redemption as "an interposition to prevent the destruction of human kind, *whatever that destruction unprevented would have been.*"

It is clear, I think, from these passages (1) That Butler rejected the mediæval dogmatism which, following Augustine, limited salvation to the baptised, and (2) the more or less prevalent Protestant dogmatism which limits it to those who know and believe in Christ. (3) That he carefully avoids pronouncing on the nature of the future punishments of evil, and never from first to last dwells on the pictures of material horrors in which so many have delighted. (4) That looking to the whole drift of his argument that future rewards and punishments come by general laws, and as the natural consequences of the good or bad deeds to which they are attached (part i. chap. 3; part ii. chap. 1), it is probable, from the *Analogy*, that he thought of the latter as consisting mainly in the "uneasiness, disturbance, apprehension, shame," which follow on evil now, and will hereafter be felt with a new and terrible intensity; just as in *Sermon XIV.* he dwells, with what is, for him, a marvellous eloquence, on the blessedness of the saints as consisting in "the perception of God's presence with us in a nearer and stricter way" than is now possible. But the passage with which I began this letter opens, I think, a wider view. There is, from Butler's point of view, a field for "*combat*" after death as well as now. There are, or may be, "*orders of vicious creatures*" in God's kingdom who may yet be "*capable of amendment, and of being recovered to a just sense of virtue.*" And in yet another passage (part i. chap. 5) we have the same thought developed. "Nothing which we at present see would lead us to the thought of a solitary unactive life hereafter." Analogy and Scripture alike teach us that "it will be a community." For aught we know, the life of that community may "give scope for the exercise of *veracity, justice,* and *charity.*"

Combine this passage with the other, and is not the inference almost irresistible that Butler was tentatively feeling after, and all but absolutely grasping, the truth that the energies of the saints made perfect will be, as analogy suggests, exerted in the same direction and for the same ends as they are now on earth? And if the highest object of such energies now be to rescue those who are perishing from lack of knowledge, and who yet are capable of recovery, then the whole drift of the argument of the *Analogy* suggests the continuance of that highest energy in the unknown spheres of action after death. I have ventured to express that thought in some lines in memory of one who occupied a high place in the lot of the saintly sufferers of whom the world knows little, and they are, I think, in harmony with Butler's teaching.[2]

He, too, is there; and can we dream
  Their joy is other now than when
  They dwelt among the sons of men,
As walking in the eternal gleam?

Are there no souls behind the veil
  That need the help of guiding hand,
  Weak hearts that cannot understand
Why earth's poor dreams of Heaven must fail?

Are there no prison-doors to ope,
  No lambs to gather in the fold,
  No treasure-house of new and old,
To meet each wish and crown each hope?

We know not: but if life be there
  The outcome and the crown of this,
  What else can make their perfect bliss
Than in the Master's work to share?

Resting, but not in slumbrous ease,
  Working, but not in wild unrest,
  Still ever blessing, ever blest,
They see us, as the Father sees.

The view thus suggested by the *Analogy* is, as might be expected, wiser and deeper than Paley's rough and ready way of dealing with this great question; but his words too are worth quoting, as showing how his robust practical sense of justice shrank from the common forms either of mediæval

(2) *Things New and Old*, p. 143. The words, "He, too, is there," refer to Frederick Denison Maurice.

or Protestant dogmatism on this matter. "It has been said, that it can never be a just economy of Providence to admit one part of mankind into Heaven and condemn the other to Hell, since there must be very little to choose between the worst man who is received into Heaven and the best who is excluded. And how know we, it might be answered, but that there may be as little to choose in their conditions?" (*Moral Philosophy*, book i. chap. 7.)

You will see that I have confined myself to the task which I had undertaken of clearing the teaching of Butler from prevalent misconceptions. I will not enter into any full discussion of the whole question. I have not shrunk from placing before those who care to know, what I hold and teach as to its momentous issues. Now in one form, now in another, I have endeavoured to show that a wider hope than that of mediæval Catholicism or popular Protestantism is in harmony with the analogy of Nature, with the teaching of Scripture, with the thoughts of the "masters of those who know" in the Christian Church. I have not read your sermons, and do not know how far I should accept your conclusions, or how far you adopt mine. But as this letter is to be printed with them, and as you tell me that you wish to connect my name with the volume—an honour which, on personal grounds, as having been once the master of a scholar from whom I have since been glad to learn, I have thankfully accepted—I think it may be well to make my own position clear by stating, without discussing. the conclusions to which I have been led.

On the one hand, I have never been able, in spite of the apparent sanction given to it by such passages as Rom. v. 19, 20, xi. 32, Isaiah liii. 11, to accept the theory of Universalism. (2) I have as little been able to accept the theory of Annihilation as the ultimate portion of all but the elect in Christ. It seems to me to have no grounds in Scripture, or reason, or the analogy of Nature, and to be at variance with our fundamental conceptions, as shown in the *consensus* of mankind, as to the soul's immortality. (3) I have never been able to attach any great importance to the discussions that have turned upon the meaning of the word *αἰώνιος*. I cannot, on philological grounds, agree with Mr. Maurice in thinking that our Lord's teaching in John xvii. 3 excludes from it the idea of duration, and the whole history of the word shows that it cannot, of itself, denote, though it may suggest, the idea of endlessness. (4) I do not hesitate, however, to accept the thought of the punishment of evil as being endless. If that punishment comes, as Butler teaches us, as the "natural consequence" of sin, if the enduring pain be

> "Memory of evil seen at last
> As evil, hateful, loathsome,"

then I cannot see how it can be otherwise than everlasting. Christian theology knows no water of Lethe to steep the soul in forgetfulness of its own past; and if the sin is not forgotten, then the remembrance of it must throughout the ages be an element of pain and sorrow. Experience, indeed, teaches that the penitent, in whom that sorrow is keenest, finds it not incompatible with peace and joy even now, and the extension of that experience beyond the veil suggests the thought that there may be a retributive element mingling with the blessedness of the highest saints; and, by parity of reason, as in the view maintained by Mr. Birks, Mr. E. H. Bickersteth, and, in his later years, by Mr. Erskine of Linlathen, that the acceptance of the punishment, the admission that it is inseparable from the righteousness of God, may bring hereafter, as it brings with it now, a mitigation of the anguish. (5) While I reject the Romish, and even the Augustinian view of purgatory, as not only without any certain warranty of Scripture, but as a "fond thing vainly invented," resting on the radically false conception that a quantitative amount of physical pain has in itself any power to purify the soul from a proportionate quantity of evil deeds or their results, I hold that it is at variance with our belief in the eternal love and righteousness of God to assume that any created will can be fixed in evil by a Divine decree, coming at the close of a few months or years of an imperfect probation, and therefore that Scripsure, and reason, and analogy alike lead to the belief that we must supplement the idea of probation by that of a discipline and education which is begun in this life, often with results that seem to us as failure and a hopeless waste, but to which, when we look before and after, we can assign no time-limits. The will, in the exercise of its imperishable gift of freedom, may frustrate that education hereafter, as it frustrates it here; but if it does so, it is because it "kicks against the pricks" of the long-suffering that is leading it to repentance; and there, as here, it may accept even an endless punishment, and find peace in the acceptance. Lastly, I will quote words which seem to me to go almost to the root of the whole matter, and which need only to be extended beyond the limits that the narrowing system to which the writer has bound himself attaches to them, to be the last words that I need now write on this great question.

> "And these two pains so counter and so keen,
> The longing for Him when thou seest Him not,
> The shame of self at thought of seeing Him,
> Shall be thy keenest, sharpest Purgatory."
>
> J. H. Newman, *Dream of Gerontius.*

XIII.

CORRESPONDENCE WITH A ROMAN CATHOLIC PRIEST.

(Reprinted from the *Contemporary Review* for May, 1878.)[1]

I DO not feel called upon to review a book (Dr. Farrar's *Eternal Hope*) with which my own name has, through the kind feeling of the author, been very closely connected, nor to restate the views which I have expressed in the volume itself as to the great question of which he treats. I propose accordingly, confining myself in the present paper to some of the collateral issues which are involved in it, and shall be content if, by such side-lights as I am able to throw on them, I can help those who are, each of them, seekers after truth and eager to "vindicate the ways of God to man," if not to a *formula concordiæ*—I do not profess to believe in the possibility of a "short and easy" *Theodikœa*—yet at least to a tolerant understanding.

I. It will be felt, I imagine, that the most telling argument on the side of the popular belief that there is no room for an extension after death of the long-suffering of God, which we acknowledge as leading

(1) The article which is here in part reprinted was one of a series of short papers on Dr. Farrar's *Eternal Hope.*

men, during this life, to repentance through the discipline of suffering—that then all punishment, however equitable, must be simply retributive and not reformatory—is found in the thought that in so doing you weaken the assurance of the penitent and the righteous that their trials are over when they sleep the sleep of death. As Keble has put it, in words which embody a widely spread conviction,

> "But with the sinners' fear their hope departs,
> Fast linked as Thy great Name to Thee, O Lord."
> (*Christian Year, Second Sunday in Lent.*)

As bearing on this question, I purpose laying before the readers of this paper some private letters which passed between myself and a Roman Catholic priest, to whom I was led to send the sermon on the "Spirits in Prison," which I preached at St. Paul's, and published in 1871. It will be admitted, I think, that the objection is stated by him with a force and subtlety to which my own style of thought and writing can make but distant approaches, and that, if my answers carry conviction with them to any thoughtful mind, as I venture to hope they may do, it is rather through their intrinsic force than through any skill in the advocate.

Omitting portions of the letter which are strictly personal, my friend begins thus:—

I.

"My dear Sir,—You will wish me, I think, to say how your sermon has struck me, and therefore, at the risk of being officious, I will venture to do so. It seems to me that you do not deny eternal punishment; but you aim at withdrawing from so awful a doom vast multitudes who have popularly been considered to fall under it, and to substitute for it in their case a purgatorial punishment, extending (as in the case of the antediluvians) through long ages; at the same time avoiding the word 'purgatory' on account of its associations.

"There is nothing, I think, in this view incompatible with the faith of Catholics.

"What we cannot accept (any more than the mass of Protestants and of divines of the Ancient Church) is one of your incidental statements, that man's probation for his eternal destiny, as well as his purification, continues after this life.

"Nor does this doctrine seem necessary for your main point; for Catholics are able to hold purgatory without accepting it, merely by holding that there are innumerable degrees of grace and sanctity among the saved, and that those who go to purgatory, however many, die one and all with the presence of God's grace and the earnest of eternal life, however invisible to man, already in their hearts—an assumption not greater than yours, for it is quite as great an assumption to believe, as you do, in the *future happiness* of those who die and make no sign, as to believe, as I may do, in the present *faith and repentance* of those who die and make no sign.

"And further still, I almost think that you yourself hold as well as we this connexion of grace with glory; for you say the 'Spirits in Prison' 'had not hardened themselves in the one irremediable antagonism to good which has never forgiveness' (p. 20); 'had not hardened themselves against His righteousness and love, and therefore were not shut out utterly from hope' (p. 7).

"Excuse the freedom of these remarks, and believe me to be,

"Yours very truly,

"July 26, 1871." "* * * * *"

I have not kept a copy of the whole of my answer to this letter, but I dwelt in it, as I have done in my letter to Dr. Farrar, on the fact that for a large number of human souls, whom the great mass of Christians recognise as heirs of immortality, there has been absolutely no possibility of any action that could test or develop character:—

"As yet I am compelled to believe that where there has been no adequate probation, or none at all, there must be some extension of the possibility of development or change beyond the limits of this present life Take the case of unbaptised children. Shall we close the gates of Paradise against them, and satisfy ourselves with the *levissima damnatio* which gained for Augustine the repute of the *durus pater infantum*? And if we are forced in such a case to admit the law of progress, is it not legitimate to infer that it extends beyond them to those whose state is more or less analogous to theirs?"

II.

"Aug. 1, 1871.

"My dear Sir,—Thank you for your very kind answer to my letter. My apology for writing to you again lies in the importance of the question which is opened in your sermon.

"Let me ask, then, will it be *possible* to extend the period of probation of any man beyond this life without extending it to all? and is not this a cruel prospect for all of those who are trying to live a good life with the hope of having done with sin and spiritual peril once for all, as the gain of dying? Also, is it not a suggestion cruel to all of us, who lose dear and virtuous friends, if we cannot rest in the security that they are beyond harm and reverse.

"And next, the barrier being once broken down between our present state and our future, are we not at once forced on to the further conclusion, to which the present day so much inclines already, that our future state is only a continuation (that is, so long as the soul endures) of the same sort of world as that in which we are now, to the disavowal of that series of catastrophes (resurrection, general judgment, heaven, and hell) which in physical matters is so contrary to the ideas of some of the most eminent physical philosophers of the day, who refer everything to the action of gradually operating laws? But if supernatural agency has no place in the future world, who will believe that it exists, or has existed in this? And so Christianity ceases to be a direct Divine revelation.

"I know you will pardon my pertinacity for the motive which causes it.

"Very truly yours,

"* * * * *"

III.

"Aug. 5, 1871.

"My dear * * * * *,—You urge as against the hypothesis that there may be, on the other side of the grave, a trial time of some kind for those who have had no adequate probation, or none at all, here, that if there is a probation for any, it must extend to all, and that this is 'cruel' to those who have rejoiced for others, and who find hope for themselves, in the thought that death frees them from all the conflict and the danger which they have had to encounter during life. The logical force of this objection is, I apprehend, this, that it is improbable, whatever seeming evidence, or counter-probabilities there may be on the other side, that a theory involving such 'cruelty' as its consequence can be a true one.

"I will be bold to ask (1) whether, on the assumption that this consequence were involved in the view which I have maintained, the balance of 'cruelty' would be altogether on its side. If it were given to one of the blessed to elect between having the possession of eternal life in fee, on the one hand, or accepting it, on the other, as the saints of God accept

His favour now, with the feeling that nothing but their own sin can separate them from it, but that they need to watch and pray lest sin should separate them, with the condition attached to the latter alternative, that those who have failed to attain holiness here should not be shut out from hope, and to the former, that the door should be closed on them for ever, which choice would be most in the spirit of St. Paul (Rom. ix. 3), most after the mind of Christ (Gal. iii. 13)? Would not the decision, 'Let *me* be safe, safe for ever, and let them perish,' seem to us as a concentrated egoism raised to its highest power? Would not the word 'cruel' rise to our lips as applicable to the temper that could make such a choice? And if this be so—if the natural instincts which fill us with a glow of admiration as we hear of some heroic self-sacrifice wrought by one who loves his neighbour better than himself, echo that judgment—then may we not ask whether the charge of 'cruelty' can legitimately lie against a theory because it involves as a *possible* consequence that what we admire, rather than what we loathe, is the law of God's dealings with the spirits of the righteous?

"2. But I question whether the inference is a necessary one. It assumes that there can be no probation but under conditions identical with those under which we now live, the presence of temptations from without and from within to which all men are equally exposed. But that assumption is surely arbitrary. In the range of God's kingdom there may well be conditions, other than those which we now experience (such, for example, as the manner in which punishment is accepted), which may yet test whether the will is loyal, loving, obedient, or self-centred and rebellious. And if we were to reason from the analogy of our own experience, and the law of tendencies which is already partially developed, would it not seem natural to infer that, as we see here, in the ἕξις (*habit*) as distinct from the ’ενέργεια (*energy*), an ever-increasing fixity of character, so that with many a falling away from grace is a moral impossibility, so when death brings them nearer to the presence of God, that fixity may become absolutely irreversible, with no more fear of change than is felt by the spirits around the throne? And if, after the law of our nature, the habit reproduces itself in the energy, may we not, must we not, think of that character, which has been formed on earth by labours of love as well as by prayer and praise, as neither sleeping nor otiose while it waits for the Resurrection, but finding there also, in that other world, some scope for a like action?

"3. But the argument from continuity, you urge further, tends to subvert the Christian's faith in events which are not continuous, but catastrophic, in their character, such as the Resurrection and the Last Judgment. The answer, however, is not far to seek, and it is (1) that our faith in those events, as such, rests on grounds altogether distinct from any argument drawn from analogy or experience, and that, if the grounds warrant our belief in them, the faith remains unshaken, whatever conclusions we may draw from analogy as to the intermediate state of souls; and (2) that the theory which I am now defending gives a significance to the Final Judgment of which the popular belief, in great measure, deprives it. Protestants and Catholics alike, for the most part, think of that judgment as passed, irrevocably passed, at the moment of death. The soul knows its eternal doom then, passes to heaven or hell or purgatory, has no real scrutiny to expect when the Judge shall sit upon the Throne; while, on this view, the righteous award will then be bestowed on each according to the tenor of his life during the *whole* period of his existence, and not only during the short years or months or days of his earthly being. This gives, I venture to think, not a less, but a more, worthy conception of that to which we look forward as the great completion of God's dealings with our race.

"Yours, very faithfully,

"E. H. Plumptre."

IV.

"Aug. 9, 1871.

"My dear Sir,—I feel the force of your answer to my objections, viewing both the objections and the answer in a strictly logical view, though in one respect I have misled you by omitting to state, as I had fully intended, what I meant by their logical issue.

"I meant to have stated it before concluding, and then forgot to do so, my letter having run to a greater length than I wished; and now, if I state it, or otherwise attempt to clear my meaning, I am sure you will not think I do so in a controversial spirit.

"Let me observe, then, that your argument in behalf of what I venture to call the 'cruelty' of teaching that the probation (to stand or fall) of good men does not end with this life, may avail, in my opinion, with men of subtle intellects or of heroic natures (such as St. Paul, whom you instance), but will not serve for the run of men, or support them in their struggle here with evil. What's the good of my striving so hard to keep from sin and temptation if I am not safe when I die, and my neighbour who gives himself to the world, the flesh, and the devil, and so dies, may, for aught I know, after this life get to heaven and I fail of it? Is it not best to go my own way here and chance the life to come? Men in general take broad practical views, and are moved by imagination rather than by speculation. Arguments after Butler's manner of what is unrevealed but possible, used by way of explanation of the great balk which the doctrine in question would be to them, will not meet their needs. It is hard enough to bear the view, as at present, of virtue suffering, evil triumphant. Would it not be a second trial, quite as great, nay, greater, because unexpected, to have to believe that, this weary life passed, the end does not come after all? Such a teaching I have called cruel, unsettling as it is both to faith and to hope. Of course I cannot prove all this, but I submit it to your judgment.

"I grant, indeed, that if your view be revealed truth, then my argument about cruelty and unsettlement goes for nothing; and this is the very point to which I omitted to proceed in my letter to you. I meant the logical drift of what I urged to be this: is this novel doctrine, or is it apostolic? There are many truths which may be startling and even dangerous in places where they have been long forgotten; but, if apostolic, we must return to them, and preach them at whatever cost. *Is this one of them?* Must it be *preached?* Certainly it has a heavy *onus probandi* on it, both as 'cruel' and as novel, and requires good evidence in order to be allowed. I had intended to have said with what interest I looked out for the testimonies of approved early writers in its behalf, which I understood you to promise in your advertisement, an interest founded on doubts whether you can fulfil your intention. Of course I was aware that several of the Fathers are in favour of a restoration of all things; but such a restoration does not imply probation to stand or fall continuing beyong this life, and this is the point which I doubt of your finding in the Fathers. I trust I have said nothing out of character with the sincere respect and goodwill with which I subscribe myself,

"Sincerely yours,

"* * * * *"

I left my courteous antagonist in possession of the

last word, and contented myself with thanking him for his letter. Nor do I wish now to enlarge on that special point of the "cruelty" which it is alleged is involved in the idea of the extension, in some instances, of the probation or discipline, which in this life has been inadequate, beyond the limits of the grave. It is, however, I think worthy of note (1) how wide a hope, extending to those who "die and make no sign," as well as to the unbaptised and the heathen, the Catholic priest holds to be compatible with Catholic theology; and (2) that he admits, what some divines of his Church have denied, that the doctrine of a restoration of all things was held not by Origen only, but, by "several of the Fathers." It is, I submit, obvious that although this theory of a restitution of all things is not identical with that which I have maintained, it is, at least, as compatible with the idea of probation after death as it is with the acknowledged fact that the present life is a time of trial and probation. Not the most fervent advocate of Universalism dreams of an absolute equality of blessedness. He is content to hope for a victory over sin, for the acceptance by each created spirit of the will of the Father as absolutely righteous, for the cessation, or at least the mitigation, of the sufferings of body and of mind which sin has caused. But if so, then the thought of an universal restoration is compatible with the belief in infinite grades of capacity for knowing God, yet more so with infinite variations in the effect produced on each separate consciousness by the memory of its own past; and thus, as this life is a probation for the next stage of our being, that in its turn may be a trial-time also, and the "lowest place" will differ from the highest, as the result of the total aggregate of the past; and so, strange as the paradox may seem, the belief even in an universal restoration is compatible with a belief also in the eternity of punishment.

[Part of the article is omitted, as dealing with the subject of *Conditional Immortality*, treated elsewhere (Study XI.) in this volume. I give the concluding paragraph.]

We need, I will venture to add in conclusion, in discussing this momentous question, compared with which all other controversies within the Church that are now raging round us sink into the category of the "infinitely little," the temper of calmness and moderation. We see but a little way into the great mystery of permitted evil and of the ultimate victory of good, and our words should be wary and few. We need to remember that each of our systems of thought has commended itself to men of truest faith in God, and deepest love, and holiest lives; that each has drawn souls from darkness to light, and from the power of Satan unto God. If we are tempted to speak of those who preach the popular eschatology as placing a Moloch in the place of God, the names of Dante and St. Francis de Sales and Archbishop Leighton should rebuke the rash and ill-advised utterance. If we condemn those who proclaim the wider hope as subverting the sanctions of personal and social morality, and leading men to an antinomian indifference, the names of Origen and Gregory of Nyssa, of Maurice and of Erskine, should bid us hold our peace, lest we condemn the righteous whom God has not condemned. The want of formulated system on which second-rate critics have dwelt as the characteristic defect of Dr. Farrar's sermons is to me their chief charm, the witness to a calmness and sobriety of thought underlying all his passionate and glowing eloquence. He has given utterance to a protest against human exaggerations or distortions of a Divine truth, and such a protest on behalf of our instinctive convictions in the righteousness and love of God can, for the most part, only express itself in the language of indignant horror. So it is indeed with other truths and other human inferences from them. We follow the sacramental teaching of Augustine and the mediæval Church until we find ourselves lodged in the conclusion that unbaptised infants are excluded from salvation. We accept the truth that eternal life depends on our knowing God as He is, until we stand face to face with the dogma that all who do not "keep the Catholic faith," as man has formulated it, shall "perish everlastingly." We receive the thoughts of grace, election, predestination, until they land us in the *horribile decretum.* We believe that man is justified by faith in Christ, until men press the conclusion, on the one hand, that we may continue in sin that grace may abound, and on the other that the millions of the heathen world are shut out from hope. We welcome the thought of a purifying discipline after death till it finds its practical outcome in the indulgences of Tetzel. Against these conclusions we feel that argument is at once needless and useless. The reason and conscience of mankind, in proportion as they are enlightened, protest against them. The teacher of a theology that shuns the falsehoods of extremes may well be content, in the question before us, to take refuge in that protest, and to echo St. Paul's cry—if you will, St. Paul's *scream*,—of horror. "God forbid!" Μή γένοιτο! may well be with us, as with him, the end of controversy. Commending what we have been led to think ourselves to the calm thought of others, we may rest, as the patriarch rested of old, in the question, "Shall not the Judge of all the earth do right?"

XIV.

THE WORD "ETERNAL."

THE questions which are discussed in this volume are so closely connected with the words which in various languages have been used to convey the idea of eternity, that an inquiry into the significance of those words seems an almost indispensable complement to any complete treatment of them. Such an inquiry is in its nature both etymological and historical. We have to ask, as in the discussion as to the meaning of the words "destruction" and "perdition,"[1] what was the original connotation of the words employed, and how far that connotation has been modified by the thoughts of individual men who have used them.

It may be well, for some at least who may read these pages, to note, at starting, the fact that the word "eternal" is not only a translation of the Greek *αἰώνιος* (*æônios*), but is absolutely identical. The Greek *αἰὼν* (*æon*) is one and the same with the Latin *ævum*, and from this we get *ævitas* and *æviternus*, with their shortened forms *ætas* and *æternus*. For

(1) See Study XI. on *Conditional Immortality.*

the sake of clearness, however, I shall in dealing with the Greek words use the terms *æon* and *æonian* instead of their Latin equivalents.

In its earliest use, then, *æon* seems to convey the thought of a period complete in relation to the object with which it is connected, and in particular of the period of man's life. When a man dies his *æon* fails or leaves him (Hom. *Il.* v. 685; *Od.* v. 160), or he brings his *æon* to a close (Herod. i. 32). The vengeance of the gods upon the evildoers descends even to the third *æon* or generation (Æschyl., *Theb.* 144). Men say of human life, "Who except the gods lives all the time of his *æon* without suffering?" (Æschyl., *Agam.* 554).

In Plato, as might be expected, we find a more subtle and transcendent conception of the word. He rises to the thought of an absolute *æon* as belonging to the Father and Creator of the universe which He has framed after the pattern of the eternal idea. To attach that *æonian* nature (this is the first instance I know of in which the adjective appears) to created things was in the nature of things impossible, and so He formed the heavens as an image of the *æon;* and time, as measured by the motion of the heavens, with its past, present, future, its years, months, days, is an *æonian image* of the absolute *æon*, which remains evermore in its simple unity (*Tim.* p. 37). Time has thus come into being with the heavens, and will endure as long as they endure, and perish, according to the pattern of the *æonian* nature—*i.e.* as I understand the passage—when the heavens, which are relatively *æonian*, shall themselves cease to be (*Tim.* p. 38).

With this twofold connotation, the highest mingling with the lower, and tending to raise its meaning, the word passed into the hands of the Hellenistic Jews, to whom we owe the Septuagint version of the Old Testament. They found in it what they wanted for the Hebrew *ad* (עד) in the sense of duration, perpetuity (Isa. lvii. 15 ; ix. 5 ; Hab. iii. 6 ; Deut. xxxiii. 15) ; for *olâm* (עוֹלָם) which, with a primary significance of "the hidden, the obscure," was used for the remote past (Ps. cxxxix. 24 ; Jer. vi. 16 ; Deut. xxxiv. 7), the remote and sometimes the never-ending future (Gen. xvii. 7 ; Jer. li. 39 ; Dan. xii. 4 ; Gen. iii. 22) ; or for the world in its completeness (Eccles. iii. 11). The noun is used accordingly, as in its earlier classical meaning, for the period of man's life (Deut xv. 17 ; 1 Sam. xxvii. 12 ; Ps. lxxviii. 1), for the entirety of a nation's life, or for one complete period of that life. The ceremonial statutes of Leviticus are thus an ordinance *for ever*, *i.e.* for the *æon* (Lev. iii. 17). It is used further for the period of the created world's existence (Job xx. 4), or for the remotest prehistoric stage of that existence "*of old*" (Gen. vi. 4 ; Job xx. 4 ; Mic. v. 2 ; Deut. xxxii. 7), for the whole world itself in its relation to time (Eccles. iii. 11 ; Wisd. xiii. 9 ; xiv. 6). The grave is the "long home," the "*æonian* house" of men (Eccles. xii. 5). The covenant made with Noah is an "*æonian* covenant" (Gen. ix. 12, 16). Canaan is given to Abraham for an "*æonian* possession" (Gen. xvii. 8). The mountains of Israel are the "*æonian* hills" (Gen. xlix. 26; Hab. iii. 6). The gates of Zion are the "*æonian* doors" (Ps. xxiv. 7, 9). The days of old are the "*æonian* years" (Ps. lxxvii. 5; Eccles. i. 10). The ancient cities that lie in ruins are "*æonian* foundations" (Isa. lviii. 12). A time may come when a man may forget even an "*æonian* shame" (Isa. liv. 4, "shame of thy youth" in A.V.) Here it is obvious we have the sense of long, undefined duration, not of absolute endlessness.

On the other hand, there is a manifest drift throughout towards the higher Platonic sense of the word. God inhabits the *æon* (Isa. lvii. 15). He reigns "for the *æon*" (Exod. xv. 18), is indeed "the king of all the *æons*" (Tobit xiii. 6, 10; Ps. cxlv. 13). The extremest conception of duration that man can form is for "the *æon*," or "the *æons*" (Deut. xxiii. 3, 4; 2 Sam. vii. 13), for the "*æon* of the *æons*" (Dan. vii. 13), "for the *æon*, and yet further" (Mic. iv. 5; Dan. xii. 3). Men strive in this way to express their sense of the absolute infinite Being, of Him whom they worship as God. He himself is the Eternal, the *æonian* (Job xxxiii. 12; Bar. iv. 10, 14, 20). It is noticeable that the combination of "*æonian* life" which was to be so prominent in the teaching of the Christ and the phraseology of Christendom does not appear in the Septuagint.

In the teaching of the New Testament we come for the first time, as far as the Greek words are concerned, upon another thought connected with the words. The whole course of the world's history was divided into (1) "this *æon*," or "this present *æon*," the whole visible world in its present evil state (Matt. xii. 32; xiii. 32; Luke xvi. 8; xx. 34; 1 Tim. vi. 17; Eph. i. 21), and "the *æon* that is to come," this being thought of, not wholly or chiefly as the life after death, but as the kingdom of God, existing and partially manifested now, but to be revealed in its fulness at the close of "this *æon*" (Matt. xiii. 49; xxiv. 3; xxviii. 20). The times in which the Apostles lived were those upon which "the ends of the *æons*" had come (1 Cor. x. 11). Where this distinction does not appear the old significance (with one possible exception, to be discussed hereafter) appears to be retained. "Unto the *æon*," or "the *æons*" (Matt. xx. 19; John. vi. 51, 58; xii. 34; 1 Cor. viii. 13, *et cet.*), or, in the fuller form, "unto the *æons* of *æons*" (Phil. iv. 20; 1 Peter iv. 11; v. 11; Rev. x. 6, *et cet.*), is the equivalent for perpetual duration. "Before *æonian* times" represents the whole period of the world's history prior to the revelation of Christ (Rom. xvi. 25; 2 Tim. i. 9; Tit. i. 2). "Unto the *æons* that are to come" (Eph. ii. 7) represents, in like manner, all that was to follow that revelation. The adjective "*æonian*" is joined with "fire" (Matt. xviii. 8; xxv. 41), with the "weight of glory" (2 Cor. iv. 17), with "destruction" (2 Thess. i. 9), with the "house not made with hands" (2 Cor. v. 1), with "might" (1 Tim. vi. 16), with "glory" (2 Tim. ii. 10), with "salvation" (Heb. v. 9), with "judgment" (Heb. vi. 2), with "redemption" (Heb. ix. 12), with "covenant" (Heb. xiii. 20), with "inheritance" (Heb. ix. 15), with "kingdom" (2 Peter i. 11), with "gospel" (Rev. xiv. 6), with the "Spirit" (Heb. ix. 14). God Himself, as in the Old Testament, is the "*æonian*" (Rom. xvi. 26). It might seem as if this were a sufficient induction to establish the conclusion that the word served to express the fullest thought that man could grasp of absolute limitless duration.

The exception to which I have just referred is the combination of "*æonian* life" upon which the whole question at issue turns. That combination meets us in well-nigh every portion of the New Testament (forty-three times in all, twenty-three of which are in the writings of St. John); and it has been urged that in order to determine the significance of that combination we must look to the writer of whose thoughts it was conspicuously the key-note. St. John, it is said, uses the words "*æonian* life," both in recording his Master's teaching and in his own writings with an altogether different connotation, and that must govern its use throughout the New Testament. Thus Mr. Maurice wrote :—

"The word eternal, if what I have said be true, is a key-word of the New Testament. To draw our minds from the temporal, to fix them on the eternal, is the very aim of the Divine economy. How much ought we then to dread any confusion between thoughts which our Lord has taken such pains to keep distinct—which our consciences tell us ought to be kept distinct? How dangerous to introduce the notion of duration into a word from which He has deliberately excluded it! And yet this is precisely what we are in the habit of doing; and it is this which causes such infinite perplexity in our minds. 'Try to conceive,' the teachers say, 'a thousand years. Multiply these by a thousand, by twenty thousand, by a hundred thousand, by a million. Still you are as far from eternity as ever.' Certainly I am, quite as far. Why then did you give me that sum to work out? What could be the use of it except to bewilder me, except to make me disbelieve in eternity altogether? Do you not see that this course must be utterly wrong and mischievous? If eternity is the great reality of all, and not a portentous fiction, how dare you impress such a notion of fictitiousness on my mind as your process of illustration conveys? 'But is it not the only process?' Quite the only one, so far as I see, if you will bring time into the question—if you will have years and centuries to prevent you from taking in the sublime truth, 'This is life eternal, to know God'"—and so further on, as explaining what is left when the idea of duration is excluded. . . . . "The eternal life is the perception of His love, the capacity of loving; no greater reward can be attained by any, no higher or greater security. The eternal punishment is the loss of that power of perceiving His love, the incapacity of loving; no greater damnation can befall any."—*Theological Essays*, pp. 436—438.

I need scarcely remind the readers of this volume that this was the passage which more than any other led to the controversy that ended in Mr. Maurice's expulsion from King's College. It seemed to Dr. Jelf and to the Council to "cast an atmosphere of doubt about the word 'eternal'" (*Reasons*, &c.) Mr. Maurice protested again and again against this conception of eternity as only a "very, very long time," and urged that the word *æon* "expresses a permanent fixed state, not a succession of moments—that it does not convey so much the idea of a line as of a circle; that it does not suggest perpetual progress, but fixedness and completeness" (*Letter to Dr. Jelf*, p. 6). Mr. Mansel wrote a pamphlet (some years before the controversy with Mr. Maurice which followed on the publication of his Bampton Lectures) to show that it is incompatible with the conception of the next life as a continuation and development of the present, or of the present life as a discipline and preparation for the next, to believe that our future consciousness will be exempted from the law of succession. He admits it is objectionable to assert that eternity *considered as an attribute of God* is identical with endless duration, but holds, in his characteristic phrase, that this is the "regulating idea" which man is bound to act on in thinking of that attribute (*Man's Conception of Eternity*, pp. 22, 23).

I have no means of judging what impression Mr. Maurice's account of eternity made on the minds of those who came more or less closely under his teaching. Some, perhaps, tried to grasp the thought of an existence in which there was no succession, as the disciples of Plato may have tried to grasp the thought of an "*æonian* being" of which time was the "*æonian* image." Judging by the comparative absence of reference to it in later writings of thinkers on either side, it seems natural to conclude that the whole discussion lay in a transcendental region into which none but those endowed with special gifts for subtle speculation could be bold enough to enter.

If the authority of a great name were sufficient to decide such a question, it will be admitted that Mr. Maurice's position has received a reinforcement, the strength of which it is difficult to over-estimate, in the adherence of Dr. B. F. Westcott. Unrivalled as an exegete of Scripture, a profound student of the Fathers, devout, contemplative, growing by years of unwearied study as into the very likeness of St. John, the divine, the theologian, he too has travelled, apparently in entire independence of Mr. Maurice, and perhaps by a different path, to the same conclusion.

He is dealing with "The Nature of Life" in St. John's Epistles, and brings together the various terms in which the Apostle speaks of it, and then proceeds :—

"In considering these phrases it is necessary to premise that in spiritual things we must guard against all conclusions which rest upon the notion of succession and duration. 'Eternal life' is that which St. Paul speaks of as ἡ ὄντως ζωή, 'the life which is life indeed' (1 Tim. vi. 19), and ἡ ζωὴ τοῦ Θεοῦ 'the life of God' (Eph. iv. 18). It is not an endless duration of being in time, but being of which time is not a measure. We have, indeed, no power to grasp the idea except through forms and images of sense. These must be used; but we must not transfer them as realities to another order" (*Epp. of St. John*, p. 205). And again: "The life which lies in fellowship with God and Christ is, as has been seen already, spoken of as 'eternal life' in order to distinguish it from the life of sense and time, under which true human life is veiled at present. Such a life of phenomena may be 'death' (1 John iii. 14; comp. v. 16). But 'eternal life' is beyond the limitations of time; it belongs to the being of God (1 John i. 2; ἦν πρὸς τὸν πάτερα), and its consummation is the transforming vision of the Son seen as He is (1 John iii. 2; John xiv. 23). For us now, therefore, it is spoken of as both present and future. . . . . essentially present, so far as it is the potential fulfilment of the idea of humanity (John iii. 36; v. 24; vi. 47, 54; xx. 31; 1 John v. 12), and the possession of life may become a matter of actual knowledge (1 John v. 13; comp. 1 John iii. 15). . . . . This thought of the present reality of 'eternal life' is characteristic of St.

John, and in its full development is peculiar to him (but comp. Gal. ii. 20)."—*Ibid.* p. 207.

It will be admitted that Dr. Westcott's train of thought in this matter runs on the same lines as Mr. Maurice's, if it is not absolutely identical with it. It may seem almost to savour of presumption to sum up the case as it is thus presented by two teachers at whose feet I have for the most part been glad to sit as a disciple, and whom I have learnt to regard as conspicuously Masters of our Israel. But having entered on the inquiry, I feel that I ought not to shrink from the task of saying, even if I do not venture fully to discuss their reasoning, how far their position seems to me tenable.

The conclusions to which I have been led may accordingly be briefly stated as follows :—

(1.) That it is not proved that our Lord excluded duration from the idea of "*æonian* life." The definition, or description, of John xvii. 3 seems to me to give the true, highest meaning of the noun, leaving the adjective with its received connotation of indefinite duration raised in this instance at least to that of perpetuity. "The eternal life, the life which knows no ending, is to know God and Jesus Christ whom He has sent."

(2.) In every book of the New Testament, except the writings of St. John, I find this connotation as the obvious and natural meaning of the word "*æonian.*"

(3) In St. John I find, with Mr. Maurice and

Dr. Westcott, the effort to make men realise the thought that the eternal life, being eternal, exists in the present, has existed always in the past. Men may enter into that life now, have it as their possession, be conscious that they have it, when they are one with Christ, who is the Life as well as the Light of men, in whom the light and the life were manifested. They may, through the act of their own will, choose darkness rather than light, death rather than life, even after they have "tasted of the powers of the world to come" (Heb. vi. 4, 5). In the end, when character is formed and discipline has done its work, it shall be, for those who accept the discipline, as a perpetual possession. The weak beginnings of the knowledge of God in this life leave men, for a time at least, open to temptations which may obscure it. When they have been perfected by the discipline appointed for them in it, as in the intermediate state, the beatific vision becomes for them, as well as in itself, eternal.

(4.) Æonian *death* is, it may be noticed, a phrase which, though it meets us in the Prayer Book, is not found in Scripture. What we find there as the ultimate revelation of the state of those who harden themselves in evil is the æonian *fire*, the wrath of God revealed against all unrighteousness (Rom. ii. 5), the *æonian* destruction (not in the sense of annihilation) (2 Thess. i. 9), and the *æonian* chastisement (*kolasis*) (Matt. xxv. 46), which, if we take the word with its received connotation, implies a punishment for the sake of the sufferers, and therefore in some measure corrective in its purpose, even where that purpose is frustrated by the creature's obduracy of will (Aristot., *Rhet.* iii. 10).

(5.) I find it impossible to conceive of life, either human or divine, apart from the idea of duration. This may, of course, be a personal infirmity of brain-power, like the incapacity to take in the combination of consciousness and unconsciousness supposed to be implied in the Buddhist *Nirvana,* or to grasp the idea of a world in which space should be thought of as of $3+n$ dimensions; but I apprehend that the infirmity is common to many minds besides my own. If there be something in the Divine Existence which transcends that conception, we have still to remember that that existence is revealed to us, apart even from the word "*æonian,*" under the regulative idea (I venture to adopt Dean Mansel's phrase) of duration. The eternal is not only the *I AM*, but the Alpha and the Omega, the beginning and the ending, the first and the last. He "was, and is, and is to come" (Rev. i. 8). His mercy "endureth for ever," throughout all generations, to *æons* of *æons* (Ps. cxxxv. 13; cxxxvi. 1—26). I fail to find, as it is used by the Greek Fathers, any instance in which the idea of duration is eliminated. The two *æons*—the one present, visible, dealing with things transitory, belonging to sensual pleasure and pain; the other future, invisible, with spiritual blessings as the reward of righteousness—are contrasted by Chrysostom as they had been contrasted by the writers of the New Testament (*Orat.* περὶ τῆς τῶν μελλόντων ἀπολαύσεως, tom. viii. p. 73 ; Hom. xcii. tom. v.). An attempt to distinguish between the *æon* in its highest sense and time as measured by man is found in Gregory of Nyssa (*Orat.* xxxvi. p. 616 , *Orat.* xlii. p. 678), followed almost *totidem verbis* by John of Damascus. (See Suicer. *Thes.*, *s.v.* ἀιώνιος). What the former says is that "the *æon* is not time nor a part of time, nor is it measurable. What to us is time measured by the movement of the sun, that the *æon* is to those that are everlasting, ever coextensive with the things that absolutely are, as a kind of temporal motion and interval." We are reminded as we read his words of the source from which they probably flowed—the language in which Plato speaks of time as an *æonian image* of the *æon* which belongs to the things eternal. In one remarkable passage Gregory of Nyssa speaks of the chastisement of the wicked as doing its appointed work "for a certain *æonian* interval" (ἐις ἀιώνιον τι διάστημα) before they are brought to the restoration on which he loved to dwell (*de Animâ et Res.* Opp. ii. p. 659). For the most part, however, the sense of indefinite duration predominates, it must be admitted, throughout the Greek Fathers.

As regards the Latin equivalent we start with the connotation which the word *æternus* conveyed in the language of pre-Christian writers. Lucretius is exulting in the thought of the victory over superstitious fears to which his philosophy will lead. Those fears tend to disturb the order and tranquillity of life.

> "Not without cause, for could men but perceive
> A limit fixed of woes, they might have strength
> To hold their own against the fears and threats
> With which the seers affright us. As it is,
> There is no power, no way to meet them left,
> Since we in death eternal pain must bear."
>
> *De Nat. Rer.* i. 107—111.

He, of course, looked on these terrors as the dreams which it was his work to dispel. But when we come to what was his solution of the problem of life, as it has been that of other materialists, the word *æternus* still meets us with the same significance. Here there is a "fixed limit" of life, and that limit is what we call death. But of death there is no limit.

> "Let thy life last long ages as thou wilt,
> Yet all the same eternal death remains."
>
> *De Nat. Rer.* iii. 1090, 1091.

With one exception it will be found, if I mistake not, that this notion of limitless duration attached to the word *æternus* through the long succession of Christian writers in the Western and African Churches. That exception is, however, a very notable one. Augustine's mind was led alike by his study of Plato and by his sympathy with St. John to strive after a profounder thought than that which satisfied other thinkers. The distinction between past, present, and future was one of the conditions of human thought, but was not to be transferred to our conception of the Divine eternity. That was to be thought of as an everlasting present, in which there is no succession and nothing transitory, the "to-day" of the eternal Father and of the co-eternal Son, begotten, not in time, but before all time (*Confess.* xi. 10). In that fixed and stable eternity, which was thus one with the light, truth, love of the Divine Nature, men might find a refuge from the mutability of time (*Enarr.* in Ps. lxxxix. c. 3). Compared with it all the ages in their limitless succession are as nought (*de Civ. Dei.* xii. 12). We attain to eternal life by entering into fellowship with the eternal God (*de verâ Rel.* 19). Passages like these are to be found, not only in the works referred to, but scattered throughout Augustine's writings. On the other hand, when he is in the attitude, not of a thinker contemplating the mysteries of the Divine Being, but of a preacher to other men who have no power of thought to qualify them for such speculations, he too adopts the current connotation of the word "eternal" as applied to life, to death, to punishment. He could hardly be cited fairly as one who excluded "duration" from the conceptions which the word involved, though, as the above extracts show, he felt that endless duration was but a partial and incomplete notion of all that it conveyed.

NOTE.—Ken may be added to the list of those who have sought to grasp the higher significance of the eternal. He quotes the old legend of the monk whom the bird's song, compressing three centuries into three hours,

"Duration boundless, unsuccessive, taught."

Farther on he sums up his train of thought—

"Ideas, Glories, Joys, Decrees,
All Futures which Omniscience sees,
All Possibles contain'd in boundless Might,
In fix'd Eternal standing NOW unite."

—*Hymnarium*, p. 11.

XV.

THE DAMNATORY CLAUSES OF THE ATHANASIAN CREED.

I CONFINE myself in the present Study to a discussion of the clauses which have for some generations past been a stumbling-block to many devout souls, who have yet accepted, in substance, the teaching of the Creed itself. I shall assume that that Creed represents faithfully the teaching of the Catholic Church, that it is a legitimate development of the Nicene and therefore of the Apostolic Creed, that that development was necessitated or made expedient by the heresies and speculations which had presented themselves prior to its composition. The one question on which I now care to touch is the meaning of the so-called damnatory clauses.

Did we know with any certainty who had written the Creed we might infer something as to the intention of the author from his character or from his other writings. As it is, the evidence in favour of Vigilius of Thapsus, or Hilary of Arles, or Vincent of Lerins, is too slight to warrant any induction from what we know of their mind or temper. We must be content to deal with the Creed itself, and to construct, as it were, an ideal biography. And here we are met with two opposite conceptions, each of which is within the limits of possibility. We may picture to ourselves a trained controversialist, a *malleus hæreticorum*, writing, in Dean Stanley's language, his "triumph psalm" over those he has confuted, exulting in the doom which he assigns to those who have opposed the Church's teaching, making the path to life as narrow and as difficult as possible, multiplying the snares and pitfalls into which the unhappy victims who refused his guidance might fall, and placing himself as on the throne of judgment to pronounce sentence on all who, during the limits of this life, had failed to attain, or had refused to assent, to the truth as he defined it. Or, on the other hand, with Mr. Maurice, we may believe that it is "simply impossible that any good man who wrote such a Creed in any age intended this; that it cannot mean that any one who does not hold certain intellectual notions about the Trinity must without doubt perish everlastingly" (*Life*, ii. p. 413). On this assumption we may picture to ourselves a profound thinker, a devout soul, one of whom we may think as uniting the characteristics of Aquinas and à Kempis, who rested in the faith that to know God is eternal life, who felt by his own personal experience, or by what he had observed in others, that every denial or obscuration of that knowledge involved the loss of an inestimable blessing, and who therefore, surveying the history of the speculations which thus distorted or obscured the truth, traced, for the guidance of his own age and for future generations, the path which the most devoted servants of Christ, which the Church Catholic at large, had taken in the labyrinth of bewildering error. We may think of such an one as judging no individual man or classes of men, affirming only that unless they came to the knowledge of the truth they could not know God as indeed He is, nor therefore share the blessedness of eternal life, setting no limit to the time within which an apprehension of the truth was possible, making all allowance, such as the Divine equity would make, for sins of ignorance and involuntary error.

We have, as I have said, no adequate *data* for determining which of these pictures is historically true. I venture to point out what may, I think, be legitimately said in favour of the latter. I would plead in favour of the unknown writer that he deliberately avoids what had been the favourite formula of councils and controversialists, "let him be anathema," expanded sometimes (I take, almost at random, an example from the fourth Council of Toledo, c. 75), into "let him be anathema, maranatha — that is, let his lot be perdition at the coming of the Lord, and let him and his companions have their portion with Judas Iscariot." "Let him be condemned with the devil and his angels to eternal tortures." It would have been so easy for one who wrote, so to speak, with the *animus damnandi* to follow in the track of these and other like formulæ, that his choice of another, implying no imprecation, may legitimately be treated as evidence that he had not that *animus*. And if this be so, then, whether we think it expedient or inexpedient, right or wrong, that a creed should be fortified with a threat, the clauses in question are minatory rather than damnatory, in the sense in which the latter word is commonly used of them. They are in the region of dogmas what the Commination Service is in the region of ethics. In neither case are we, as is often said, cursing our neighbours. In both we proclaim the conditions of a true blessedness. As the sentences which define who are "accursed" are the legitimate expansion of the law, a moral and not a positive law, that "without holiness no man shall see the Lord" (Heb. xii. 14), so the minatory clauses of the Athanasian Creed set forth that the condition of eternal life is to know God, that that knowledge *is* eternal life, and therefore that not to know God and Jesus Christ whom He hath sent is to lose that life so long as the ignorance continues.

It will be instructive in this as in other matters to trace the history of English thought since the Reformation. It is noticeable that up to the time of Hooker no objection had been raised to the "damnatory clauses" as such. He has, it is true, to defend the Creed (which, by the way, he assumes to have been written by Athanasius *circ.* A.D. 340) as against his

Puritan antagonists; but the only objection which he notices is that which was urged on the ground that the danger of the heresies it condemns was past, and therefore that it was superfluous. The recitation of the Creed was an "unprofitable labour" (*Eccl. Pol.* v. 42, § 11, 12). So, in like manner, there is no trace of any wish for an alteration or even an explanation on this point expressed at the Hampton Court Conference (A.D. 1604). The two leading parties of the Church were, as parties, on this point, of one mind. The change which was to come over men's feelings was in this, as in other things, to be the work of individual thinkers, who were in advance of their own age, whom we have seen before as the fore-runners of the wider hope. Among these Chilling-worth occupies a foremost place. So far as I can trace, he was the first to whom the damnatory clauses presented a stumbling-block so serious that for a time they hindered his seeking orders in the English Church. To him it seemed—to use a favourite phrase of his—a "high and schismatical presumption" for any man to pronounce the sentence of judgment which the Creed pronounces (Chilling-worth, *Works*, i. p. xxvi. *ed.* Oxford). A reference to the passage from *The Religion of Protestants*, quoted in p. 160, will show how naturally Chilling-worth's temper of mind would lead him to this con-clusion.

The free license given to the discussion of religious questions in the first half of the seventeenth century, the tendency to indifference or latitudinarianism which was its natural result, descended from the universities to the society of towns, from scholars to laymen in general. Dryden, in his *Religio Laici*, may be fairly looked on as, in this respect, the spokesman of a class. He had spoken of his hope that the righteous heathen—

> "With Socrates may see their Maker's face,
> While thousand rubric martyrs want a place."

He adds—

> "Nor doth it baulk my charity to find
> The Egyptian bishop of another mind;"

and proceeds to argue against the clauses as dooming to "endless pains" all who did not accept the Creed.

Taylor, in the stage of thought represented by his *Liberty of Prophesying*, a work which may be described as a theologian's attempt to look at theology from a lay standpoint, throws out a doubt parenthetically as to the authorship of the Creed, and speaks much in the same tone as the *Laicus* of Dryden. He cannot see in the preface and conclusion of the Creed "that moderate sentence and gentleness of charity" which he finds in the Nicene. "Nothing there but damnation and perishing everlastingly, unless the article of the Trinity be believed, as it is there with curiosity and minute particularities explained. . . . For the articles themselves I am most heartily persuaded of the truth of them, and yet I dare not say all that are not so are irrevocably damned" (*Liberty of Prophesying*, § 2, *Works, ed. Heber*, vii. pp.

491—3). Assuming this to be the natural and necessary meaning of the clauses, Taylor proceeds to argue for two or three pages on the familiar topics of the wisdom of charity, the distinction between the error and the man holding it, the pleas of ignorance and prejudice, much in the same tone as Chillingworth.

It is clear that the clauses thus interpreted would clash with the wider charity of which I have traced the growth, as far as the English Church is concerned, in a previous Study. It is a noticeable fact that the question is as conspicuous by its absence in the Savoy Conference as it had been in that of Hampton Court. The interval between the Restoration and the Revolution of 1688 was, however, one of rapid transition, and the change showed itself in the Church and out of it. The Presbyterians of the Commonwealth began to shade off into the Unitarianism with which they have since been identified. The objections urged by Chillingworth and Taylor were felt more widely, and the subject cropped up at the Conferences which were held for the revision of the Prayer Book under the Royal Commission of 1689. The Commission proved abortive, but there is evidence that two proposals were made to meet the difficulties that were felt by many: (1) that the use of the Creed should be left optional at the discretion of the minister; (2) that an explanatory rubric should be added "declaring the curses denounced therein not to be restrained to every particular article, but intended against those that deny the substance of the Christian religion in general" (Cardwell, *Hist. of Conferences*, pp. 432, 433). The latter alternative seems to have been adopted by the majority of the Commissioners. Of those who took part in the Commission Tillotson is reported to have said (I am unable to verify the tradition by a reference) that "the Church were well rid of the Creed." Burnet in his work on *The Thirty-nine Articles* discusses the question, and falls back upon the answer given "by the most eminent of this Church," that the clauses apply only to those who, "having the means of instruction, have rejected them, and have stifled their own convictions and loved darkness rather than light." "We do not limit the mercies of God towards those who are under such darkness as not to be able to see through it and to discern and acknowledge these truths." He adds—and the addition shows probably the part he had taken in the discussions of the Commission—that "it were indeed to be wished that some express declaration to this purpose were made by those who have authority to do it" (Burnet, *Art.* VIII.). The growing tendencies to what looked like Arianism within the Church—as in Clarke's *Scripture Doctrine of the Trinity*—and Socinianism outside it, gave occasion to Waterland to come forward in his *Critical History of the Athanasian Creed*, a work which takes a high place in theological literature as the first scholarly, and for the time exhaustive, inquiry into the authorship and history of that document. Vossius in his *De tribus Symbolis* (1642) and Usher in his *De Symbolis* (1647) had indeed led the way; but their treatment of the question was comparatively meagre, and their books were so little known that even a man of Taylor's exceptionally wide reading does not seem to have been acquainted with them. Waterland enumerates the various conjectures that have been started as to authorship—Vigilius of Thapsus, Vincentius of Lerins, an Athanasius, Bishop of Spire (642), Hilary of Poictiers—and gives reason for his own conclusion in ascribing it to Hilary of Arles. In expounding the damnatory clauses he follows Burnet. They are to be understood, "like all such general propositions, with proper reserves and qualifying conditions." They "do not exclude any such merciful abatements or allowances as shall be made for men's particular circumstances, weaknesses, frailties ignorance, inability, or the like" (*Works*, iv. p. 299). Dissenters who had had "long scruples against them were now well reconciled to them modestly expounded" (*ibid.* p. 307). In a later work, *The Importance of the Doctrine of the Trinity* (1733), written in answer to *A Sober and Charitable Disquisition on the Doctrine of the Trinity*, an anonymous pamphlet, of which he speaks with respect as "written in a Christian spirit," and in which the old objections had been urged afresh, he takes the same line and quotes with approval a remarkable passage from Salvian (*de Gubernat. Dei*, p. 100) in regard to those who err in ignorance. "They are heretics, but do not know that they are so. . . . They esteem themselves such good Catholics that they even throw on us the charge of heresy. . . . They err therefore, but they err with an honest mind; not out of any hatred in God, but with affection to Him, designing thereby to show their love to the Lord. . . . How they shall be punished at the day of judgment for this their error of a false persuasion, no one can know except the Judge" (*Works*, v. p. 119).

From the time of Waterland onwards the controversy has been renewed at intervals on much the same lines, and it would be a task beyond my present limits to follow it step by step. I content myself with noting some of the more significant facts. In 1789, after the separation of the United States of America from England, the Church of the former country had an opportunity for revising its Prayer Book, and deliberately dropped the Creed altogether, not retaining it even as a document for reference. In 1794 Dr. Hey, Norrisian Professor of Divinity at Cambridge, the broadest of all Broad Churchmen, published his *Lectures on the Articles*, and declared his belief that the "damnatory clauses" had "occasioned much needless uneasiness." That such men as Chillingworth, Clarke, Tillotson, Secker should have felt scruples as to using them could be ascribed only "to the influence of religious terror," which made them unable to admit in matters of religion "the limitations which common sense suggests in the application of every general proposition" (iii.p. 102).

Dr. Arnold, on the other hand, though he speaks of Hey's *Lectures* as "the best and fairest book on the Articles" which he knew (Stanley's *Life*, i. p. 150), was unable to accept what seemed to him a non-natural interpretation. "I do not believe the damnatory clauses in the Athanasian under any qualification given of them, except such as substitutes for them propositions of a wholly different character." He was ready, however, to read the Creed and to renew his subscription to Art. VIII. as "not conceiving the clauses in question to be essential parts of it," or "to have been deliberately retained by our Reformers after the propriety of retaining or expunging them had been deliberately submitted to their minds" (*ibid.* ii. p. 120). Later on, when a "petition on subscription" was being pushed forwards by his friend Mr. W. W. Hull, who carried on an almost life-long warfare against the Creed, he writes that he would like to "petition specifically for the direct cancelling of the damnatory clauses of the anonymous Creed vulgarly called Athanasius' (*ibid.* ii. p. 204).

It was not to be wondered at that Arnold's biographer, with liberal tendencies that carried him yet further than his master, should carry on the conflict which was thus opened. Now in one form, now in another, he appeared as the champion of liberalism in its warfare against the clauses. The warfare culminated in his volume on the *Athanasian Creed*, published in 1871. He maintained, in the strongest terms, that the clauses are not a "mere separable adjunct of the Creed," but are "firmly incorporated at the beginning, the middle, and the end. 'Necessary to everlasting salvation' . . . clenches and nails every single part together into one indissoluble whole" (pp. 27, 28). His strategy was, apparently, to attack the Creed itself through the "damnatory clauses." The controversy, as most of us will remember, waxed fierce and hot. There were memorials (one against the clauses signed by seven thousand laymen) and counter memorials.[1] Dr. Pusey and Dr. Liddon led the hosts on one side, and the latter threatened to "reconsider his position" if the Church of England ceased, in this respect, to be that with which he had entered into covenant. Bishop Magee (*Charge* in 1872) and Dean Perowne (*Sermon in Peterborough Cathedral*, 1872), were conspicuous on the other side, the former analysing, with his wonted masterly incisiveness, what seemed to him the inconsistent explanation of the clauses put forward by their defenders, the latter urging the disuse of the Creed on the ground that it was a stumbling-block to a large number of our "most intelligent and conscientious laity," who "refuse to utter the clauses which consign the vast majority of mankind to everlasting perdition" (p. 26), but being content to leave it in the Prayer Book as "an exposition, orthodox and useful, of great and blessed verities" (p. 27).

The most notable results of the controversy were

(1) Two of the chief memorials on each side may be found in the Fourth *Report* of the Ritual Commission, pp. 158, 159.

found, however, (1) in the wide extension of the plea of ignorance to "all who repented of their sins and sought to do right" in Dr. Pusey's *Sermon on Responsibility for Religious Belief*, already quoted on p. 184 of this volume; (2) in the fact that the explanations which had been given before by individual divines were now formally ratified by the Convocations both of Canterbury and York, in 1876, in the following terms:—

(1.) "That the Confession of our Christian faith, commonly called the Creed of St. Athanasius, doth not make any addition to the faith as contained in Holy Scripture, but warneth against errors which from time to time have arisen in the Church of Christ."

(2.) "That as Holy Scripture in divers places doth promise life to them that believe, and declare the condemnation of them that believe not, so doth the Church, in this Confession, declare the necessity, for all who would be in a state of salvation, of holding fast the Catholic faith, and the great peril of rejecting the same. Wherefore the warnings in this Confession of Faith are to be understood no otherwise than the like warnings of Holy Scripture; for we must receive God's threatenings even as His promises, in such wise as they are generally set forth in holy writ. Moreover, the Church doth not herein pronounce judgment on any particular person or persons, God alone being the Judge of all."

Not without significance was another explanatory

document, drawn up by the Oxford Professors of Divinity, in which amplest allowance was made, as in Dr. Pusey's sermons, not only for "involuntary ignorance" but for "invincible prejudice." The same line of defence was followed by Mr. (now Canon) Malcolm MacColl (*Damnatory Clauses Vindicated,* 1872), who maintains that the Creed does not affirm of any heretic—not even of Arius—that he has "perished everlastingly." "Have the scales fallen from his eyes, and does he see the truth at last? Were there any extenuating circumstances which the eye of man could not detect, but for which He who 'knoweth all things,' and 'willeth not the death of a sinner,' made due allowance?" All that he will say is that "a heretic, *as such,* shall not inherit the kingdom of God" (p. 46).

Still more significant was the new attitude taken by one conspicuous section of the defenders of the Athanasian Creed. Mr. F. D. Maurice had for some years previous to this stage of the controversy, *i.e.* in 1852, applied a new method of interpretation to the damnatory clauses. He could not tell whether the writer of those clauses "reconciled them with his obedience to Christ, who had said, 'Judge not, that ye be not judged.'" He "could, and could lead others to do so." The thoughts of Eternal Life to which he had been led made him see in the Creed the full statement of that knowledge of what God is which *is* eternal life. "The language of the Creed often startled him. It would outrage his conscience and his faith to condemn any human being" (*Life*, ii. p. 148). Ten years later he sought to remove the scruples of inquirers with the thought that the power to return to the "Infinite Charity, the Eternal Love," which was one with "the Name of the Trinity, the Father, the Son, and the Holy Ghost," is not limited to the three score years and ten of men's pilgrimage here; "that the Creed had taught him not to condemn others, but to examine himself, lest he might be confounding the persons and dividing the substance" at the very moment when he was "arguing ingeniously and triumphantly for the terms that denote distinction and union" (*Life*, ii. pp. 413—415.)

What Mr. Maurice thus taught was reproduced by others who were, in greater or less measure, under the influence of his teaching. Professor J. S. Brewer entered the lists as against Dean Stanley in *The Athanasian Creed Vindicated* (1871). He too defends the damnatory clauses, partly on the ground taken by Waterland and the Oxford Professors. "We leave it to God's mercy alone to determine how any man has kept the faith—what are his shortcomings, his difficulties, and his obstacles—God alone can determine the strict adjustment between the will and the deed" (p. 85). But he, with Mr. MacColl, goes further. "He (Dean Stanley) will claim that men holding these errors (as *e.g.* the Sabellian, or Arian, or Greek) may be everlastingly saved, and need not hold the Catholic faith, because God, out of His mercy and consideration for the general piety of such men, will pardon their deflections from the right path. I ask, How will He pardon? By opening their eyes, or by allowing them to remain in ignorance? If by opening their eyes, then we come back to the assertion of the Creed: 'Whosoever will be saved before all things it is necessary that he hold the Catholic faith.' How or how long it shall be held the Creed does not define, nor is that material. . . . Either those who are worthy of that life" (the life eternal) "must learn and take up that song with the Catholic Church or be excluded from it; or more correctly, exclude themselves from it by their unbelief, so long, at least, as they continue in that unbelief. If Dean Stanley says God will open their eyes and take away that unbelief, I hope so too" (pp. 81—93).

The course taken by Mr. Charles Kingsley was still more noticeable. He had signed two addresses to the Archbishops asking for relief from the damnatory clauses, or for an authoritative explanation of them. His name suddenly appeared on the Committee which was formed by the leading theologians of the High Anglican School for the defence of the Creed. His friends expressed their surprise at this apparent change of front. He explained that his purpose was to lead the defenders to "construe the Athanasian Creed not in the light of Puritan eschatology, *i.e.* of the doctrine which the Puritans (so far as I know) introduced first, namely that the fate of every man is irrevocably fixed at the moment of death," but in that of the Catholic doctrine of an "intermediate state." In an elaborate memorandum addressed to the Committee he set forth his belief as to that state. "The Creed says, and says truly, that the knowledge of God and it alone is everlasting life. It does not say that that knowledge may not be vouchsafed hereafter to those who have sought honestly for it in this life, but through unfortunate circumstances have failed to find it. Provided the search be honestly continued in the unknown realms beyond the grave, the Athanasian Creed does not deny that the seeker, it may be after heavy pains and long wanderings, shall at last discover his Saviour and his God." "Such an interpretation of the Athanasian Creed would relieve the consciences of thousands, and make it tolerable to those to whom it is now intolerable." This seemed to him the only way to avoid the loss, "to our extreme injury, not only of the so-called 'damnatory clauses,' but (for all practical purposes) of the Creed itself." Of that Creed he holds that "the maintenance of it by the Church of England will exercise a most potent and wholesome influence not only on the theology but on the science, both physical and metaphysical, of all English-speaking nations for generations to come" (*Life*, ii. pp. 396—398). Mr. Kingsley's *Life* does not state what was the result of this communication, but I am informed by a member of the Committee (Canon MacColl) that a resolution was passed thanking him for his memorandum, and that it was received with general sympathy and approval.

It remains only to note the fact that the questions connected with the Athanasian Creed were brought under discussion in the Ritual Commission of 1869, and that, though the official report did not go beyond recommending an explanatory note, "That the condemnations in this Confession of Faith are to be no otherwise understood than as a solemn warning of the peril of those who wilfully reject the Catholic faith," seventeen of the Commissioners expressed their dissent from that recommendation, of whom several, including Archbishop Tait and Bishop Thirlwall, Dean Stanley and Dean Payne Smith, Professor Jeremie and the Rev. W. G. Humphry, recommended the entire disuse of the Creed in the public worship of the Church (*Report*, pp. viii. xi.), the greater part of them urging strong objections to the Creed itself, and treated the explanatory note as "illogical and unsatisfactory."

It seems right, lastly, that I should not shrink from stating what seem to me the legitimate conclusions from this historical survey.

(1.) That the Creed, almost every sentence of which implies a reference to heresies, the history of which is known only to professed students of theology, is not adapted for the public worship of the Church.

(2.) That explanations of the damnatory clauses such as have been proposed will always appear to the great majority of mankind to present a non-natural interpretation, and are therefore insufficient as a remedy for the difficulties which many thousands feel in accepting, or repeating without accepting them, in what seems their obvious and natural meaning.

(3.) That the Creed itself, as a concise and well-defined statement of the doctrine which the Church has gathered from Scripture as to the Trinity in Unity and the Incarnation of the Eternal Word, is a document of great value, and ought therefore to find a place among the formularies of the Church of England.

(4.) That the case of the Church of the United States of America and of the Irish Church, with both of which our own Church is in full communion, shows that the removal of the Creed from the public worship of the Church would not in itself affect the catholicity of any Church that adopted the same course.

(5.) That to make the use of the Creed optional, *i.e.* to leave it to the discretion of the minister or congregation, would be attended practically with insuperable difficulties.

(6.) That so long as the Creed is retained in the public worship of the Church, clergy and laity may use it with a safe conscience, putting on the damnatory clauses whatever interpretation seems to them most agreeable to the equity and the charity of God. Whatever may have been the intention of the writer —and the extracts given from Augustine in p. 162 and from Salvian in p. 380 of this volume show that the wider and more charitable judgment as to those who err in ignorance was not impossible even in the period when the controversies with which the Creed deals were at their hottest point—there is now at any rate a *consensus* of expositions all but formally authoritative in favour of such a judgment, and at any rate sufficient to prove that the *animus imponentis, i.e.* that of the existing Church of England, is distinctly on its side.

XVI.

THE ACTIVITIES OF THE INTERMEDIATE STATE.

I KNOW nothing in the records of the deathbeds of great teachers more touching or more characteristic than the words which fell from the lips of Frederick Maurice, when he was told that his life's work on earth must be looked upon as ended, that he must never preach again. "If I may not preach here," he said, "I may preach in other worlds" (*Life*, ii. p. 636.) I do not know whether Mr. Maurice had in his thoughts at the time a passage in the writings of one of the Fathers of the Church whom he seems to have regarded with a special reverence and affection (Maurice, *Lectures on Ecclesiastical History*, pp. 231—239; *Moral and Metaphysical Philosophy*, i. pp. 307—315.) Twice over does Clement of Alexandria in his *Stromata* (ii. 9, vi. 6), following in the steps of the *Shepherd* of Hermas (*Past.* c. xv. 1), dwell on the thought that in the work of "preaching to the spirits in prison" (Clement takes the words in their natural and obvious meaning) the Apostles were followers of their Lord. "It was requisite, in my opinion, that, as here, so also there, the best of the disciples should be imitators of their Master," proclaiming the Gospel to the souls of the heathen, as He had proclaimed it to those who had perished in the flood, to patriarchs and kings and prophets.

The thought thus brought before us suggests many questions—many more than we can hope to answer—as to the activities of the intermediate state. Is such a work possible or conceivable? How have men thought in the past as to the conditions of that life after death? What is the drift of the conclusions of more recent psychology? What light is thrown upon the perplexities of human questionings by the teaching of Him who brought life and immortality to light? or by that of the Church which His spirit has been guiding? There is scarcely a page in the history of the literature of any nation that has risen out of the crudest barbarism that does not bear witness to the eager desire of men to get some glimpses of the undiscovered country that lies behind the veil. They would fain believe that it was not altogether "the bourne from which no traveller returns," the eternal dwelling-place of the dead, and welcomed anything that professed, whether it came in the dreams and visions of the night, or in the pictures of the creative imagination of the poet, which professed to solve the mystery. The Egyptian *Book of the Dead* represented the soul of the dead as brought before the judgment of Osiris, to have its deeds weighed in the balance, and to receive his sentence on them (see p. 35 of this volume). The mysteries of the Greeks owed their attractiveness and influence in part at least to this, that the hierophant professed to lead the initiated on to the contemplation of the things after death. Popular mythology spoke of Minos and Rhadamanthus, and the Elysian Fields and Tartarus and Acheron and Phlegethon, the fiery river and the Lethe of forgetfulness. The eleventh book of the *Odyssey* brought before men the thought that in that other world they would recognise those whom they had known on earth and "see the great Achilles whom they knew." The elegiac song on Harmodius led them to think of the souls of patriots and heroes as in "the island of the blessed." Plato, who saw in these popular legends at least the parables and symbols of eternal truths, was never weary, as in the *Republic* (x. pp. 614—621), the *Timæus* (p. 42) the *Gorgias* (pp. 523—6), the *Phædon* (p. 113), and the *Apologia*, of bringing them before men's minds as being more than merely mythical. Cicero, in the grand passage with which the *De Senectute* ends (c. xxi.—xxiii.) and in the *Somnium Scipionis* (c. iii.), contemplates, at least for the superior souls among mankind, an immortality of development and growth in their converse with the spirits of the wise and good, and looks forward to meeting once again the Cato whom he had known and loved. Tacitus (*Agric.* c. 46) cannot remember the virtues of Agricola without cherishing the hope (though, as the "*si quis piorum manibus locus*" shows, not without a touch of the scepticism of his age) of some communion between the living and the dead. The sixth book of the *Æneid* gave to Virgil the influence which he exercised, when other Latin poets were forgotten, over the mind of mediæval Christendom, and led to his acceptance by the great Florentine as his master and guide in the regions of the unseen (Dante, *Inferno*, c. i.). Visions like those of Alberico, Walkelin, St. Brandan (see the *Illustrations to the Inferno* in Longfellow's *Dante*), and Cunningham of Melrose (Bede, *Eccl. Hist.* v. 12) were reproduced in a thousand forms in the mysteries and miracle-plays which fed the imagination of our forefathers. In our own time, to group together works of most unequal calibre, the insatiable eagerness of men to look into the unseen world has been met by such poems as Cardinal Newman's *Dream of Gerontius* and Mr. E. H. Bickersteth's *Yesterday, To-day, and for Ever*, by such spiritual romances as *The Little Pilgrim* and *Gates Ajar*.

The almost infinite variety of thoughts which are brought before us in this rapid survey of the past warns us that it is well that our words should be wary and few; that we should not seek to advance too far into the things that we have not seen or be wise above that which is written; that here also it is right to endeavour to restrain our knowledge within the limits of the knowable. But are we therefore forced to the conclusion that the veil which hides the unseen is, like that of Isis in the temple at Sais, one which no man has ever lifted? Has He who brought life and immortality to light through His gospel left us still in clouds and darkness as to the conditions of that immortality? That question I purpose endeavouring to answer as far as the guidance of the teaching of Scripture, or the consent of Christendom, or the thoughts of the wise of heart may suggest probable conclusions in which we may rest with at least an approximate certainty.

(1.) Nothing in Scripture suggests the thought of a suspension of conscious existence at the moment of death. Whatever latitude of interpretation we give to the framework of the parable (if it be a parable, and not rather a history) of the Rich Man and Lazarus (Luke xvi. 19—31), it suggests the thought of a continuity of consciousness. The promise to the repentant robber who sought to be remembered in the far-off coming of the kingdom of the Christ, "This day thou shalt be with me in Paradise" (Luke xxiii. 43), assumes that continuity. St. Paul rests in that belief when he judges it "far better" to "depart and be with Christ" (Phil. i. 23) than to continue his labours upon earth. St. John assumes it throughout the Apocalypse. The souls that are under the altar cry out, "How long, O Lord, how long?" (Rev. vi. 10). The four-and-twenty elders are round about the throne and lift up their voices in praise (Rev. iv. 10). The hundred and forty-four thousand of the sealed ones, the great multitude that no man can number, that came out of great tribulation, are guided by the Lamb to the living fountains of waters (Rev. vii. 17). Our Lord and the writers of the New Testament in this instance reproduce the belief which they found current among their countrymen. It seems idle to set against this evidence of their belief the language of those who, like Hezekiah and the Psalmist and the Preacher, lived with a less definite vision, who complained that the dead could not praise God, that they who went down to the pit could not hope for His truth (Isa. xxxviii. 18), or who asked, "Who shall give Thee thanks in the pit?" (Psa. vi. 5; xxx. 9; lxxxviii. 11); or declared, in tones borrowed from the scepticism of Greek thought, that there was no wisdom, or device, or knowledge, or counsel in the grave (Eccles. ix. 10). Still less can the clearer teaching of the New Testament writers be balanced by the fact that they speak of death as a "sleep" (John xi. 13), that the faithful dead are those who "have fallen asleep in Christ" (1 Cor. xv. 18; 1 Thess. iv. 14, 15). Such language was natural enough as men looked upon the calm face of the dead and compared it with the face of the sleeper. They would say—

> "After life's fitful fever he sleeps well."

For those who have no clearer hope the sleep might seem to be eternal. But even within the limits of our experience sleep is a modification, not a suspension, of the continuity of consciousness. And the word, as used by Christian writers, does not imply more than such a modification.

The history of Christendom shows that it has, on the whole, been faithful to the tradition which it thus received. With here and there an exception which proved the rule, it has maintained the continuity of consciousness in the intermediate state. When the opposite opinion appeared in the East and West, it was branded, even though in the latter it had the sanction of Pope John XXII., as the heresy of the Psychopannychii (those who taught the all-night slumber of the soul), and rejected, in their decrees on purgatory, by the representatives of the Greek and Latin Churches who met at Ferrara (1438) and Florence (1439), and that rejection was renewed in the Council of Trent (*Sess.* xxv.). The liturgies of the East and West have been consistent in their witness against it. The teachers of our own Reformation condemned it in the Forty-two Articles of 1552 in the following terms, when it had been reproduced by some of the German Anabaptists (I modernise the spelling): "They which say that the souls of such as depart hence do sleep, being without all sense, feeling, or perceiving until the Day of Judgment, or affirm that the souls die with the bodies, and at the last day shall be raised up with the same, do utterly depart from the right belief declared to us in Holy Scripture." The teaching of Calvin and the leading Lutheran theologians was in the same direction Herzog., *Theol. Encyklop.* Art. *Seelenschlaf*).

Looking to the psychology of the case, our choice seems to lie between the materialism which looks on thought and consciousness as only a function of our animal organisation, and therefore ceasing with the cessation of its working, and the belief to which Christendom has thus borne its continuous witness. There may be something plausible and scientifically tenable in the thought that death is an eternal sleep, rounding our little life. But if this conclusion be not accepted, then there seems something, if not inconceivable, yet at the least in a very high degree improbable, in the thought of the existence of the soul during a thousand or ten thousand years in a state of absolute unconsciousness, then to be waked up as by the sound of the last trump to start on the new stage of its existence, as though the whole period between death and the resurrection had not been at all. The fact that in very many if not in most instances consciousness continues in unabated activity up to the moment of death, supplies the argument which Butler presses (*Analogy*, part i. ch. i.), that unless it can be shown that it is only a function of our bodily organism, it is probable that it should continue after death has removed it from the sphere of our observation.

(2.) Assuming, then, the continuance of consciousness, we have to ask whether any light is thrown on the energies which belong to it under the new conditions involved in its separation from the material body. Difficulties may perhaps be found in the conception of an absolutely disembodied spirit, and the thoughts of men, from Homer to Dante, in Judaism and in Christendom, have for the most part got over the difficulty by imagining a subtle attenuated corporeity as investing the soul and as being the condition of its retaining a distinct personality, the *simulacrum* or *eidôlon* of what its body was on earth, not of flesh or blood, or depending on the laws of nutrition or decay. Some support for that belief is found in tho phenomena of our Lord's body after His resurrection (John xx. 19; Luke xxiv. 31, 36); in the appearance of the bodies of the saints that slept in Matt. xxvii. 52, 53; in St. Paul's desire not to be unclothed, but to be clothed upon "with the house which is from heaven" when the earthly house of this tabernacle is dissolved (2 Cor. v. 1—4). What are the conditions of that body, whether it is after the likeness of the man when he dies in infancy, or maturity, or age, or represents, so to speak, the ideal of his personal humanity, are questions which we may ask but cannot easily answer. We must be content to say, as of the future spiritual body of the resurrection, that "God giveth it a body as it hath pleased Him" (1 Cor. xv. 38).

Starting, then, from the continuity of consciousness, we may ask what are its main activities. It lies in the nature of the case that there is a cessation of the manifold impressions which we have received through the senses as they now are. The pains and pleasures of the body, such as they are, belong to the past, though new pains and pleasures may take their place. The hints of Scripture point to memory as the chief energy of the soul under its new conditions of existence. The words of Abraham to the rich man in Hades were, "Son, remember" (Luke xvi. 25). He was to survey the whole extent of that life in which he had received his good things and had cared for little or nothing else. And those words at least fall in with some of the known facts of consciousness in this life. To many—notably, it is said, to those who have been in the peril of sudden death by drowning, and have, as it were, tasted its experiences—there comes, as in a moment of time, the unrolling of the scroll of their whole past lives. Their memory acts with a new intensity and with an almost inconceivable rapidity. It becomes (to borrow a phrase from the *Dream of Gerontius*) the "standard of its own chronology." Even under the conditions of a calmer death we note often something of the same kind. The mind goes back to the remote past of its life, and the scenes of childhood and the old familiar faces come back with a long-vanished distinctness.

It is almost inconceivable that such a retrospect should not affect every soul in which there is any capacity for growth. And so far as our knowledge extends, we cannot pronounce of any individual soul that it has lost all such capacity. The conception of a state in which the soul, being conscious, *must* remain absolutely in the same ethical state as that in which it left the body, clashes, I venture to think, with all true psychology, and has no ground to stand upon in the teaching which is the basis of the beliefs of Christendom. In that act of memory, when the impressions of the outer world are withdrawn, consciousness passes into conscience. The thoughts that accuse each other may then come to exercise a terrible retribution. The criminal or vicious acts, the bitter words that can never be recalled, the impurity which tainted the life of another as well as our own, the greed of gain, the life that fared sumptuously every day, the dishonesty and the fraud which passed for wisdom, the zeal for God that was not according to knowledge, the hollow formalism, the life self-centred in its love of praise or power—all these may come to be seen then as God sees them now. There will be no water of Lethe to narcotise the agony of that remembrance, no faint vibration of the *mala mentis gaudia,* such as comes now at times to the memory of the sensualist. In this sense it may be true that the repentance that comes after death for those in whom the capacity for it has not been extinguished may be more deep and agonising than any that has been known in life. The worm that dieth not, the flame that is not quenched, may begin to do their strange and terrible work. If the repentance be a true repentance, a sorrow for the sin as sin, it lies in the nature of the case that it must lead on not only to an objective forgiveness, but to the subjective sense of being forgiven. But, as in Ezekiel's searching analysis of the state of one who is restored after apostasy and alienation, the pain and the shame and the self-loathing which the memory of the past brings with it are not incompatible with, are, it may be, rather the indispensable condition of, all true growth in holiness and, therefore, in blessedness (Ezek. xvi. 60, 61; xx. 43; xxxvi. 31). By the soul's accepting that as the punishment which it has deserved, the torturing scourge may wound only to heal, and develop an ever-increasing sense of the everlasting covenant of peace.

May we not think that the new conditions of the life after death will be, for those who have in any measure sought, and are still seeking, for light, favourable also to the larger knowledge of Divine truth? The soul may not as yet be ripe for the beatific vision, and may have to wait for the time when it shall know even as also it is known. But the transition from our present partial to that complete knowledge may legitimately be thought of as gradual rather than instantaneous. The law that "whosoever willeth do the will of the Father shall know of the doctrine whether it be of God" (John vii. 17), gives a basis for the hope which the wisest of our teachers, not of one school only but of all, have in these latter days led us to cherish as to those whom involuntary ignorance or invincible prejudice has kept during life from the full apprehension of revealed truth, or indeed from any knowledge of that truth at all. There those whose life has been spent in mutual bitterness, or ceaseless controversy, or cankering distrust, or pitiless persecution, denouncing each other as blasphemer, infidel, heretic, may find themselves at once in the wrong and in the right, and dwell together under the shadow of the wings of God. There the eyes that were dim shall see, and the deaf ears shall be unstopped, and the tongue of the stammerer shall be ready to speak plainly. The promise that he that seeks shall find, that to him that knocketh at the gate of the Father's house it shall at last be opened, which seemed during life to tarry so long for its fulfilment, shall be seen at last not to fail. Men shall see that systems which were only partially true, which contained a large admixture of weak and beggarly elements, have yet been as a schoolmaster, a *pædagôgos* (the trainer, rather than the instructor, of the child), leading men to Christ as the true Teacher. He has yet "many things to say unto us" which now we cannot bear (John xvi. 12), partly because our organs of spiritual discernment have been more or less atrophied by disease, partly also because, so far as they have been exercised at all, it has been in an environment that was unfavourable to their expansion.

Will that growth in knowledge be limited to what we commonly speak of as religious knowledge, the truths which concern us as to God's being and our own nature, and the relations between the two? May we cherish the thought that the man of science shall know more of the laws which govern the forces of the material universe, of the evolution of life in its higher or its lower forms, of the education of the human race, and the work assigned to each portion of it in the history of the world? We may well shrink from over-bold conjecture in answering that question, but unless we draw an altogether arbitrary line between knowledge secular and religious, and think of the laws that cannot be broken, and the times before appointed, and the bounds of men's habitation, as belonging altogether to the former, as forming no part of the works of God which have been from the beginning, as not His laws at all, but only formulated statements of the sequence of phenomena which exist apart from Him, I cannot see that we can limit the words "then shall I know even as also I am known" to the mystic contemplation of the Divine perfections, and not rather extend them so as to take in those perfections manifested in act. With the vast majority who pass out of this life with the merest elements of human or divine knowledge, stunted, enfeebled, almost in the stage of child-like ignorance, it is manifest that, if they are to be fitted for the apprehension of the truth in its completeness, there must be (I say not how, or through what discipline or help) a development of capacities that are now latent, as well as the extension of the range of action of capacities that are now vigorous and strong. We find it hard to picture to ourselves the future life of one who dies in infancy, or idiocy, or the ignorance which seems to us to reduce the life of man almost to the level of the brute, still more, perhaps, that of one who has passed away in violent or chronic insanity. All that we can do is to cling to the belief that the Christ is now what He was when He laid His hands upon the little ones of Galilee, and took them up in His arms and blessed them; as He was when He cast out the evil spirit from the frenzied Gadarene, so that he sat at the Master's feet clothed and in his right mind. "In the Father's house there are many mansions" (John xiv. 2), many resting places which He has gone to prepare for them, according to their character and capacities. We may well leave the lambs of the flock, to whatever fold they may belong, under the guidance of the Good Shepherd. The little ones, of whom He said that of such is the kingdom of Heaven, are safe in the school of the Great Teacher.

Will there be in that region of preparation, or in the ultimate blessedness of the saints, a mutual recognition among those who are thus partakers of the inheritance of the Kingdom? That is, perhaps, of all questions that rise up in men's minds, as they look forward into the dim unseen, the one on which they most crave for certainty. The hopes of men, in Christian or pre-Christian times, have for the most part made answer to themselves. They have cherished the belief, as they laid their loved ones in the earth, that the parting was not to be for ever, that they should meet again under better and happier conditions, that misunderstandings and mistakes should no longer cloud the communion of soul with soul. They look back on the friendships of their lives or the relationships which are closer than friendships and feel how little they have really known of those even with whom they were in daily converse—

> "Not e'en the tenderest bosom, next our own,
> Knows half the reason why we smile or sigh."

Every poet who has ever ventured to picture to himself the dwelling place of the dead, from Homer to Dante, has shown that for him an immortality without recognition was a thing hardly conceivable. It is probably true of most Christians that, if they would utter truly what was in their hearts, they would confess that for them it would be hardly a thing to be desired. They would crave, even in the joy of the beatific vision, and still more in that which is preliminary and preparatory to it, for the joy, at once natural and spiritual, of the Communion of Saints.

And it is clear, I think, that, though we cannot point to distinctly revealed declarations that so it shall be, the whole drift of the teaching of the Scriptures tends in that direction. That teaching at least does not clash with the consentient hope of humanity. That hope may be found colouring its language, underlying its formal or informal statements. When David faces the death of the child for whom he had fasted and prayed with a restored cheerfulness, it is because he can say, "I shall go to him, but he shall not return to me" (2 Sam. xii. 23). In the parable which above all others is fruitful in its suggestiveness, Abraham and Lazarus and the rich man identify each other (Luke xvi. 19—31). Those who love darkness rather than light shall *see* men coming from the east and from the west, from the north and from the south, and sitting down with Abraham and Isaac and Jacob in the kingdom of God (Luke xiii. 28). Philemon was to receive back the fugitive Onesimus no longer as a slave, but as a brother beloved, *for ever* (Philem. v. 15). The seer of the Apocalypse recognises the four-and-twenty elders and the hundred and forty-four thousand, and those whose names were in the Lamb's book of life, and those that were slain for the Word of God (Rev. iv. 4; vi. 9; vii. 4; xxi. 27). Can we form any conception of the life after death which shall include the idea of the communion of saints, the consciousness of belonging to the great family of God, of being members of the body of Christ, and yet exclude the thought of recognition? Are the personal affections, the love strong as death, the friendships stronger than death, that are the mightiest elements in the formation of our character now, to be cast aside when they have done their work, and leave us in an isolation that either knows no affections or finds no scope for their activity? Are the children of the Father to cease to know each other precisely at the moment when they enter into the Father's house?[1]

(1) The fact that the probability of such a recognition is maintained in Bishop Mant's *Happiness of Heaven* is probably the ground of the general acceptance which that book has met with. Mr. Birks, on the other hand (*Victory of Divine Goodness*, p. 60), postpones the recognition till the time that follows the resurrection, the intermediate state being one of communion with Christ alone.

It is easy, of course, to ask hard questions, after the manner of the schoolmen, as to the nature and extent of this recognition. Will it be confined to those we have known on earth, or extend to all whom we have wished to know or who may have wished to know us? Will it be limited to those who are sharers, in greater or less measure, in the blessedness of the Kingdom? Or shall we, as the Lazarus parable suggests, recognise also those that are in the darkness and the fire? If the latter, shall we be able so to acknowledge the righteousness and love of God that even that knowledge will not shake the firmness of our faith that He doeth all things well, that not without cause has He manifested His eternal love as being also the eternal wrath? Shall we bear to contemplate the evil that has entered into the life of those whom we have known and loved, or the more terrible discovery to them of the evil which has been in us? Will the perception of identity be through the medium of something analogous to human vision or through some more immediate act of consciousness and spiritual presence, of which even in this life we have sometimes, as in what we have learnt to call telepathy, foretastes and forebodings? I formulate these questions because, as a matter of fact, they are those which constantly present themselves to men's mind as they look across the valley of the shadow of death to the region that lies beyond it. I do not venture to formulate an answer. We know not what we shall be. Now we see, as in a mirror, darkly. Then we shall know even as also we are known (1 John iii. 2; 1 Cor. xiii. 12). Is there room, to come round to the question with which we started, in our conceptions of the future life for the activities of the love of man as well as for the energies of the love of God which show themselves in contemplation and in praise. For the most part we dwell almost exclusively on the latter, on the endless Hallelujahs and the song of the victors and the ceaseless hymns and the golden harps. But does not the assumption that this is all involve the frustration in the life to come of the noblest elements of character that have been formed on earth? Have we been trained here as members of a society resting upon the idea of altruism and mutual service to find ourselves, when we have passed into a region of higher development, in a state in which all such service is impossible? If the supremest joy of those who were most like Christ on earth has been to minister to their brethren for His sake, to help them to follow in His footsteps, to teach, comfort, guide, to bring them to Christ, and Christ, as it were, to them, is it a natural or legitimate conclusion that all that thus ties men to their fellows will be rudely snapped off and that they will find their occupation gone? Looking to the infinite variety of characters and capacities among those who are admitted within the gates of the Father's house, is it not conceivable that there also there may be joy, as there is in the presence of the angels of God, over one sinner that repenteth

(Luke xv. 7, 10); that it may be ours to feed those who are still as babes in Christ with the pure milk which their souls need (1 Peter ii. 2); to remove the lingering prejudice, to help forward the expanding soul in its progress to the truth, to "wash the feet of the disciples" from the stains which they have contracted during their pilgrimage on earth (John xiii. 14, 15)? May not the masters of those who know find their joy and crown of rejoicing in bringing forth treasures, new and old, from the house of the Interpreter? Was it not the reward of the servant who was faithful over few things, not only to enter into the joy of his Lord, but to be made ruler over many things (Matt. xxv. 21), over ten cities or five (Luke xix. 17—19), according to his capacity and faithfulness? If we again shrink from formulating a dogmatic answer, enough remains to show that we need not banish the hope that was expressed by Clement of Alexandria and Frederick Maurice to the region of cloudland and delusions.

Yet again we ask in our restless eagerness, Do the souls of the righteous know what is passing on the earth? Do they think of and pray for those they have left behind them? Are the prayers of the invisible Church offered for the visible, of the triumphant or the expectant Church for that which is still militant? Here also we dare not speculate over-boldly. Memory of what has been does not necessarily involve the knowledge of what is, still less of that which shall be. It may be that there are things which the souls of the dead, though they are equal to, like unto, the angels (Matt. xxii. 30 ; Luke xx. 36), still "desire to look into" (1 Peter i. 12), that the events of this visible world, or of other regions of the invisible, lie beyond their ken. But this much may at least be said with but small chance of error, that if they remember (and the consciousness of personal identity is, as we have seen, inseparable from memory), then, if we believe in the communion of saints, if the perfected Christian character does not lose that which was the crowning grace and excellence of the imperfect, they cannot but pray for those whom they have loved on earth, for the whole Church militant in its temptations and its conflicts. If they are in any sense with Christ, they must be one in spirit with Him who is our Advocate with the Father (1 John ii. 1), and ever liveth to make intercession for us (Heb. vii. 25). Of this, indeed, we have something like an assurance in the cry of "How long, O Lord?" which went up from the souls beneath the altar in the apocalyptic vision (Rev. vi. 10). It was with a profound insight that Dante placed the Lord's Prayer in the lips of the souls who were on the Mount of Purification, emphatically in its character as a prayer of intercession, and, in part, at least, for others rather than themselves (*Purgat.* xi. 1—24). Nor can we, looking to the faith of Christendom as traced in the Study on *Prayers for the Dead*, believe that the souls of the departed are unaffected by the prayers of the living. This also is involved in the very idea of the communion of saints. If their state is not absolutely unalterable, if there is any capacity for growth and improvement, then, apart from the mystery which attaches to all intercession in its *modus operandi*, there is nothing to suggest the thought that our prayers for them are profitless or ineffectual.[2] We offer those prayers now up to the moment of death; we pray, even when consciousness seems extinct and the whole probation of life all but over, that the soul that is on "the point of its departure," "may be washed in the blood of the immaculate Lamb, that whatsoever defilements it may have contracted in the midst of this miserable and naughty world, through the lusts of the flesh or the wiles of Satan, being purged and done away, it may be presented" before the throne "pure and without spot" (*Visitation of the Sick*). Is it more in accordance with the teaching of Scripture or with the laws of spiritual growth to limit the possible answer to that prayer to an instantaneous act of sanctification, wrought by the Divine Omnipotence in the very moment of death, on the soul that at least seems unconscious, or to leave it, as we leave the answer to other prayers, to the "manifold," the "very varied" wisdom (πολυποίκιλος σοφία, Eph. iii. 10) which is wonderful in its working and its ways past finding out?

(2) I may refer on this point to an interesting article *On the Letters of the Princess Alice*, by Canon Malcolm MacColl, in the *Fortnightly Review* for July, 1884, and to a paper on *Prayers for the Dead*, by the same writer, in the *Contemporary Review* for Jan., 1871.

I have no wish, in giving utterance to these thoughts as to the possibilities of the intermediate state, to rest in an unreal optimism. The vision, seen through the uplifted corner of the veil, is not without its terrors. The flames of Hades in which the rich man was tormented are the symbols of a dread reality. There is the sin that hath never forgiveness (Matt. xii. 31), that is liable to the sentence of an "æonian judgment" (Mark iii. 29), the "sin unto death," of which St. John cannot say that a man should pray for it (1 John v. 16) as he prays for the sins not unto death of which a brother may be guilty, which at least seems in its own nature to exclude forgiveness just because it has extinguished all the last germs of the promise and potency of spiritual life, and therefore excludes repentance. There is the working of the eternal laws of retribution, for those who are saved as well as for those that are lost, recoverably or irrecoverably, that "whatsoever a man soweth that shall he also reap" (Gal. vi. 7). There is the sense of loss and shame that follows on the memory of deeds, words, thoughts of evil which cannot but be, in its nature, terrible, the self-loathing which may accompany even the restoration to the everlasting covenant of peace (Ezek. xvi. 60, 61). St. Paul did not cease to remember, with humiliation and contrition, the days when he was a "blasphemer, and a persecutor, and injurious" (1 Tim. i. 13), even though he knew that he had obtained mercy, because he did it "ignorantly and in unbelief," and that "henceforth there was laid up for him a crown of righteousness" (2 Tim. iv. 8). And experience shows that there is even on earth a stage in the growth of evil which, at least, seems incurable, in which punishment restrains but does not soften, which does not accept its punishment but rebels against it, which is to the last defiant. The history of the criminals of all ages, of the vices which in the righteous judgment of God "seal the eyes" of those who yield to them, of the fatal hypocrisy which does not know itself to be hypocritical, brings us fearfully near to the possibilities of such a state. We may not dare to affirm that it has been reached in any individual case, not even, as some have thought, in that which Christendom has accepted as the representative instance of perdition without hope, the sin of Judas.[3] In the murderer at the gallows as in the robber on the cross, there may be that which we know not, but which makes salvation possible. *Meliora latent.* "The things that are

(3) Hammond (*Commentary on Acts* i. 25) contends earnestly against the interpretation which sees in St. Peter's words, "to his own place," an assertion of the damnation of Judas. Chrysostom (*in loc*) praises St. Peter for dwelling on the temporal not the eternal punishment of his sin. Origen (*Tract.* xxxv. *in Matt.*) suggests that the motive for his suicide was that he might pass into Hades, and there, in his unclothed soul, implore his Lord's forgiveness, and is followed in this view by Theophanes (*Hom.* xxvii. p. 202) and Theophylact (*Hom. in Matt.* xxvi.; Suicer. *Thesaurus*, *s. v. Judas*). Our Lord's words in Matt. xxvi. 24, John vi. 70, xvii. 12, remain, of course, in all their dread significance as speaking of a loss irrecoverable, a throne left vacant, the memory of a sin which would for ever deprive life of all that gave it nobleness; but do they affirm that his sin was identical with that which hath never forgiveness?

impossible with men are possible with God." "Better than the seen lies hid," may be true of the roughs and the prostitutes of our great cities, as it was of the publicans and harlots of Judæa and Galilee. There may be capacities for growth in such as these, as in the rich who neglect or the Pharisees who condemn them, which escape our most microscopical analysis. And in any case we know that the punishment, whatever it may be, will be measured out with what the conscience of illumined and redeemed humanity will recognise as an absolute and perfect righteousness, not without mercy except for those who have shown none, nor without love except for those who have themselves shut love out. In the end we may be sure, though we shrink from the fierce exultation, or the material horrors, or the narrow limitations of the poet who wrote the words, that we shall be able to see written over the gates of the city of great woe, into which no hope enters—

> "Giustizia mosse il mio alto fattore,
> Fecemi la divina potestate,
> La somma sapienza e il primo amore."

> "Justice it was that moved my Maker high,
> The power of God it was that fashioned me,
> Wisdom supreme, and primal charity."
>
> Dante, *Infern.* iii.

P. 69. The parable of the potter, as first presented to Jeremiah's mind, was, it should be remembered, something more than the assertion of an arbitrary will. It was spoken, as in Jer. xviii. 1—12, as a message of comfort to a people who said "There is no hope." The potter could fashion the vessel that had been marred into another vessel, could mould a nation or individual man that had failed to attain the perfect form into another vessel, for other, though, perhaps, lower uses. The thought has been expressed in striking words, by two very different writers.

(1.) Theophilus of Antioch. *Ad Autolycum.*

"As a vessel which, when it is formed, is found faulty, is re-cast, or re-fashioned, to the end that it may become perfect and complete, so it comes to pass with man also by means of death."

(2.) Robert Browning. *Rabbi ben Ezra.*

"So take and use thy work;
Amend what faults may lurk,
What strain o' the stuff, what warpings past the aim:
My times are in thy hand
Perfect the cup as planned;
Let age approve of youth, and death complete the same."

P. 74. Comp. Westcott, B.F., *On the Apostle's Creed.* "If called upon to decide between the endlessness of evil and sin, and their ultimate disappearance from the universe, I should unhesitatingly decide for the latter."

P. 83. I am indebted to Prebendary E. C. G. Gibson, Principal of the Theological College, Wells, for the following additional references.

i. 1. Ignatius, *Ad Magn.* ix., as referring to the descent into hell (Ed. Lightfoot, ii. 131).

l. 16. Two other quotations from Irenæus, who gives the passage quoted in iv. 33, as from "*alii autem dicentes,*" in v. 31, as "*quemadmodum propheta ait,*" and in iv. 27 as having heard it, "*a quodam presbytero,*" the last carrying the chain of testimony to the immediately sub-apostolic period.

Other patristic references may be noted.

Hippolytus, *ad Antioch.* c. 45.

Cyprian, *Testim.* ii. 24.

Hilary of Poictiers, *Tract. in* Ps. cxxxviii. 22.

Basil M. *in* Ps. xlviii.

P. 93, note 8. Add to references Jerome, *in Esai.* c. xiv.

L. 18. It ought in fairness to be added that Aquinas (*Summ.* iii. qu. 52, art. 2, 3) adopts Augustine's interpretation of 1 Pet. iii. 19., as does Bede, quoted by Alford *in loc.*

P. 96, l. 2. So Calvin had written, "We are instructed by the Descent into Hell, not only that the body of Christ had been delivered up as the price of our redemption, but that a greater and more excellent price had been paid, to wit, that He had undergone in His soul the entire tortures of a man damned and lost." *Institt.* ii. 16. 10.

P. 100. Four other witnesses from the present generation of Anglican theologians may be added.

(1.) T. S. Evans, D.D., Professor of Greek in the University of Durham, who, in a sermon on 1 Pet. iii. 18, in the *Anglican Pulpit of To-Day*, 1886, adopts without reserve the Catholic interpretation which I have followed.

(2.) Rev. H. E. Head, in *The Ultimate and Proximate Results of Redemption*, 2 vols. 1854—7. I quote a single sentence, but the whole work is worth studying.

"Who can tell what gulfs were not passed over when the Redeemer went and preached to the spirits in prison?" I. p. 154.

(3.) F. C. Cook, M.A., Canon of Exeter, in his Notes on 1 Pet. iii. 18, iv. 6, in the *Speaker's Commentary*.

(4.) A. J. Mason, M.A., Canon of Truro, in his Notes on the same passages in Bishop Ellicott's *New Testament Commentary for English Readers*.

(1), (3), (4), as coming from some of the most profound and devout interpreters of our time, are specially commended to the reader's attention.

On the other hand, as these notes are passing through the press, a volume of *Biblical Essays* by the Rev. C. H. H. Wright, D.D., comes into my hands, in which Augustine's interpretation is elaborately defended in an Essay on *The Spirits in Prison*, to which I gladly refer such readers as wish to hear both sides. Dr. Wright looks on *The History of the Exegesis of the Passage*, as presented in this volume, as "far from complete," "only an outline," as it professes to be—as an outline "faulty and misleading."

All that comes from Dr. Wright's pen bears the stamp of a wider and fuller scholarship than my own, and I readily accept the criticism of a superior person who remarks, in the language of Goldsmith's art-critic, that "the author might have done better if he had taken more pains." I am compelled, however, to demur to the exception which he takes to the manner in which I have spoken of Bishop Horsley's "masterly treatment" of the passage under discussion. Dr. Wright urges, that this "masterly treatment, when that which is common to all interpreters is excluded, occupies less than four pages" (p. 144), a standard of measurement which is, I confess, new to me. I have read Dr. Wright's fifty-eight pages, and am constrained to adhere to the adjective which I have bestowed on Horsley. So I leave my readers to compare and judge.

P. 131. I translate the first of the two passages for readers who cannot read the Latin.

(1.) Virg. *Æn.*, vi. 743—746.

> "Beneath the whirlpool vast
> The deep-stained guilt of others is washed out,
> Or burnt out in the fire. So we each
> Dree our own weird, and then, albeit but few,
> We through the wide Elysian plains are sent,
> And gain possession of the joyful fields."

A translation of Lucretius *De Nat. Rer.*, i. 107—111, will be found in p. 370.

P. 135, l. 6. περὶ Ἀρχῶν = *De Principiis.* A treatise on the First Principles of the Doctrine of Christ.

P. 183, l. 14. Cardinal Manning has indeed not only not recalled his earlier teaching on this point, but has finally and emphatically reproduced it. It is instructive to note how the Church which claims to be the representative of an infallible and immutable theology has, as in spite of itself, been carried onwards to a wider hope than that of mediæval theology, and I therefore begin with a striking passage from St. Francis Xavier's *Letters from Japan* (*Ep.* 86.)

"One of the things which most of all pains and torments these Japanese is that we teach them that the prison of hell is irrevocably shut, so that there is no egress. For they grieve over the fate of their departed children, of their parents and relatives, and they often show their grief by their tears. So they ask us if there is any hope, any way to free them by prayer from that eternal misery, and *I am obliged to answer that there is absolutely none.* Their grief at this affects and torments them wonderfully: they almost pine away with sorrow. They often ask if God cannot take their fathers out of hell, and why their punishment must never have an end; but they do not cease to grieve, and I can sometimes hardly restrain my tears at seeing men so dear to my heart suffer such intense pain about a thing which is already done and can never be undone."

Such thoughts have, I imagine, often risen in the hearts of missionary preachers of all Churches. I quote from a letter from the friend to whom I owe the quotation from Xavier. "Now I had exactly the same experience during the nine years I was labouring in Japan. Again and again I and my brother missionaries were questioned by people about their dead parents and forefathers who had not heard the gospel. Could they pray for them? What would I do on the anniversary of my father's funeral? Long after the idols were cast away, the household ancestral shrines were clung to. I have had most painful scenes. They would not forsake their parents. I think that all the S.P.G., and many American Church Missionaries, even as Russian missionaries and Bishops, and our Bishops and missionaries in North China also, came to the conclusion to allow prayers. I pointed to the litany, 'Remember not the offences of our forefathers.'"

Happily in the case of Xavier's followers, the hope was given which threw light upon those who were thus sitting as in the valley of the shadow of death, first, as we have seen, in the writings of the Jesuits, and then in that of other Roman Catholic theologians, till it is at last proclaimed by her most conspicuous teachers as a doctrine of which the Church of Rome has always been the witness. This leads me to Cardinal Manning's *Temporal Mission of the Holy Ghost*, p. 80. "God is infinite in His mercy to those who have never heard the words or the name of Jesus Christ. . . . . Assuredly He will take care of the nations and races who, through no rejection of His truth have never known His name. They will obtain, in some way secret to us, the benefit of His infinite mercy."

The same thought is stated more fully in a second edition of the same work with the altered title of the *Internal Mission of the Holy Ghost* (1875), p. 6.

"There are men so narrow as to say that no soul among the Heathen can be saved. The perfections of God, the attributes of mercy, love, tenderness, justice, equity, all rise up against so dark a theology. The word of God declares that the Son of God is the true light that enlighteneth every man that cometh into the world. Every soul created in the likeness of God is illuminated by the light of God even in his creation. . . . Two Pontiffs have condemned as heretical the two following assertions: that the heathen and the Jews and heretics receive no influence from Jesus Christ, but that their will is without help, that is, without grace, was condemned as a heresy by Alexander VIII. Again that there is no grace given outside the Church was also condemned as heresy by Clement XI. The work, therefore, of the Holy Ghost, even in the order of nature, so to say, that is, outside the Church of God, and the revealed knowledge of Jesus Christ among the heathen,—that working is universal in the soul of every individual human being, and if they who receive the Holy Ghost are truthful in corresponding with it, God in His unrevealed mercies will deal with them in ways secret to us. His mercies, unknown to us, are over all His works, and the infinite merits of the Redeemer of the world are before the mercy-seat of our heavenly Father for the salvation of those who follow even the little light which in the order of nature they receive."

I add two more quotations even more striking in their width of thought, from French Roman Catholic writers of some authority, which I owe to the Rev. Charles Bodington.

(1.) The Abbé Gabriel, *Le Monde et le Christ*, ch. x. p. 24. "L'Eglise en effet ne commence pas à Bethlehem, mais elle remonte jusqu'au premier homme, ou-plutôt, eternelle dans ses dogmes, dans sa vie, elle est avant tous les siècles. C'est le Verbe, qui, avant son Incarnation, est la vraie lumière qui eclaire tout homme venant en ce monde. C'est lui qui illuminait Adam et ses descendants, les patriarches, avant et après le deluge. . . . Tous ils faisaient parte de l'Eglise. Bien plus, toutes les verités, d'ailleurs si nombreuses, eparses parmis les paiens, n'etaient encore que les rayonnements de ce Verbe Divin. . . . Tous les justes de Paganisme en tant qu'ils professaient les verités, etaient donc membres de l'Eglise. Vous le voyez, l'Eglise résume en elle toutes les verités avant, comme après, les predications de l'evangile."

(2.) The Abbé Bauhier, *Cours d'Instruction Pastorale*, iii. p. 18. "Dieu seul sait le qui se passe dans l'âme de l' Eglise. Aucun regard humain ne peut penetrer dans ce sanctuaire. . . . Il peut donc y avoir, et il y a certainement, soit parmi les infideles, soit parmi les hérétiques, des hommes que l'âme de l'Eglise penetre de divines influences, quoiqu'ils n'appartiennent pas à son corps."

The teaching of the French divines goes beyond that of the English Cardinal. With him the heathen and the heretic are outside the Church. They see in the heathen, and even in the heretics who err in ignorance, members of the Church belonging to its soul, though outwardly separated from its body.

P. 196, l. 8. I am enabled, through the kindness of a correspondent, to give the passage from Baxter. It is found in the *Reliquiæ Baxterianæ*, published by Matthew Sylvester in 1696, p. 75. Sterry is described as "so famous for obscurity in preaching that Sir Benjamin Rudyard said he was too high for this world, and too low for the other." He was "an intimate of Henry Vane the younger," and "vanity and sterility were never so happily combined."

P. 200, l. 13. Young's sneer, in his Sixth Satire, at Tillotson's liberality is, perhaps, worth quoting, as showing the impression which it made on the narrower theologians of his time :

"Dear Tillotson, be sure, the best of men,
Nor thought he more than thought great Origen;
Though once upon a time he misbehaved,
Poor Satan! doubtless he'll at length be saved."

P. 208, l. 2. A correspondent calls my attention to the fact that Wesley, four years before his death, published an Universalist tract by the Swiss philosopher, Bonnet.

P. 214, l. 5. A favourite text with Mr. Erskine, into which he read his own belief, was Ps. lxxx. 4. "There is forgiveness with Thee, that Thou mayest be feared."

P. 222, l. 1 from bottom. Bishop Blomfield's son, the present Bishop of Colchester, recollects nothing. This is but negative evidence, but it is, perhaps, worth stating.

P. 229, l. 18. Some of Professor Birks' friends have asked me to reconsider the language which I have used as to the parallelisms which seemed to me so striking between his thoughts and words—I do not say his conclusions—and those of Mr. Maurice. I will content myself, in replying to that request, with printing the passages in the *Theological Essays* (p. 442) of the latter writer, and leaving the reader to compare it with the words which I have quoted from Mr. Birks.

"What dreams of ours can reach to the assertion of St. John, that death and hell themselves shall be cast into the lake of fire. I cannot fathom the meaning of such expressions. But they are written: I accept them and give thanks for them. I feel there is an abyss of death into which I may sink and be lost. Christ's Gospel reveals an abyss of love, below that; I am content to be lost in that."

I should have thought it unnecessary, had I not been told by some of Mr. Birks' friends that my language seems to suggest a charge of plagiarism, to repeat my disclaimer of any intention to make such a suggestion. Whatever other faults of style and manner I may be guilty of, I may, I hope, claim to be free from the fault of insinuating covertly what I shrink from stating openly. I do not "just hint a doubt, and hesitate dislike." I should have thought, indeed, that it was obvious that the case which I was putting depended largely for its force on the unconsciousness of the parallelism which I pointed out. The noticeable thing was that two minds trained in such different schools of religious thought as Mr. Maurice and Mr. Birks, were alike, yet independently of each other, influenced by the reaction which they felt against the eschatological teaching of popular Protestantism. I gladly comply with another request of Mr. Birks' friends. They tell me that the *Victory of Divine Goodness*, from which I have quoted, is out of print, and ask me to refer such readers as may wish to make themselves better acquainted with his teaching to the *Difficulties of Belief* which embodies that of the earlier volume (Macmillan & Co., 1876).

P. 232, l. 11. It is due to the writer of *Yesterday, To-day, and for Ever*, now Bishop of Exeter, to state that his convictions also were the result of an independent inquiry, beginning in 1861, and were matured and actually published in 1866, before the appearance of Mr. Birks' *Victory of Divine Goodness* in 1867. The latter, however, as the "Letter to a Friend," in pp. 41—49 of that work shows, had entered on his own course of thought about the same time as the future Bishop. Here again we have another instance of parallelism, not of derivation.

P. 236, l. 20. The list ought to have included the *Salvator Mundi* (Kegan Paul, Trench, & Co.) of the Rev. S. Cox, the late Editor of the *Expositor*. Few living writers equal Mr. Cox in the life and originality which he has brought to his work as an interpreter, and the volume which I have named well deserves attention as possessing those qualities in a more than usual measure.

P. 280, l. 22. It is worth while noticing one or two special instances. I owe the following to the Bishop Suffragan of Colchester. It is the epitaph of Richard Watson, Bishop of Llandaff, best known as the writer of an *Apology for the Bible* (D. 1816).

"Quod mortale fuit Ricardi Landavensis juxta cœmeterium habet. Quod immortale est, faxit Deus ΕΝ ΧΡΙΣΤΩ cœlum habeat."

Bishop Barrow's epitaph is noted in the *Diary of Philip Henry* (ed. M. H. Lee, 1882, p. 291), as having been found written in his own hands. He refers also to Thorndike's tomb in Westminster Abbey as containing the words "*requiem ei in Christo et beatam resurrectionem precare*," or to that purpose; but Archdeacon Farrar informs me that he has not succeeded in finding the inscription.

My attention has been also called by the Rev. J. A. Paynter, Minister of Christ Church Congregational Church, Oswestry, to the following interesting passage from a recently published work on the *Old Stone Crosses of the Vale of Clyd*, p. 22.

"In Corwen churchyard there are gravestones of a very peculiar form, evidently pointing to the old custom of praying for and over the dead. They are only a few inches above the ground, placed at the head and foot of the grave, with holes for the knees of those who pray." The writer quotes from Pennant (ii. p. 353) that "it was customary for the friends of the dead to kneel and say the Lord's Prayer for several Sundays after the interment, and then to dress the grave with flowers," and adds his own belief (p. 23) that "the probability is that even so late as the beginning of the present century, people prayed for, or over, their dead in and about Corwen."

P. 286, l. 22. Ken's epitaph was written by himself (Bowles, in his *Life of Ken*, vol. ii., gives a fac-simile) but was not put upon his tomb in Frome churchyard.

P. 328, note. The passage to which I refer is found in Maurice's *Theological Essays* (2nd ed.) pp. 469, 470.

Comp. also Kingsley's Preface to *Alexandria and her Schools.* "Let a man fear him, the destroying devil, and fear therefore cowardice, disloyalty, selfishness, sluggishness, which are his works, and to be utterly afraid of which is to be truly brave."

P. 371, *ad fin.* I note one or two passages which illustrate the craving for some other definition of eternity than that of infinitely prolonged duration.

(1.) Boethius *De Consolatione Philosophiæ*, B. v., discusses the whole question in connection with God's foreknowledge, and comes to the conclusion that strictly speaking God does not foresee—*providet*, not *prævidet*,—there being for Him no past or future. To Him all things in the history of the universe are ever present in the eternal Now. He is *æternus*, the world is only *perpetuus*.

Boethius is reproduced by

(1.) Cowley.

> "Nothing there is to come, and nothing past,
> But an eternal Now doth ever last."

(2.) Henry Vaughan. *Silex Scintillans*, p. 91.

> "I saw Eternity, the other night,
> Like a great thing of pure and endless light,
> All calm as it was bright:
> And round about it Time, in hours, days, years,
> Driven by the spheres,
> Like a vast shadow moved, in which the world
> And all her train were hurled."

(3.) Carlyle. *Sartor Resartus.*

"Time and space are not God, but creatures of God. With God, as it is an universal Here, so it is an everlasting Now."

P. 379. The phrase is found in Burnet's *History of his Own Time*, ii., p. 719 (ed. 1734) in a letter from Tillotson to Burnet. "The account given of Athanasius' Creed seems to me nowise satisfactory. I wish we were well rid of it."

P. 406. The following passage on Mutual Recognition, from Cardinal Manning's *Sermons* (published before his change), is, I think, worth quoting: I am indebted to the Bishop Suffragan of Colchester, for calling my attention to them.

"O dull hearts and slow to believe what Christ Himself has spoken. 'God is not the God of the dead,' of nameless, obscured, obliterated spirits, of impersonal natures, beings robbed of their identity, spoiled of their consciousness, of blinded eyes, of marred aspects. The law of perfect recognition is inseparable from the law of perfect identity. Our individual knowledge must be eternal. We should not be what we are to ourselves if we were not so to others. They would lose their identity if they were not the same to us."

In another striking passage (i. 373) he dwells on the same thought in its darker aspect, as pointing to one element of retributive suffering for the spirits of the lost. They too will recognise those with whom they have sinned, or whom they have led to evil.

P. 416. I ought not to close without referring to the exhaustive volume, *A Critical History of the Doctrine of a Future Life*, by William Roundeville Alger (Tenth Edition, Boston, Roberts Brothers, 1880), and to express my regret that I had not met with it at an earlier stage of my own studies, which could not fail to have been enriched by it.

INDEX OF SUBJECTS AND NAMES.

INDEX OF GREEK WORDS.

INDEX OF SCRIPTURE TEXTS.

St. Matthew—(continued).

St. Mark.

St. Luke.

St. John.

Acts.

Romans.

ROMANS—*(continued)*.

1 CORINTHIANS.

2 CORINTHIANS.

2 CORINTHIANS—*(continued)*.

GALATIANS.

EPHESIANS.

PHILIPPIANS.

COLOSSIANS.

1 THESSALONIANS.

2 THESSALONIANS.

1 Timothy.

2 Timothy.

Titus.

Philemon.

Hebrews.

St. James.

1 St. Peter.

1 St. Peter—*(continued)*.

2 St. Peter.

1 St. John.

St. Jude.

Revelation.

CPSIA information can be obtained
at www.ICGtesting.com
Printed in the USA
BVOW08s0709120418
513141BV00018B/244/P